Water:
Its Spiritual Significance

Rivers, ponds, lakes and streams. They have different names but all contain water. Religions have different names, but all contain truth.
Muhammad Ali, US boxer (1942 -)
Louisville, Kentucky

"Ohio" is the Iroquois word for "fine" or "good" river.

Water:
Its Spiritual Significance

Edited by
Elena Lloyd-Sidle and Gray Henry-Blakemore

FONS VITAE

First published in 2009 by
Fons Vitae
49 Mockingbird Valley Drive
Louisville, KY 40207
http://www.fonsvitae.com
Email: fonsvitaeky@aol.com

Copyright Fons Vitae 2009
Library of Congress Control Number: 2009934944
ISBN 9781891785412

This book was typeset by Neville Blakemore, Jr.

Printed in Canada

I sailed up a river in a pleasant wind
New lands, new people, and new thoughts to find;
Many fair reaches and headlands appeared,
And many dangers were there to be feared;
But when I remember where I have been,
And the fair landscapes that I have seen,
THOU seemest the only permanent shore,
The cape never rounded, nor wandered o'er.

Thoreau's dedication in
A Week on the Concord and Merrimack Rivers

Table of Contents

An ancient people tells us that when the moment of a great teacher's death was near, the disciples said, "What is it we will see when you are gone?" And the master said, "All I did was sit on the river bank handing out river water. After I'm gone I trust you will notice the water."

Recounted by Joan Chittister in
The Rule of Benedict: Insight for the Ages,
New York: Crossroad, 1997, p. 137

Dedication

We dedicate this book to our friends who,
this summer, returned to their Maker,

Ewert Cousins, Thomas Berry and Carmen Blacker

Acknowledgements

We would like to thank Christy Brown for originating the theme, 'Sacred Water: Sustaining Life,' for Louisville, Kentucky's 14th Annual Festival of Faiths, for which this volume has been prepared, and for her unfailing enthusiasm and inspiration. Thanks to the Center for Interfaith Relations, which undertakes this festival every year. Also to Stewart Lussky, Shane Spaulding, and Kendra Foster for their hard and creative work on the festival.

John Faulkner of the Muhammad 'Ali Center of Louisville, KY, Mustafa Gouverneur of Ten Thousand Films, Owsley Brown III, Maria Montes Spaggiari, and Barry McDonald. To Mary Evelyn Tucker and John Grim, co-directors of the Forum on Religion and Ecology at Yale University, for their presences which were felt throughout this project.

We thank the following institutions: Counterpoint Publishing for permission to include poems of Wendell Berry; Islamic Texts Society, Cambridge, England; New Directions for permission to include the writings of Thomas Merton; Linda Lloyd-Jones and Chrysanthe Constantouris at the Victoria and Albert Museum, London, for facilitating the permission to use the cover images; World Wisdom, Inc. for permission to include the essays by Titus Burckhardt and Ananda K. Coomaraswamy.

Members of the Fons Vitae staff and board. Neville Blakemore for his typesetting against daunting odds, Eli Brown V and Anne Ogden for their proofreading of often complex texts, and Becca Heiser for her invaluable help in the production.

The best way to live
is to be like water
For water benefits all things
and goes against none of them
It provides for all people
And even cleanses those places
A man is loath to go
In this way it is just like Tao
Live in accordance with *the nature of things…*
One who lives in accordance with nature
Does not go against the way of things
He moves in harmony with the present moment
Always knowing the truth of just what to do

Tao Te Ching, Verse 8

Introduction[1]

Elena Lloyd-Sidle

All that exists, in whatever mode this may be, necessarily participates in universal principles, and nothing exists except by participation in these principles, which are the eternal and immutable essences contained in the permanent actuality of the Divine Intellect. Consequently, it can be said that all things, however contingent they may be in themselves, express or represent these principles in their own way and according to their order of existence, for otherwise they would be purely and simply nothingness. Thus, from one order to another, all things are linked together and correspond, to come together in total and universal harmony, for harmony is nothing other than the reflection of principal unity in the manifested world; and it is this correspondence which is the veritable basis of symbolism.

René Guénon[2]

The symbol is not based on man-made conventions. It is an aspect of the ontological reality of things and as such is independent of man's perception of it. The symbol is the revelation of a higher order of reality in a lower order through which man can be led back to the higher realm. To understand symbols is to accept the hierarchic structure of the Universe and the multiple states of being.

S.H. Nasr[3]

Our Waters

In planning our Festival of Faiths, we learned that before the first mirror was ever fashioned, water served as the original, primordial mirror. In Kentucky we currently suffer, not from scarcity of water, but from water pollution. Thus one member of our community responded, "The notion of water as the first mirror makes me think that even today, a community's values are reflected in its water. What are our polluted rivers and streams saying about us? And does that match what our Faith instructs us to be?"[4]

---

1. This essay results from various conversations with Wendell Berry whose approach and honesty have challenged me to learn more so that I may write more clearly, and whose humility has been and continues to be exemplary. I am also deeply indebted to conversations with Barry McDonald from whose fineness of doctrinal understanding I have benefited beyond measure.

2. R. Guénon, *Fundamental Symbols*, Louisville, KY: Fons Vitae/Quinta Essentia, 1995, p. v.

3. S.H. Nasr, *Sufi Essays*, London: Allen & Unwin, 1972, p. 88.

4. Richard M. Gula, S.S. writes of the relationship between the inward and outward in discussing ethics: "Spirituality is concerned with the wellspring of our actions. If we focus only on the actions that get done, then we neglect what nourishes and sustains those actions. There is more to us, and more to life, than what we do. Our

Essays and poetry in this volume attempt to address these questions on various levels. To what dimension within us does water correspond? Why does water play such a central role in the rituals of the world's religions? How is the water imagery of Thoreau and Rumi able to affect us? To what higher planes of reality does water refer? That is, what is the spiritual significance of water? In learning about these significances we hope that reverence for both creation and Creator will increase in the reader, as well as greater clarity for the 'work' that stands before us.

The Introduction which follows intends to provide the reader with a basis for understanding how symbolism and spirituality relate—in the most profound sense—to our responsibility for and appreciation of the natural world in general, and water in particular, on which existence depends entirely. Offered here are some of the spiritual and metaphysical principles and concepts which underlie the issues at hand, as understood by some of the most brilliant minds within the great faith traditions, from the time of Plato until today.

Divine Plenitude in Nature

Not that the One is two, but these two are One.

Hermes Trismegistos

Our beloved friend Wendell Berry, whose work appears in this volume, added this observation to the writing he contributed: "I am unsure about the spiritual nature of my work. I swore off that word 'spiritual' a long time ago because I so dislike its supposed separation from 'material'." We share Wendell's concern about spirituality's "supposed separation from [the] 'material'" as the natural world is in fact understood by all the great faith traditions to be a theophany, that is, a manifestation of the presence of God.

Wisdom excerpts from various traditions confirm the universal understanding of creation as a theophany:

God made this (terrestrial) world in the image of the world above; thus, all which is found above has its analogy below…and everything constitutes a unity.

The *Zohar*[5]

Crazy Horse dreamed and went out into the world where there is nothing but the spirits of things. That is the real world that is behind this one, and everything we see here is something like a shadow from that world.

Black Elk[6]

---

interior life affects our exterior behavior…. Virtues link us to action by providing a sensitivity to what is right and a motivation to do what human well-being demands…With virtue, we act naturally." (R. Gula, *The Good Life: Where Morality and Spirituality Converge*, Mahwah, NJ: Paulist Press, 1984, pp. 3-5.)

5. *Spiritual Ascent: A Compendium of the World's Wisdom*, presented by Whitall Perry, Louisville, KY: Fons Vitae, 2008, orig. *Treasury of Traditional Wisdom*, Fons Vitae, 2000, p. 306.

6. Black Elk, J. Neihardt's, *Black Elk Speaks,* London: Abacus, 1974, p. 67.

Form is a revelation of essence.

Meister Eckhart[7]

The Sages have been taught of God that this natural world is only an image and a copy of a heavenly and spiritual pattern; that the very existence of this world is based upon the reality of its celestial archetypes.

Michael Sendivogius[8]

All forms of being in this corporeal world are images of pure Lights, which exist in the spiritual world.

Shihab al-Din Suhrawardi al-Halabi[9]

...if a world did not cast down shadows from above, the worlds below it would vanish altogether, since each world in creation is no more than a tissue of shadows entirely dependent on the archetypes in the world above....There is not the least thing in existence which is not such a shadow....*Verily God disdaineth not to cite as symbol even a gnat or something smaller.* (Qur'an II:26) Nor is there anything which is any more than a shadow...

Martin Lings[10]

When we speak of 'seeing God everywhere', and perceiving the natural world as a manifestation of the Qualities of God, it is important to say at the outset that there must be a balance in our understanding of the two aspects, Divine immanence and Divine transcendence. God is immanent in all of nature in that it is permeated with the Divine Presence. There is nothing that lies outside of the Divine Presence. God is also transcendent—expressed in Islam by the saying *Allāhu akbar*, "God is greater"—in that the Reality of the Divine is incomparably greater than ourselves, or anything else of the creation.

We have seen the dire consequences of views that are unbalanced and extreme in either aspect. Emphasis on the transcendence of God has led to a focus on "the path of personal salvation, which frequently emphasize[s] otherworldly goals and reject[s] this world as corrupting."[11] This 'otherworldly' focus has often resulted in a vision of the natural world as part of the 'realm

---

7. *Spiritual Ascent*, p. 673.

8. *Spiritual Ascent*, p. 672. Orig. source: 'The New Chemical Light', *The Hermetic Museum*, Vol. II, London: John M. Watkins, 1953 (reprint from edn. 1893), p. 138.

9. *Spiritual Ascent*, p. 673. Orig. source: M. Horten, *Die Philosophe der Erleuchtungnach Suhrawardi*, Halle a.S. 1912, p. 44; in *Hermetica* (see under Hermes), IV, p. 268.

10. M. Lings, *Book of Certainty*, Cambridge, England: Islamic Texts Society, 1996, p. 37.

11. Mary Evelyn Tucker and John Grim, "Series Foreword," *Religions of the World and Ecology Series*, see for example volume on *Islam and Ecology*, p. xxv.

   In Arabic there is a difference between *dunya* (meaning the worldly world, the herebelow, the separation that human beings imagine and live by due to our 'fallen nature', comparable to the Buddhist *dokkha*) and *'ālam* (meaning the world that God created, the earth and all that is upon it).

of the flesh' as opposed to the 'realm of the spirit' and thus devalued in one's personal, religious life. Incredible damage has occurred due to this disregard of the natural world and its being seen as 'separate' from the religious life.[12] We see many religious practitioners involved professionally in the destruction of the natural world without any ethical concern. It is this divorce between the spiritual and material which is so harmful.

Too great a focus on divine immanence has fostered unbridled love of, reverence for, dependence on and, thus deification of, the material realm. We end up loving things in and of themselves—the physical forms exclusively—and building a life around them. We thus forget that it is the Spirit that gives us life.[13] This is a worldview founded on a myopia and it is what the monotheistic religions refer to as idolatry. Every age and people have fallen into idolatry in some form or another. The present manifestation of this is the materialism we see rampant today and which characterizes modern society. We love 'stuff', want more and more of it, and yet are never satisfied. This is partly because our souls are made instead to be filled with the Divine. Something deep within us is unsatisfied by the material with which we fill our lives. It is by nature un-satisfactory.[14]

Both aspects, Divine immanence and Divine transcendence, are essential for understanding 'the nature of things'. The Platonic view of reality as emanating from the Source, first as 'universals' or 'ideas', and then in successive levels of creation, occurs in all traditions in some version or another.[15]

---

12. We suffer today from this pandemic of supposed lack of responsibility. How often have we heard, "I'm just doing my job," as if work ethic were somehow magically separate from all other ethics and in fact took precedence over them; and as if within the realm of 'work', if you fulfill the terms of a job description, your soul will be untouched by any havoc you may have wreaked in the world while 'just doing your job.' There is no tradition which does not have a doctrine of being held accountable for what we have done or put in motion. Likewise, there is no tradition which does not teach that our actions affect the state of our soul, thus the importance of honor, justice, and upholding truth and goodness in every facet of out lives.

13. As Elihu says to Job, "The spirit of God has made me, and the breath of the Almighty gives me life." [Job 33.4]

14. This being seen in the doctrine of *dokkha* in Buddhism. For more on this 'filling of the spiritual vacuum' see Hamza Yusuf's essay "Climbing Mount Purgatorio."

15. The following delineation provided by HRH Dr. Ghazi bin Muhammad of Jordan helps us to understand more clearly what these different levels of reality are: "According to the traditional cosmological scheme of creation, manifestation as such comprises three great Worlds created successively by God (in descending order of ontological reality and 'closeness' to God): 'the World Spirit,' 'the World Soul,' and 'the World Body.' Now the World Spirit, or the World of the Spirit, is also called the 'World of Ideas' (by Plato); the 'World of Archetypes'; the Universal Spirit; the Kingdom of Heaven; the Realm of Supra-formal Manifestation; the World of Essences; the World of the Domination (in Christianity); the *'Alam al-Jabarut* or *'Alam al-Ruh* (in Islam); the *Olam Haberiyah* (in Judaism); *Svar* (in Hinduism), and so on. It is said to 'contain' the Archangels, the eternal Archetypes

The system we in the West may be most familiar with is the *scala naturae* or Great Chain of Being.[16] There are levels of the reality of the Spirit, thus unchanging and immutable; and there are levels of the Earth, which thus are changing and mutable. However, in addition to the aspect of *gradation*, the aspects of *plenitude* and *continuity* are also fundamental. That is, the entire chain is marked by a Divine *plenitude* due to the *continuity* of the Divine Presence which makes the very existence of the chain possible. "If He should take back His Spirit to Himself, and gather to Himself His breath, all flesh would perish altogether, and man would return to dust." [Job 34.14-15]

The language of 'higher' and 'lower' levels of reality invokes an image which can be used as a tool for understanding and for inciting in the human being a desire for greater proximity to the Divine.[17] But this image can be misunderstood. Reality is a continuum of levels of proximity to the Divine. Some things and some people more clearly reflect the Divine Presence than others. In the Great Chain of Being for example, gold and silver are the pinnacle of metals and thus 'closer' to the Divine, likewise the eagle and the lion are the kings of their respective realms and are thus considered 'closer' to the Divine than are the other animals. However, any separation that might be imagined or seen is a type of mirage. For it is precisely this imagined separation—a result of our veiled sight—which is illusory.

---

of all things in Creation, and the 'individual' spirits of men, but strictly speaking it *is* each spirit, each Archetype, and each Archangel, for in it there is no 'separation' or 'difference' (although of course there are 'distinctions')…"

He goes on to explain the subsequent, 'lower' levels: "The World Soul, or the World of Souls, is also called the World of Formation; the Subtle World; the Psychic World; the Grave; the World of the Imagination; the World of Exemplars; the Intermediary World; the Isthmus; the World of the Dominion (in Christianity); the *'Alam al-Malakut* or *Barzakh* (is Islam); the *Olam Hayetsirah* (in Judaism); *Bhuvas* (in Hinduism), and so on. It is ordinarily hidden to (fallen) man, but it contains the individual souls of all men (as well as the genii or *jinn*, the fairies, and the other 'psychic beings') *distinctively* in much the same way as individual bodies are contained in that third great World, the World Body or Physical Universe (the Corporeal World; the *'Alam al-Mulk wal Shahadah* in Islam; *Olam Ha'asiyah* in Judaism; *Bhu* in Hinduism) which is obviously none other than the world that all men ordinarily know through their physical, bodily senses." (G. bin Muhammad, "The Traditional Doctrine of Symbolism," *The Underlying Religion*, ed. M. Lings, C. Minaar, Bloomington, IN: World Wisdom, Inc. 2007. p. 158.)

16. This idea has its roots in Platonic thought, was systematized by Aristotle, adopted by various philosophers and theologians of the Middle Ages, and later, by thinkers of the Renaissance. According to Arthur Loveyjoy it was " the most widely familiar conception of the general scheme of things, of the constitutive pattern of the universe" until approximately the end of the 18th century. (A. Lovejoy, *The Great Chain of Being: A Study of the History of an Idea*, Cambridge, Mass.: Harvard University Press, 1936, p. vii.)

17. "But it is the spirit in a man, the breath of the Almighty, that makes him understand." [Job 32:8]

In many traditions we are taught that we have two kinds of sight: the physical eyes of the outward, and the 'eye of the heart' which is the 'inward eye'.[18] Our outward eyes see things as separate, seeing material things. Our inward eye sees all things as coming from, part of, and returning to the Divine Source. Our outward eyes are veiled in their sight, seeing only duality: 'this is separate and different from that'. Our inward eye sees Oneness, that there is nothing but God.

As we live in this world, we see with both inner and outer vision: the vision of separation and the vision of union. That is, the vision of creation as incomparably less than the Ineffable Divine (transcendence), and the vision of all things as permeated with the Divine and communicating various aspects of It (immanence).

In the end, Divine Reality is ineffable, that is, it cannot be described. We will always run into difficulty in trying to express divine realities and truths with human language, for they can only be properly seen by the eye of the heart, which lies in unity, while human perception and language convey duality.

Confucius said to Lao-tzu, 'Today you are at leisure. Pray tell me about perfect *Tao*.' 'Purge your heart by fasting and discipline,' answered Lao-tzu, 'Wash your soul as white as snow. Discard your knowledge. *Tao* is abstruse and difficult of discussion. ...Attainment implies non-discussion: discussion implies non-attainment.'

Chuang-tzu (ch. XXII)[19]

Returning to 'the Nature of Things'

The spectrum of cosmologies, myths, symbols, and rituals within the religious traditions will be instructive in resituating us within the rhythms and limits of nature.

Mary Evelyn Tucker and John Grim[20]

Environmental concerns are often treated as ethical questions. Honorable scholarship in religious studies increasingly highlights the ethical demands on the human being vis-à-vis the natural world—of which he or she is an integral part—as delineated by the world's great faith traditions.[21] Ethical

---

18. In Arabic this is differentiated by the terms *baṣar* and *baṣīra*.

19. *Spiritual Ascent*, p. 575.

20. "Series Foreword", *Islam and Ecology*, p. xxiii.

21. The most notable example of such current scholarship is the Forum on Religion and Ecology directed by Mary Evelyn Tucker and John Grim, out of which has come the Religion and Ecology series edited by the same and published by Harvard's Center for World Religions and Harvard Divinity School, distributed by Harvard University Press. See www.yale.edu/religionandecology. Also, see Appendix in this volume, "The Emerging Alliance of World Religions and Ecology."

The scholarship of Seyyed Hossein Nasr has included this focus for decades. See for example, *Man and Nature: The Spiritual Crisis of Modern Man*, Chicago: Kazi Publications, 1997, first pub. 1968.

prescriptions in the faith traditions however must be understood in the context of the essential function of religion: to provide a spiritual framework and vision of the Real, which guides individuals back to 'the nature of things'.[22] Ethical prescriptions in religion include the guidelines provided by legal prescriptions for outward action as well as the exemplary models that its founders, prophets, saints, and sages provide for inward attitude or state of being. These guidelines are like garments which are too big for us, but into which we must grow.[23]

In Islam, for example, it is this state (*fiṭra*), precisely, which Muslims strive to truly embody. Seyyed Hossein Nasr writes, "In a profound sense one might say that the whole of nature is *muslim*, meaning that it has surrendered itself totally to the Will of God. All creatures follow the nature which God has given to them. A pear tree always bears pears, a fish always remains true to the nature of a fish and a bird to that of the bird. It is only man who has been given the freedom of rebellion against his own primordial nature."[24] Man, in his perfect, primordial state is in fact *muslim* in its universal meaning of 'in harmony with his nature', in harmony with the will of heaven, and in harmony with 'the nature of things.'

In order to live and act in accordance with 'the nature of things', we must first have some knowledge of 'the nature of things' itself. This Knowledge includes, essentially, knowledge of the Origin and End of creation (metaphysics), the emanation of creation from the Origin in stages, or levels of reality (cosmology), and the essential nature and purpose of the human state. In his *Universal Meaning of the Kabbalah*, Leo Schaya writes, "The principal aim of tradition in regard to the forms and laws of the cosmos is to connect all

---

22. Contemporary Quranic commentator, Muhammad Mitwaly Sha'rawy uses the Arabic word *ṣawāb*, meaning the correct, upright or proper way, or sense, of things, as being the goal to which 'right guidance' will deliver the believer. For example, "Then they realized their error and returned to the right way, or sense, of things (*ṣawāb*)." (commentary on Maryam 19:46) Also, "...one considers these truths and looks into all of the different opinions in order to be rightly guided, by one's own [discernment], to the proper [understanding of] way of things (*ṣawāb*)..." (commentary on 19:48. See the Royal Aal al-Bayt Institute for Islamic Thought's online *tafsir* database at www.altafsir.com)

23. "The religious world-view points to a kind of mystery...the mystery of the relationship between laws that should govern us morally and spiritually and the laws that govern the universe. ...From *Tao* to *dharma*, to *rta* to *Shari'ah*, to *nomos*, whatever term is used to designate this reality [of law or order] in different traditions... they all demonstrate that there is an order that governs man as well as nature, from which comes our modern word 'cosmos.' The Greek word *cosmos* means both order and beauty, which is extremely significant..." (S.H. Nasr, "The Spiritual and Religious Dimensions of the Environmental Crisis", *Seeing God Everywhere*, ed. Barry McDonald, Bloomington, IN: World Wisdom, Inc., 2003, pp. 91-92.)

24. S.H. Nasr, *A Young Muslim's Guide*, Chicago: Kazi Publications, 1994, p. 38.

things with their first and divine cause and thus show Man his true meaning, the sense of his own existence being likewise revealed to him thereby."[25]

The Science of Symbolism

As many of the individual articles and poetry included in this volume deal with water as a metaphor or symbol, we offer the following passages to be considered on the nature of symbolism itself.

Martin Lings writes in *The Book of Certainty*, "Symbols...have already been referred to as being guides and incentives to the traveler upon his journey, and they have power to remind him of their counterparts in higher worlds not through merely incidental resemblance but because they are actually related to them in the way that a shadow is related to the object which casts it."[26]

In his book, *Alchemy: Science of the Cosmos, Science of the Soul*, Titus Burckhardt writes that "a symbol is not a mere allegory.... True symbolism depends on the fact that things, which may differ from one another in time, space, material nature and many other limitative characteristics, can possess and exhibit *the same essential quality. They thus appear as diverse reflections, manifestations, or productions of the same reality* – which in itself is independent of time and space. It is thus not quite right [for example] to say that gold represents the sun and silver the moon; rather is it the case that the two noble metals and the two luminaries are both symbols of the *same two cosmic or divine realities*."[27] (italics ours)

On the universality of symbolism, Lings writes, "...there is no traditional doctrine which does not teach that this world is the world of symbols, inasmuch as it contains nothing which is not a symbol."[28] HRH Dr. Ghazi bin Muhammad of Jordan elaborates: "The first thing to be said about the traditional doctrine of symbolism is that it is a single doctrine, which is to say that despite vast theological, cultural, social, racial, linguistic, and historical differences there was more or less one common, unified understanding of the question of symbolism the world over in all non-secular—'traditional' precisely—societies up to the time of the Renaissance. Now this is perhaps not as surprising as it might initially seem, for three obvious reasons: first, because man was (and still is) everywhere essentially the same. Second, because the world was (and still is) everywhere essentially the same. Third, because belief in the Creator necessarily imposes a hierarchical worldview or *Weltanschauung*: that is, a cosmology which comprises varying ontological degrees, from Absolute Reality 'down' to the material world. Indeed, such a traditional cosmological scheme can be independently found, *muta-*

---

25. L. Schaya, "Creation, The Image of God," *The Universal Meaning of the Kabbalah*, trans. Nancy Pearson, Louisville, KY: Fons Vitae, 2004, p. 52.

26. M. Lings, *Book of Certainty*, p. 37

27. T. Burckhardt, *Alchemy: Science of the Soul, Science of the Cosmos*. Louisville, KY: Fons Vitae, 1997, p. 2.

28. M. Lings, *Symbol & Archetype: A Study of the Meaning of Existence*, Louisville, KY: Fons Vitae Publishing, 2005, p. vii.

tis mutandis, in most ancient religions—from Platonism to the three great Monotheistic religions (Judaism, Christianity, and Islam) to Hinduism—and it is above all precisely this which enables one to speak of 'a traditional doctrine of symbolism' for ... traditional symbolism relies upon the correspondences between the different levels of reality."[29]

Thus it is that Martin Lings prefaces his *Symbol and Archetype: A Study of the Meaning of Existence* "with a statement which would once have been a platitude, but which now, to say the least, needs no apology: symbolism is the most important thing in existence; and it is at the same time the sole explanation of existence."[30]

Ritual and the Environmental Crisis

Once we have shut our hearts to God, darkness spreads over the whole world....

Seyyed Hossein Nasr[31]

We might ask, how does this traditional view of things relate to the 'environmental crisis'? It does so in innumerable ways. When one sees the natural world as a concretization of meanings and thus a book to be read, one's relationship to it changes completely. One consequence is seeing ritual as the tool with which to maintain or re-establish cosmic harmony, that is, harmony with all of the levels of the continuum of reality.[32]

Among the many knowledgeable participants in Louisville, Kentucky's 2009 Festival of Faiths, 'Sacred Water: Sustaining Life', will be Dr. Masuru Emoto, who is best known for his experiments demonstrating the effects of thoughts, words, music, recitation of sacred texts, and prayers on water. A global movement to pray over the earth's waters was inspired by his work. Dr. Emoto's work only gives a glimpse through science of what traditional peoples have always known: prayer has an actual impact on the physical realm.

Seyyed Hossein Nasr writes, "Now, these [God-given] rites, by virtue of their re-enactment on earth, link the earth with the higher levels of reality. A rite always links us with the vertical axis of existence, and by virtue of

---

29. G. bin Muhammad, "The Traditional Doctrine of Symbolism", *The Underlying Religion*, pp. 157-8.
30. M. Lings, *Symbol & Archetype,* p. vii.
31. S.H. Nasr, "The Religious and Spiritual Dimensions of the Environmental Crisis", *Seeing God Everywhere,* p. 81.
32. "Now, this idea is meaningless in the context of modern thought, where ritual seems to have no relation or correspondence with the nature of physical reality. In the modern world-view, rituals are at best personal, individual, subjective elements that create happiness in the individual or establish a relationship between him or her and God. That much at least some modern people accept. But how could rites establish cosmic harmony? From the modern scientific point of view such an assertion seems to make no sense at all. But it is not nonsense; it is a very subtle truth that has to be brought out and emphasized." (S.H. Nasr, "The Religious and Spiritual Dimensions...", *Seeing God Everywhere,* p. 80.)

that, links us also with the principles of nature. This truth holds not only for the primal religions, where certain acts are carried out in nature itself—let us say the African religions or the Aboriginal religion of Australia, or the religions of the Native American Indians—but also in the Abrahamic world, in the Hindu world, and in the Iranian religions."[33] We may recall here, for example, the rain-dance of the American Indians, the performance of communal prayers in the face of drought in cities across the Muslim world, and the recitation of scripture in various traditions in face of natural disasters.

All of this helps to "recreate balance and harmony with the natural world by calling upon Divine Mercy. ...If we do not have this relationship, nature is reduced to an 'it', to a pure fact, to a material lump... [and] we must bear all the consequences which such a view entails. ...Of course, such a thing is laughed at by official science, but that does not matter for such a science neglects the *sympathaeia* which exists between man and cosmic realities."[34]

,You cannot omit the outward if you wish to know the inward. The inward is reflected in the outward world.

Ananda Moyi[35]

Man himself as he was created—True Man as the Taoists name him—is the greatest of earthly symbols. The universal doctrine that he was made in the image of God (Genesis 1:27) signifies this pre-eminence: man is the symbol of the sum of all the attributes, that is, of the Divine Nature in its Totality, the Essence, whereas the animate and inanimate creatures that surround him reflect only one aspect or certain aspects of that Nature.

Martin Lings[36]

The original disposition (*fitra*) of Adam is the original disposition of all the cosmos...; it is the Self-disclosure of God.

Ibn al-'Arabi[37]

Hamza Yusuf Hanson in his lecture series on al-Ghazali's *Alchemy of Happiness* speaks from the perspective of the correlation between the outer and the inner when he asks us to take note of which animals are becoming extinct. He points out that it is not the rats, cockroaches and pigs that are disappearing, but the animals of high and noble natures. In recent years our attention has been called to the disappearance of honey bees, but certainly not flies or mosquitoes. "Why? Because [certain noble] qualities in human beings are going extinct. We are the reflection; all of creation is in us. These creatures [are disappearing]—whales, falcons—because these qualities in

---

33. S.H. Nasr "Religious and Spiritual Dimensions...", *Seeing God Everywhere,* p. 82.

34. ibid.

35. A. Moyi, *Spiritual Ascent*, p. 306.

36. M. Lings, *Symbol & Archetype*, p. 2.

37. Cited by William Chittick, "Foreword" to T. Bayrak, *The Name and the Named*, Louisville, KY: Fons Vitae, 2000, p. 10.

us are disappearing."[38] He quotes the poem of a Moroccan poet Muhammad bin al-Habib,

> The cosmos is composed of meanings set up in images;
> whoever understands this is among the people of discernment.

Shaykh Hamza continues, "Why are we attracted to flowers? Or colors? … Because they reflect meanings. They are manifestations (*tajalliyāt*) of the Qualities of God." He goes on to speak of our attraction to beautiful things being, in essence, an attraction to the Divine Attribute Beauty (*al-Jamāl*). "Why do we not like ugliness? Because God is not ugly. …The primordial nature (*fitra*)…is attracted to those things that are beautiful and is put off by those things that are ugly. When [our] nature becomes distorted, corrupted, it is actually attracted to ugly things. …[The things people are attracted to] are all indications of their states." He asks why traditional peoples embellish clothes, carpets, and the like? Why not just make functional things? "Because these are people of *ihsan* (excellence, virtue, beautiful nature), so they make things beautiful."[39]

Dr. Reza Shah-Kazemi writes, "'Beauty is in the eye of the beholder.' This English saying accords perfectly with a key Platonic principle: the eye must itself be of a luminous nature for it to be able to register light; the truth must be immanent in the intellect for the intellect to be able to recognise truth. It is because beauty is of the essence of man's spirit that he is able to perceive and love beautiful forms."[40]

This inward-outward correspondence points to a deep correlation between the contamination and desecration of the outer world and the con-

---

38. "Since nothing can exist except in virtue of its Divine root, does that mean that everything is a symbol? The answer is yes and no—yes for the reason just given, and no because 'symbol' means 'sign' or 'token', which implies an operative power to call something to mind, namely its Archetype. In the light of the initially quoted verse *Nor is there anything but glorifieth Him with praise*, we could say that whether its 'praise' is powerful or faint. The word symbol is normally reserved for that which is particularly impressive in its 'glorification'. …The lion, the eagle and the bee are all true symbols, each being a summit in its own domain…" In an endnote he continues, "…On the other hand, in contrast with these sacred animals, the hippopotamus, the giraffe and the hyena are uninspiring, by which we mean, to revert to our liminal quotation, that their 'praise' is too 'faint' to earn for them, as such, the title of symbol in the higher and more exclusive sense of the word…" (M. Lings, *Symbol & Archetype*, pp. 5-6, 133.)

39. *Imam al-Ghazali, The Alchemy of Happiness, translation and commentary by Hamza Yusuf*, Hayward, CA: Alhambra Productions, 2006-07.

40. He continues, "…but it must be added that this capacity to intuit the essence in forms depends not only upon one's contemplativity, but also on the degree to which the individual's inherent beauty of soul is actualized: in other words, whether virtue and piety adorn the soul." (R. Shah-Kazemi, "Divine Beatitude: Supreme Archetype of Aesthetic Experience," *Seeing God Everywhere*).

tamination and desecration of our souls. Beyond pointing to a certain causal relationship, this correspondence also implies that each of us has a great opportunity and role to play in the rectification of our world, and even a responsibility to do so.

A member of our community said to us recently, "When an injustice is committed, there are cosmic effects. Likewise there are cosmic effects when an injustice is redressed, a wrong righted." Each of us has a particular nature, leading us naturally to work in various aspects of this struggle for rectification. The role of each individual is important and far from insignificant.

Regardless of our vocation, personality, affinities, physical strength, articulateness, political opinion, or wealth, our faiths call *all of us* to work to restore our inward natures, and this indeed has been said to have 'incalculable effects'.

New Haven, Connecticut
September, 2009

On mountain-tops we shine transformed in love
Yet it is here we live and not above,
And we forget that bliss and lose our sight
That even here it's true: we all shine with light.

From "All Life is Shimmering",
hymn by Phil Lloyd-Sidle

The Lakota philosophy can be understood by a review of the structure of Lakota words used in the creation story—MI or "me" and NI or "spiritual quality of life". Therefore, MINI, the word for "water" translates as "my spiritual quality of life."

Let yourself be open and life will be easier. A spoon of salt in a glass of water makes the water undrinkable. A spoon of salt in a lake is almost unnoticed.

The Buddha

As irrigators lead water where they want, as archers make their arrows straight, as carpenters carve wood, the wise shape their minds.

The Buddha

When we use water in the sweat lodge we should always think of Wakan-Tanka who is always flowing, giving His power and life to everything: we should also be as water, which is lower than all things, yet stronger than the rocks.

Black Elk, OGALA SIOUX 1863-1950

A great state is like a river basin
That receives everything flowing into it
It is the place where all things come to rest
Where all the world is welcomed

The low is greater than the high
The still is greater than the restless
The low country wins over its neighbor
The still female wins over the male

The Sage wants to uplift the people
The people want to follow the Sage
Only by being low does this come to be
The Sage bows to the people
The people bow to the Sage
And when they lift up their heads
Only greatness remains

Lao Tzu
Tao Te Ching, Verse 61

The Symbolism of Water*

Titus Burckhardt

The modern economy, in spite of all the research findings at its disposal, has for a long time almost completely left out of account one the of the most important bases of our life as well as of its own existence, namely the living purity of water. This fact bears witness to a unilateralness of development which, quite apart from the question of water, is also harmful to many other things, not the least of which is the psyche or soul. When the balance of Nature is not disturbed, the earth's waters themselves continually re-establish their purity, whereas, when this balance is lost, death and pollution are the result. It is thus not merely a coincidence that the 'life' of the waters is a symbol for the 'life' of the human soul.

When one considers whether there is anything that could possibly alert non-scientifically minded people to the menace of water pollution, one quickly realizes that the natural sense of beauty that enables us spontaneously to distinguish a diseased tree from a healthy one should also be able to sound a warning here. That it has not done so—or hardly done so—comes from the fact that modern man completely separates not only 'the beautiful' from 'the useful', but also 'the beautiful' from 'the real'. This way of thinking is like a split in one's consciousness, and it is difficult to say whether it is cause or effect of a state of affairs which, on the one hand, drives man systematically to destroy, on an ever-widening front, the natural balance of things and, on the other, impels him periodically to flee the artificial world which in this way he creates. Never before have there been such enormous concentrations of buildings of stone, concrete and iron, and never before did city-dwellers, in such enormous numbers, periodically leave their homes in order to re-discover Nature at the seaside or in the mountains—that very Nature which they themselves have so inexorably banished. It would not be true to say that, in so doing, people are merely seeking to preserve their health. Many, if not all, are at the same time seeking a relaxation of soul that is accorded only by surroundings whose still unspoilt and harmonious state has ensured the preservation of such beauty as gives peace to the soul and frees the mind from the pressure of calculating thoughts. However, the same people who, when on holiday, consciously or unconsciously seek this beauty, quickly reject it as 'romanticism' whenever it stands in the way of their utilitarian interests. In this, the good or bad intention of the individual scarcely plays a role; everyone is under the pressure of economic forces, and it is usually unconscious self-defense if one hides from oneself the destructive consequences of certain developments. In the longer view, however, such an attitude is disastrous.

---

*From *Mirror of the Intellect*, Quinta Essentia, Cambridge, 1987. Reprinted by permission of World Wisdom, Inc.

Beauty always represents an inward and inexhaustible equilibrium of forces; and this overwhelms our soul, since it can neither be calculated nor mechanically produced. A sense of beauty can therefore permit us the direct experience of relationships before we can perceive them, in a differentiated manner, with our discursive reason; in this, incidentally, there is a defense for our own physical and psychic well-being, something that we cannot neglect with impunity.

To this it may be objected that men have always distinguished between the useful and the beautiful; a pleasure-grove was always a luxury, while a wood was usually viewed in a utilitarian manner. It might even be said that it took modern education to create the desire to protect a given piece of nature on purely aesthetic grounds.

However, in earlier times there were also sacred groves, which no axe might fell. They catered neither for use in the usual sense of this word nor for luxury. Beauty and reality—two qualities which the modern world spontaneously separates—were (and, for men who have a pre-modern view regarding the sacred, still are) united. Even today there are sacred woods in Japan and India, just as there were in pre-Christian Europe; we mention them here only as one example of sacred nature, for there are also sacred mountains, as well as—and this touches us more closely—sacred springs, rivers, and lakes. Even within Christendom, which generally avoids the veneration of the various phenomena of Nature, there were and are springs and lakes—for example, the well at Chartres and the spring at Lourdes—which, because of their connection with miraculous events, have come to be regarded as sacred. What is important here is not that some particular mountain or spring is regarded as sacred, and therefore inviolable; but that one particular phenomenon is invariably an example of a whole range of related things, of a complete order of Nature, which for a larger or smaller community of men is of vital importance, and expresses a higher or supernatural reality: thus, for the ancient Germans, the forest was the indispensable basis of their very life, and at the same time something of a temple, a place that harbored the Divine Presence. All forest had this quality and, in this sense, was inviolable. Since, however, the forests also had to be used, there were special sacred woods whose function was to recall the principial and spiritually significant inviolability of the forest as such. The case of the sacred cow among the Hindus is similar: in reality, for the Hindus, everything living is sacred, in other words, inviolable and symbolical, for, according to their doctrine, all consciousness participates in the Divine Spirit. Since, however, it is impossible everywhere and always to avoid the killing of living creatures, the law of inviolability was in practice limited to a few symbolic species, amongst which the cow, as the incarnation of the maternal mercy of the cosmos, assumes a special position. By renouncing the slaughtering of cows, the Hindu in principle venerates all life and at the same time protects one of the most important bases of his way of life, which for thousands of years has depended on cultivation and the raising of cattle. Likewise the sacred springs, of which there were many in Medieval Christendom, drew attention to the sacredness of water as such; they were a reminder that water is a symbol of grace, something that can readily be seen in the symbolism of baptism. The sacred is that which is the object of veneration and awe; it is the reflection of something eternal and therefore indestructible; and the inviolability which it enjoys stems directly therefrom.

Depending on which faith a people adheres to, and depending on their hereditary mentality, there are other natural or artificial things that they may regard as sacred. The four elements—air, fire, water, and earth—which are the most elementary modes of manifestation of all matter to offer themselves to our senses, are almost everywhere—with the exception of the modern, rationalistic world—endowed with the quality of sacredness; from this point of view, earth is illimitable, air is ungraspable, fire in its very nature is undefilable; only water is open to violation, and therefore commended to special protection.

To recapitulate: for pre-modern cultures, there are realities which transcend the level of mere utilitarianism and have precedence over them. There realities are in themselves of a purely spiritual or divine nature. They are however reflected in certain sensory appearances, which may consequently become the object of veneration and awe. These are then, either completely or in part (as representative symbols), withheld from the violent interference of men. Such an attitude is naturally very different from that of aesthetic sensitivity, which may also cause us, all considerations of usefulness apart, to admire and protect a natural phenomenon. But the sense of beauty is somehow contained within the veneration of the sacred; for the truly beautiful is that which lies hidden in the inexhaustible richness of harmoniously united possibilities. The same holds true for the sacred, and indeed for all phenomena and elements pertaining to the very bases of life, so that awe of the sacred also more or less directly contributes—not always in a predictable way—to the maintenance of life itself.

A few remarks should be made here regarding the elements: these have naturally nothing to do with what are called elements in modern chemistry but, as we have already said, represent the most elementary modes of manifestation in which the 'stuff on which the world is made' communicates itself to our five senses: the solid, the liquid, the aerial, and the fiery modes of manifestation. There are indeed other liquids besides water, but none has for us the same aspect of purity, and none plays such an important role in the preservation of life. Likewise there are other gaseous substances besides air, but none of them can be breathed.

Cosmically, then, the four elements are the simplest manifestational modes of matter. From an inward point of view, on the other hand, they are also the simplest images of our soul, which as such is ungraspable, but whose fundamental characteristics can be likened to the four elements. This is what St. Francis of Assisi has in mind when he praises God for the four elements, one after the other, in his famous Canticle of the Sun. In regard to water, he says: 'Praised be Thou, O Lord, for sister water, who is very useful, humble, precious, and chaste (*Laudato si, o Signore, per sor acqua, la quale e molto utile ed umile e preziosa e casta*).' That may sound like pure poetic allegory, but in fact it signifies very much more: humility and chastity well describe the quality of water which, in a river, takes on all forms, without thereby losing its purity. Herein also lies an image of the soul, which possesses the capacity to take in all impressions and to follow all forms while remaining true to its own undivided essence. 'The soul of man resembles water,' said Goethe, thereby reiterating an image that occurs in the Scriptures of both Near and Far East. The soul resembles water, just as the Spirit resembles wind or air.

It would lead us too far to mention all the myths and customs in which water appears as an image or reflection of the soul. An awareness that the soul recognizes itself when it beholds water—finding animation in its play, refreshment in its rest, and purity in its clarity—is perhaps nowhere more widespread than amongst the Japanese. The whole of Japanese life, to the extent that it is still formed by tradition, is penetrated by a sense of purity and pliant simplicity that finds its prefiguration in water. The Japanese make pilgrimages to the famous waterfalls of their country and will gaze for hours at the unruffled surface of a temple pond. Significant is the story of the Chinese sage Hsuyu—a recurring theme of Japanese painters—who received a message that the Emperor wished to hand over his kingdom to him; he fled to the mountains and washed his ears in a waterfall. The painter Harunobu represented him allegorically in the form of a young and noble maiden who, in the solitude of the mountains, washes her ear in the vertical fall of water.

For the Hindus, the water of life finds embodiment in the Ganges which, from its source in the Himalayas, the mountains of the Gods, irrigates the largest and most populous plains of India. Its water is held to be pure from beginning to end, and in fact it is preserved from all pollution by the fine sand which it drags along with it. Whoever, with repentant mind, bathes in the Ganges, is freed from all his sins: inner purification here finds its symbolic support in the outward purification that comes from the water of the sacred river. It is as if the purifying water came from Heaven, for its origin in the eternal ice of the roof of the world is like a symbol of the heavenly origin of divine grace which, as 'living water', springs from timeless and immutable Peace. Here, as in the similar rites of other religions and peoples, the correspondence of water and soul helps the latter to purify itself or, more exactly, to find anew its own—originally pure—essence. In this process, the symbol prepares the way for grace.

Water symbolizes the soul. From another point of view—but analogously—water symbolizes the *materia prima* of the whole universe. For, just as water contains within itself, as pure possibilities, all the forms which, in flowing and sparkling, it may assume, so *materia prima* contains all the forms of the world in a state of indistinction.

In the Biblical story of creation it is said that, in the beginning, before the creation of the earth, the Spirit of God moved upon the face of the waters; and the holy books of the Hindus tell us that all the inhabitants of the earth emerged from the primordial sea. In these myths, water is not meant in the ordinary sense of the word; and yet the picture they create in our imagination is in its own way correct, and as apt as possibly can be, for nothing conveys better the undifferentiated and passive unity of *materia prima*.

The myth of the creation of all things from the primordial sea finds an echo in the Koranic words: 'We have created every living thing from water'. The Biblical allegory of the Spirit of God moving upon the waters has its counterpart in the Hindu symbol of the divine swan Hamsa which, swimming on the primordial sea, hatches the golden egg of the world; and each of these allegorical representations is finally echoed in the Koran, where it is said that, at the beginning, the Throne of God was upon the water.

The opened lotus flower, the seat of Indian divinities, is also a 'throne of God' floating upon the water of *materia prima*, or upon the water of principial possibilities. This symbol, which was transmitted from Hindu to Buddhist mythology and art, brings us back from water as the image of the primordial substance of the world to water as the image of the soul. The lotus-stream of the Buddha or Boddhisattva rises up from the waters of the soul, just as the spirit, illumined by knowledge, frees itself from passive existence. Here water represents something which has to be overcome, but in which nevertheless there is good, because in it is rooted the flower whose calyx contains the 'precious jewel' of Bodhi, the Divine Spirit. The Buddha, the 'Jewel in the Lotus', is himself this Spirit.

That must suffice as a survey of the meanings which water can have as a symbol, though many other examples of this kind could be mentioned. But it is not merely a question of demonstrating that in all cultures that can be called pre-rationalist—and the term is not used pejoratively—water has more than a purely physical or biological meaning; the spiritual realities, of which it is the symbol, are never attached to it arbitrarily, but are directly and logically derived from its essence. The contemplative beholding of Nature which, through essential and constant appearances, perceives the timeless prototypes or causes of these appearances, is not something that is merely sentimental, nor is it bound to time and place, and this despite the fact of the modern world, from which this kind of contemplation seems to have been banished. We say 'seems', for such a contemplation of things is too deeply rooted in the human heart to be able to disappear completely. It even continues unconsciously, and it would not be difficult to show how the mysterious attraction of water as something sacred, as a symbolic and manifested expression of a psychic or cosmic reality, lives on in art, especially in painting and poetry. Who, when confronted with a pure mountain lake or with a spring gushing forth from the rock, has never felt at least something of the awe and veneration that are inseparable from anything sacred? The people of earlier times knew better than we that one does not disturb the balance of nature with impunity. Our superior scientific knowledge is totally insufficient to protect us from all the effects of a negative relation on the part of the physical environment, we would still have no guarantee that the psychic or subtle world would not take its revenge on us. A glance at Asia and Africa, where the spiritual equilibrium of ancient cultures has been disturbed on all sides, and their very existence called into question, is sufficient to let us sense that it may still come to a destruction of 'living waters', in comparison with which the pollution of our physical waters will seem harmless.

In conclusion, and by way of indicating that even in modern Europe there are still sacred waters, mention should be made of Lough Derg in Donegal, the most northerly county in Ireland. In this Lough is an island on which are a number of Christian shrines dating from the Middle Ages and also a cave, which represents the entry to the underworld. It is called 'St. Patrick's Purgatory', for it is said that it was here that St. Patrick, the Apostle of Ireland, made hell and the Mount of Purgatory appear to the heathen in a vision. Since the early Middle Ages, the island has been a place of pilgrimage, with which very strict rules are associated. The pilgrims, who are brought to the island by boat, must walk on it fasting, bare-footed, and carry out certain spiritual exercises during a stay of three days. These consist principally in kneeling on the rocks and praying before a number of crosses that have been erected in honor of the most important of the Irish saints. Each time a pilgrim completes his devotion before these 'stations', set out like the beads of a rosary, he makes his way to a large rock that rises out of the water at a little distance from the shore of the island, and, after a few prayers, recites aloud the creed, looking out over the water of the lake. People who have performed this pilgrimage declare that these moments of solitude, in contemplation of the unruffled lake, surrounded by uninhabited hills, release in their hearts something that is undescribable.

Both suns shine to us.   Boehme

Sabbaths 2006
III. The Book of Camp Branch*

Wendell Berry

Camp Branch, my native stream,
forever unreturning flows
from the town down to Cane Run
which flows to the river. It is
my native descent, my native
walk, my native thought
that stays and goes, passing
ever downward toward the sea.

Its sound is a song that flings up
light to the undersides of leaves.
Its song and light are a way
of walking, a way of thought
moved by sound and sight.

It flows as deep in its hollow
as it can go, far down as it has
worn its way. Passing down
over its plunder of rocks, it makes
an irregular music. Here
is what I want to know. Here
is what I am trying to say.

O brave Ross Feld, here is
no "fortification against time."
Here the fort has fallen
and the water passes its benediction
over the shards, singing!

*

---

*This poem and the following two poems copyright 2009 by Wendell Berry from the volume *Leavings*. Reprinted by permission of Counterpoint.

How much delight I've known
in navigating down the flow
by stepping stones, by sounding
stones, by words too that are
stepping and sounding stones.

Going down stone by stone,
the song of the water changes,
changing the way I walk
which changes my thought
as I go. Stone to stone
the stream flows. Stone to stone
the walker goes. The words
stand stone still until
the flow moves them, changing
the sound—a new word—
a new place to step or stand.

                    *

In the notch of Camp Branch
the footing changes, year
to year, sometimes
day to day, as the surges
of the stream move the rocks.
Every walk, as Archie Ammons
said, "is a new walk." And so

go slow. Let the mind
step with the feet
as the stream steps
downward over the rocks
nowhere anywhere
but where it is.

                    *

In the crease of its making
the steep stream gathers
the seeps that come silently
down from the wooded slants.
Only here at the rockbed
of the branch do the waters break
into light, into singing

of water flowing over rocks
which, in its motion, the water
moves. And so, singing, the song
changes, moved by music
harsh and crude: splashes,
slubbers, chuckles and warbles,
the hollow tones of a bell,
a sustained pour, the small
fall steady as a column.

Sometimes, gentled, if you
stand while it flows, it seems
to meditate upon itself
and the hill's long changing
under sun and rain.

                    *

A changing song,
a changing walk,
a changing thought.

A sounding stone,
a stepping stone,
a word
that is a sounding and a stepping
stone.

A language that is a stream flowing
and is a man's thoughts as he
walks and thinks beside the stream.

His thoughts will hold
if the words will hold, if each
is a stone that will bear weight,
placed by the flow
in the flow. The language too

descends through time, subserving
false economy, heedless power,
blown with the gas of salesmanship,
rattled with the sale of needless war,

worn by the mere unhearing
babble of thoughtlessness,
and must return to its own
downward flow by the flowing
water, the muttered syllables,
the measureless music, the stream
flowing and singing, the man
walking and thinking, balanced
on unsure footholds
in the flowing stream.

*

"Make sense," I told myself,
the song of the tumbling waters
in my ears. The sense you make
may make its way along the stream
but it will not be the stream's sense
you make, nor yet your own
quite, for the flux of language
will make its claim too
upon your walk, upon the stream.

The words fall at last
onto the page, the turning leaf
in the Book of Camp Branch
in time's stream. As the eye,
as the mind, moves from
moving water to turning page,
what is lost? What, worse,
is lost if the words falsify
the stream in your walk beside it?
To be carried or to resist
you must be a stone
in the way. You must be
a stone rolled away.

                    *

The song changes by singing
into a different song.
It sings by falling. The water
descending in its old groove
wears it new. The words descending
to the page render the possible
into the actual, by wear,
for better or worse, renew
the wearied mind. This is only
the lowly stream of Camp Branch,
but every stream is lowly.
Only low in the land does
the water flow. It goes
to seek the level that is lowest,
the silence that gathers
many songs, the darkness
made of many lights,
and then by the sun is raised
again into the air.

Sabbaths 2006
V.

Little stream, Camp Branch, flowing
through the ever-renewing
woods on the steep slopes
by what name did the Shawnee
call you? We live briefly in time
longer than we will live to know.
When we who know you by name
are gone, what will they call you?
When our nation has fallen as all
things fall, when the Constitution
is only another paper god, prayed to
and lied to by only another
autocrat, what will they call you?
When our kind has gone
as all things go, and you remain,
your tumbles catching and returning
light to the air as beautifully
as before, will only the angels
name you and praise you then?

Sabbaths 2007
XIII.

"The past above, the future below
and the present pouring down . . ."
wrote Dr. Williams. Is that
correct? Or is the future above
and the past below?

                    The stream
that is departing from itself as
it was is above and is the past.
The stream that is coming to itself
as it will be is below and is
the future. Or:

                    The stream yet
to come is above and is the future.
The stream that has gone by
is below and is the past.

In its riddles in the world
in the mind in the world
the stream is the stream
beyond words, beginning nowhere,
ending nowhere.

                    It falls as rain.
It flows in all its length. It enters
finally the sea. It rises into the air.
It falls as rain. To the watcher
on the shore, it comes and it
goes.

The immeasurable, untestable,
irrecoverable moment of its passing
is the present, always already
past before we can say that it is
present, that it was the future
flowing into the past or is
the past flowing into the future

or both at once into the present
that is ever-passing and eternal,
the instantaneous, abounding life.

Wandering Thoughts on Rumi, Water, Music, Love, and Identity

Coleman Barks

The big collection of Rumi's odes (*ghazals*) and quatrains (*rubai*), entitled the *Divani Shamsi Tabriz* (The Works of Shams of Tabriz), is sometimes called simply *The Shams*.

Say the present moment is in motion as water is. Consciousness is also moving like an ocean, infinitely responsive. An ocean is a fluid web of interconnectivity, as is a human being, and moreso, a friendship. Say music comes from the edge where personal consciousness dissolves into soul.

Rumi's poetry in *The Shams* comes out of his friendship with Shams Tabriz, which is one of the most mysterious of all religious icons, that friendship. It feels, as it gets experienced in the poetry, very alive and free and dangerous. His image for both his poetry and the friendship with Shams is "an ocean with no shore."

Here is an ode.

Entirely Jewels

Notice how each particle moves.
Notice how everyone has just arrived from a journey.
Notice how each wants a different food.
Notice how the stars vanish as the sun comes up,
    how all streams stream toward the ocean.

Look at the chefs preparing special plates for everyone,
    according to what they need.
Look at this cup that can contain the ocean.
Look at those who see the face.
Look through Shams' eyes
    into the water that is entirely jewels.

#1910

And here is this quatrain about the nature of such friendship as a drowning of self within self that gives the wet shine of sacredness to everything.

Would you like to have revealed to you the truth of the friend?
Leave the rind, and descend into the pith.
Fold within fold, the beloved drowns in his own being.
This world is drenched in that drowning.

#330

The ocean-form of *The Shams* cares for each particular as it absorbs it into itself. As you read these poems you must leave your Whitmanic beachwalk-observer-self and dive in. This kind of self-transcendence requires risk.

You have been walking the ocean's edge, holding up your robes to
    keep them dry.
You must dive naked under and deeper under, a thousand times deeper.
Love flows down.

(Love comes with a knife....)

One of the strangest, and most original, water images is found in Book II of
Rumi's *Masnavi*, ll. 1193-1214. It is a surreal, emblematic scene. There is a
thirsty man on a wall built on the edge of a stream. He is gradually disman-
tling the wall, and *going down,* to get closer to the streamwater that his thirst
is drawing him toward. As he throws big chunks of masonry into the stream,
he falls in love with the sound. Who wouldn't? But the *water itself* is curious
about this kind of love, so it asks him, and he answers.

There is a high wall on the bank of a clear creek
    with a man sitting on top of the wall,
    a grieving, thirsty man.

The height of the wall, of course,
    keeps him from getting down to the water to drink.

Suddenly he pries loose a brick and throws it in the stream.
The sound of it plunging into water makes such delicious noise
    in his ears, he tears off another and heaves it in, another, another.

The melding waterstone sounds are like the spoken words
    of a close friend.
He begins to get tipsy with the water's talking.
Finally the water itself, apart from the bricks being thrown,
    asks him to explain himself.

I have two purposes. First, this plunging sound is rebeck and trumpet
    and drum to me.

As thunder delights a spring garden needing rain, as alms come to a
    beggar, like release to an inmate, like the wind of grace that came
    to Muhammad in Yemen, like the fragrance of Joseph to his lean
    father, Jacob.

That music is the deep reason I do this demolition.
Also, it is helping me come closer to the stream.

This deconstruction work brings me lower like full prostration
    in prayer.
The loosening of the mortar humbles me into the flow of my longing,
    and the more in love one is with the double-chunk sound that the
    masonry makes as it enters the river, the lovelier is one's ruinous
    descent.

Those not in love with this delapidation watermusic hear only
    the flat slap of brick hitting liquid.

Rumi loves the boundary, the membrane, between form and the whole (dew-drop and ocean, grape and wine). There is music there, and a kind of ecstatic hypnotic trance, as the ego dissolves and a wider self takes over, a listening, more musical, self.

    Another passage from the *Masnavi,* Book IV.

Philosophers have said that we love music
because it resembles the sphere-sounds of union.

We have been part of a harmony before, so these moments of treble
    and bass keep our remembering fresh.

But how does this happen within these dense bodies full
    of forgetfulness and doubt and grieving?

It is like water passing through us.
It becomes acidic and bitter,
but still as urine it retains watery qualities.
It will put out a fire.

So there is this music flowing through our bodies that can dowse
    restlessness.

Hearing the sound, we gather strength.
Love kindles with melody.

Music feeds a lover composure, and provides form for the imagination.
Music breathes on personal fire and makes it keener.

The waterhole is deep.
A thirsty man climbs a walnut tree growing next to the pool
    and drops walnuts one by one into the beautiful place.

He listens carefully to the sound as they hit and watches the bubbles.

A more rational, less entranced, man gives advice,
You will regret doing this. You are so far from the water
    that by the time you get down to gather walnuts,
    the water will have carried them away.

The listener replies. *I am not here for walnuts.*
I want the music they make when they hit.

                      (lines 733-751)

There is music at the verge, on the beach-edge of surrender, as particles push into and become, the whole. Remember the woman singing by the sea in Wallace Stevens' "The Idea of Order at Key West."

And when she sang, the sea,
Whatever self it had, became the self
That was her song, for she was the maker.

And Plotinus, his wonderful metaphor for what soul is. A net thrown in the sea. That is what we are with our great longing, our works of art, our civilizations, our loving. We are the net. The cosmos is the net. Soul is the substance we live within. But we cannot *own* any of it. We cannot hold it, this surround that we so love. We ache to hold it, we long to. And somehow the longing is there because of soul. As Rumi says, *The ocean swims in the fish.* We are, and we are swimming inside, a love we cannot quite hold or embody.

Here is the relevant passage from Plotinus, Ennead IV. Section 9.

The cosmos is like a net thrown into the sea, unable to make that in which is its own. Already the sea is spread out, and the net spreads with it as far as it can, for no one of its parts can be anywhere else than where it is. But because it has no size The Soul's nature is sufficiently able to contain the whole cosmic body in one and the same grasp.

(Elmer O'Brien's translation)

That's what the mystics call oneness, that grasp. Rumi dove deep into Plotinus.

So there is music flowing through us, an ocean-flood of soul-identity. That mystery is addressed in Shams' quatrain.

I/you/he/she/we/you/they
In the garden of mystical lovers
these are not true distinctions.

Here's a related quatrain of Rumi's I only recently discovered.

I am the soul in a hundred thousand bodies.
What is soul? What is body? I am both,
        and there is someone else I am as well.

In order to please that one
I take on various personalities.
I say my lines.

#1238

I cannot paraphrase the watery truth about identity here, but I feel it is so, nameless.

Rumi says *Poems are rough notations for the music we are.* But those notations cannot be *experienced* like the music can.

Poems derive from a source we cannot know. Rumi calls it *a pearl somewhere on the ocean floor.*

Poems reach up like spindrift
and the edge of driftwood along the beach, wanting.

#110

Language is like spray and the flotsam leavings, momentarily clear of and apart from the mystery of the seawater itself, which can have no name. But sometimes Rumi calls that oceanic place *love*. And of the lover's religion, he can only say what it is *not*.

Know this. A lover cannot be a muslim.
In the love religion there is no doctrine and no blasphemy.
No body, no soul, no reason, no heart.

If you are not that empty, you are not a lover.

#768

We live much of our lives (the best parts), I feel, longing and waiting for that pure absence, the emptiness of the lover, free of mental concepts, ocean with no shore. Experience indefinable, in motion, like every poem Rumi ever wrote.

The ground is turning green.
The king's drum begins. Light arrives. Get up.

Commentaries on the heart have come in seven volumes.
A love-messenger runs with his head down
    like an ink pen giving sweetness to the page.

The pure spirits gather again, the ones we thought were dead.
Planets go anywhere they want.
Venus sways drunkenly over to the North Star.
The moon holds on to Leo.

I hope everything is all right.

The host who has no self has come.

Now it is our turn to look into those eyes.

A child is still a child even after it has learned the alphabet.
Joy reaches into the mountains.
Solomon holds out a morning cup, *Welcome.*
Sit down in this dazzling pavilion.
Be silent, and let the poet sing the delight that never ends.

That is #882 in the standard Furuzanfar edition. The poems do not have titles in Persian, so they feel even more watery and elusive. I have called that one "Our Turn." In Rumi's poetic tradition it is customary for the poet to mention his own name at the end as a way of signing it. Rumi never claims authorship. Instead he mentions Shams, or sunlight (*shams* means *the sun*), or, as here, silence (*khamush),* as a way of expressing the dissolving of ego into the whole, which is the subtle, ineffable mystery of this friendship, a non-dual, non-relationship, love that widens out into weather, light, landscape, and "what anybody says."

The Japanese tea master Sen no Rikyu built a teahouse on the side of a hill overlooking the sea. Three guests were invited to the inaugural tea ceremony. Hearing about the beautiful site, they expected to find a structure that took advantage of the wonderful view. After arriving at the garden gate, they were perplexed to discover a grove of trees had been planted that obstructed the panorama. Before entering the teahouse, the guests followed the traditional custom of purifying their hands and mouths at the stone basin near the entry. Stooping to draw water with a bamboo ladle, they noticed an opening in the trees that provided a vision of the sparkling sea. In that humble position they awakened to the relationship between the cool liquid in the ladle and the ocean in the distance, between their individuality and the ocean of life.

From *The Temple in the House* by Anthony Lawlor

The Quranic Symbolism of Water*

Martin Lings

In the Qur'ān the ideas of Mercy and water—in particular rain—are in a sense inseparable. With them must be included the idea of Revelation (*tanzīl*), which means literally 'a sending down'. The Revelation and the rain are both 'sent down' by the All-Merciful, and both are described throughout the Qur'ān as 'Mercy', and both are spoken of as 'life-giving'. So close is the connection of ideas that rain might even be said to be an integral part of the Revelation which it prolongs,[1] as it were, in order that by penetrating the material world the Divine Mercy may reach the uttermost confines of creation; and to perform the rite of ablution is to identify oneself, in the world of matter, with this wave of Mercy, and to return with it as it ebbs back towards the Principle, for purification is a return to our origins. Nor is Islam—literally 'submission'—other than non-resistance to the pull of the current of this ebbing wave.

The Origin and end of this wave lie in the Treasuries (*khazā'in*) of the water which are with Us (XV:21). *The Treasuries of Mercy* are also spoken of in just the same terms; and it is clear that these Treasuries are no less than the Supreme Source of Mercy Himself, *ar-Raḥmān*, the Infinitely Good. The Qur'ān also speaks of its own Archetype, *the Mother of the Book*, which is the Divine Omniscience, nor can this Treasury be set apart from those of Mercy, for it likewise belongs to *ar-Raḥmān*, who is the Source of the Book: *The Infinitely Good taught the Qur'ān* (LV:1). We have already seen the connection between mercy and comprehension;[2] and the Treasuries of Water comprise both these aspects of *ar-Raḥmān*, for water is a symbol of Knowledge as well as of Mercy. Al-Ghazālī remarks, with regard to the verse *He sendeth down water from heaven, so that valleys are in flood with it, each according to its capacity* (XIII:17). 'The commentaries tell us that the water is Gnosis and that the valleys are Hearts'.[3]

---

1. Far from being a 'concrete' image arbitrarily chosen by man to illustrate some 'abstract' idea; a symbol is, as we have seen, the manifestation, in some lower mode, of the higher reality which it symbolizes and which stands in as close a relationship to it as root of tree to leaf. Thus water is Mercy; and it would be true to say that even without any understanding of symbolism and even without belief in the Transcendent, immersion in water has an inevitable effect upon the soul in addition to its purification of the body. In the absence of ritual intention, this effect may be altogether momentary and superficial; it is none the less visible on the face of almost any bather emerging from a lake or river or sea, however quickly it may be effaced by the resumption of 'ordinary life'.

2. See p. 44 (in *Symbol and Archetype*-Eds.).

3. *Mishkāt al-Anwār*.

Symbol and Archetype: A Study in the Meaning of Existence. Fons Vitae, 2006.

The differentiation here is in the varying capacities of the valleys, not in the water itself, which has come directly from above and has yet to undergo the influences of soil or stone or mineral. But water which comes up from the earth is in fact differentiated, so that it symbolizes different aspects of knowledge as in the following verse: *And when Moses asked for water for his people, and We said: 'Strike with thy staff the rock', and there gushed forth from it twelve springs, everyone knew his drinking place* (II:60). The differentiation here is not only in the drinkers but also in what they drink; and the last five words are quoted throughout Islamic literature to refer beyond their literal meaning, to the fact that everyone who 'drinks' from the Qur'ān is aware of the particular standpoint that has been providentially allotted to him whether it be that of ritual law, for example, dogmatic theology, or mysticism. Nor is it out of line with the literal meaning, if one remembers that in ancient Israel, each of the twelve tribes had its own particular function.

When the Qur'ān tells us that at the Creation *His Throne was upon the water* (XI:7), it affirms implicitly two waters, one above the Throne and one beneath it, since the Tenant of the Throne is *ar-Raḥmān* with Whom are the Treasuries of Water, or rather Who constitutes Himself these Treasuries. From this duality, the Waters of the Unmanifest and the waters of Manifestation,[4] is the prototype of the duality, within creation, of the two seas which are so often mentioned in the Qur'ān.[5] *These two seas one sweet and fresh, the other salt and bitter* (XXV:53) are respectively Heaven and earth which were originally *one piece* (XXI:30). Parallel to this and in a sense based on it, is the Sufi symbolism of ice, for salt water and ice, both representing the untranscendent, are both 'gross' albeit in different ways, when compared with fresh water. It is true that the ocean, as the vastest thing in the whole terrestrial globe, has an altogether transcendent significance. When the Qur'ān says: *If the sea were ink for the Words of my Lord, the sea would be used up before the Words of the Lord were used up* (XVIII:109) it is saying that the symbol is not to be compared with That which symbolizes, namely *the Mother of the Book*, the Sea which is in fact vast enough to contain the Words of God. None the less, by choosing the material seas rather than any other earthly thing for this demonstration, the Qur'ān affirms that they are, for the Infinitude of the Divine Wisdom, the symbol of symbols; but they have this symbolism in virtue of their size, apart from and as it were despite their saltness, for salt water as such is always transcended by fresh water.

The significance of a symbol varies according to whether it is considered as an independent entity or in relation to some other symbol. In relation to wine, water—even fresh water—may represent the untranscendent or the less transcendent, as for example when the Qur'ān mentions that in Paradise the elect are given wine to drink whereas the generality of the faithful

---

4. In Genesis also the pure primordial substance of the created universe is water. *The Spirit of God moved upon the face of the waters.*

5. So too in Genesis *He divided the waters.*

drink from fountains of water. This relationship between wine and water is analogous to the relationship between the sun and the moon, for wine is in a sense 'liquid fire' or 'liquid light': but fire and water, inasmuch as both are elements, are on the same plane, and it is possible to consider wine and water as equal complements. Thus in another description of Paradise, the Qur'ān mentions *rivers of water and rivers of wine* without specifying any difference of level. Here it may be said that wine, being 'warm', has the 'subjective' significance of Gnosis in relation to the cold objectivity of water which represents Truth, the Object of Gnosis. But when considered by itself, water has a total significance which transcends the distinction between subject and object, or which includes both subject and object, for inasmuch as it can be drunk, water is a symbol of Truth 'subjectivized', that is, Gnosis; and water can indeed claim to be 'the drink of drinks'. In any case, whatever the drink, water is always its basis.

The following passage, the first part of which has already been quoted in connection with Gnosis, is particularly important for its illustration of the difference between the true and the false, or reality and illusion: *He sendeth down water from heaven so that valleys are in flood with it, each according to its capacity, and the flood beareth swelling foam... thus God coineth the symbols of reality and illusion. Then as for the foam, it goeth as scum upon the banks, and as for what profiteth men, it remaineth in the earth.* In the light of this imagery of the scum which remains visible and the water which disappears we may interpret the verse: *They know only an outward appearance of this lower life* (XXX:7). The outward appearance is 'the scum of illusion', whereas what escapes us in this world is the hidden 'water of reality'. We see here the significance of the fountain which holds such an important place in Quranic symbolism. The bursting forth of a spring, that is, the reappearance of heaven-sent water that has become hidden signifies the sudden unveiling of a reality which transcends 'outward appearances', and the drinking of which is Gnosis. But in addition to this objective-subjective symbolism, the fountain has also the purely subjective significance of the sudden opening of an eye, which is implicit in the word *'ayn* which means both 'fountain' and 'eye'. This subjective symbolism is in a sense the more important, because the reason why men see only 'the scum of illusion' is that *their hearts are hardened*, or in other words that 'the eye of the Heart' is closed, *for verily it is not the sight that is blind but the hearts that are blind* (XXII:47); and in one highly suggestive passage the Qur'ān compels us to envisage the possibility of a fountain springing from the Heart: *Then even after that your hearts grew hard so that they were like rocks, or even harder, for verily there are rocks from which rivers gush forth, and there are rocks which split asunder so that water floweth from them* (II:74).

The presence between the two seas of *a barrier beyond which they pass not*, means that the waters of this world are unable to overflow into the next, and that the upper waters refrain from utterly overwhelming the lower waters and allow them to exist as a seemingly separate domain without undue interference from above, at any rate *for a while*—to use the Quranic phrase which is so often repeated to denote the impermanence of this world and everything in it. 'Undue' is a necessary reservation, because the upper waters by their very nature cannot altogether be kept out, any more than water—to revert to the Sufi symbolism—can be kept out of ice. The upper waters, being the original substance to all creation, not only surround but also penetrate this world as its secret reality to which it will eventually return. Thus although the rain, symbolizing this penetration, is only sent down *in due measure*, it is none the less a herald or portent of the *Hour*,[6] that is, the Last Day, when the barrier will be removed and the upper waters will flood this world, transforming its nature and causing the resurrection of the dead, for they are the Waters of Life.

Until then, any presence of life in this world means that a drop of these waters has passed the barrier, but this possibility is limited. *Verily this lower life is but as water which We have sent down from the sky* (X:24). Life is altogether transcendent in relation to this world, where it exists merely as a fleeting loan, ready to 'evaporate' back whence it came as water evaporates back to the sky. Life is a passing trespass of the Beyond on the domain of the herebelow, a brief penetration of soul and body by the Spirit;[7] but the Spirit is not 'at home' in this world—hence the extreme precariousness of life[8]—whereas it is indeed at home in the Beyond: *Verily the Abode of the Hereafter, that, that is Life, did they but know* (XXIX:64).

If it be asked how this symbolism can be reconciled with the earth-depopulating Flood, it must be remembered that although rainfall set the Flood in motion, the actual cataclysm is represented in the Qur'ān as a stormy sea. One of Noah's sons who was drowned is said to have been swept away by a wave, and agitated water is a symbol of vanity and illusion, the waves being images of accident and vicissitude, which are 'unreal'[9] in relation to the water itself whose true nature they are powerless to affect. It is significant that in the Verse of Darkness (XXIV:40) which follows close on the better known Verse of Light, the works of the infidels, having just been likened in their vanity to *a mirage in the desert which the thirsty man reckoneth to be water*, are then immediately likened to what is indeed water but has become 'by accident' so remote from its true nature as to be comparable to a mirage, namely a dark storm-tossed sea. This passage may even be taken as an inex-

---

6. *And thou seest the earth barren, and when We send down upon it water it thrilleth and sprouteth... that is because... the Hour is coming beyond all doubt and because God raiseth those who are in the tombs* (XXII:5).

7. To speak of death as 'a giving up of the ghost' is thus altogether correct; and it is because life is a presence of the Spirit, and therefore altogether transcendent, that it defies any scientific analysis.

8. The great symbol of life is also most precarious over much of the earth's face, especially in those regions where the Quranic Revelation was first received.

9. Ice and waves are parallel as symbols, representing respectively the rigidity (or brittleness) and instability of this form-bound world.

plicit description of the Flood. In any case, there is no doubt that the waves of the flood and the waves of the Red Sea which crashed down upon the pursuers of the children of Israel are a just 'payment in kind' for the passionate perversity of Noah's contemporaries, and of Pharaoh and his ministers. On the other hand, as regards what set the Flood in motion, the symbolism of rain is here tempered and conditioned by the number forty which signifies death[10] or a change of state. Thus the purifying aspect of water may be said to take precedence here over its life-giving aspect. The earth was to be purified for a new state just as the children of Israel were to be purified by the forty years wandering in the desert. We may compare also the purification of Lent. The waters of the Flood were an inseparable part of the Revelation made to Noah of a new religion, symbolized by the Ark, and as such they were waters of Mercy. But any manifestation of Mercy is bound to be terrible for those who refuse it, for it serves to gauge the extreme hardness of their hearts, while for those whose hearts are not hardened the Transcendent is always awe-inspiring, and this aspect of Mercy is expressed by the thunder which so often precedes the rain. *He it is who showeth you the lightning, a fear and a longing, and raiseth the heavy clouds. And the thunder extolleth and praiseth Him, as do the angels for awe of Him* (XIII:12-13).

The awe-inspiring and mysterious transcendence of the upper waters, as also their life-giving aspect, is stressed in the strange and elliptical story of Moses and al-Khiḍr (XVIII:60-82). Moses says to Joshua: *I will not cease until I reach the meeting place of the two seas.* They start out as for a long journey, but they stop for rest on a rock which is, unknown to them, the barrier that separates the two seas. Joshua sets down for a moment the provisions he has brought, which consists of a dried fish; and whether because of the extreme nearness of the Waters of Life, or because a drop of these waters actually falls on the fish, it suddenly comes to life, slips from the rock, and swims away in the sea. Moses does not notice this; and the attention of Joshua who does notice it, is immediately distracted by Satan, so that he does not even mention it to Moses, and they set off once more. At length Moses, exhausted by the journey, suggests that they stop to eat. Joshua remembers that their food has gone, and tells Moses about the miracle of the fish, and Moses understands that the rock must have been *the meeting place of the two seas*, and they retrace their steps. When they regain the rock they find there one of our slaves unto whom *We had given mercy from Our Mercy and knowledge from Our Knowledge.* This person is not named, but the commentaries tell us that it is al-Khiḍr, the immortal Prince of the Solitary Ones (*al-afrād*).[11]

---

10. The Arabic letter *mīm* stands for death (*mawt*), and has the numerical value of 40. But this letter and this number have also the sense of reconciliation and return to the Principle. It is said that Seth was able to return to the Earthly Paradise and that he remained there for 40 years: see René Guénon, The *Lord of the World* (Ellingstring, Yorkshire, 1983), chapter 5.

11. These are the few exceptional individuals who are independent of any particular religion but who represent religion in its highest aspect, being, without any effort on

The symbolism of this meeting with Moses is parallel to the symbolism of the meeting of the two seas. The salt sea of this world represents, like Moses, exoteric knowledge,[12] whereas the Waters of Life are personified by al-Khiḍr. Moses said unto him: *May I follow thee that from what thou hast been taught thou mayst teach me right guidance. He said: Verily thou canst not be patient with me, for how shouldst thou be patient in respect of that which is beyond the compass of thine experience? He said: God willing, thou shalt find me patient, nor will I gainsay thee in aught. He said: Then if thou go with me, question me of naught until of myself I mention it to thee.*

They set out together, and al-Khiḍr performs three acts of mercy in disguise, but Moses, seeing only the 'scandalous' outside of these acts, is too outraged not to expostulate each time, and the third time al-Khiḍr refuses to let him accompany him any further; but he explains, before they part company, the true nature of his actions. To consider this passage in any detail would be beyond the scope of our subject; but it has at least given us a glimpse of the deviousness of the exoteric path and the extreme nearness of the Waters of Life. For we are already, if only we knew it, at the meeting place of the two seas—witness the miracle of life which is always with us, both in us and about us, but which the powers of illusion persuade us to take entirely for granted.

In setting before us this strange example of inadvertence and forgetfulness in respect of the marvelous incident of the fish, the Qur'ān lays bare the general obtuseness of man's attitude towards Life. There is only One Life, that of the Living, in varying degrees of radiation, with a mere difference of intensity between the elixir strong enough to quicken a dried fish and the less strong elixir which suffices to enable the living to continue to eke out *for a while* their precarious earthly existence. It is thus grossly disproportionate to marvel at the one and to remain unmoved by the other. There can be no true wisdom which does not include the enlightenment of seeing life as the miracle that it is, a supernatural interference which cannot be claimed by nature as a purely natural phenomenon. The Shaykh al-'Alawī tells us that the Divine mystery and miracle of life eludes us because of its extreme transcendence. It is with us, and yet at the same time it is utterly beyond us.[13] The spiritual path is in one sense not so much a journey as a gradual attunement of the soul to the presence of the Spirit, a gradual reconciliation between the natural and the supernatural, between the lower waters and the upper waters, between mind and intellect, between Moses and al-Khiḍr.

In conclusion let us consider another relevant passage, which is from the story of Solomon and the Queen of Sheba (XXVII:20-24). Solomon sends

their part but by their very nature as it were, 'throw-backs' to the primordial state of man which it is the purpose of religion to regain.

12. The Qur'ān here as it were extracts from Moses one aspect only to correspond to the symbolism of the lower waters, passing over his more exalted aspects which are the theme of other passages.

13. See Martin Lings, *A Sufi Saint of the Twentieth Century*, p. 134, note 1.

for the Queen in order to convert her to the true religion, and while she and her retinue are on their way he says to his surrounding assembly of men and of jinn: *Which of you will bring me her throne before they come unto me in surrender?* The throne is immediately set before him, and he gives instructions for it to be disguised:

> *Disguise her throne for her; we shall see if she is on the right path, or if she is of those who are not rightly guided. And when she came it was said unto her: Is thy throne like unto this? She said: It is as if it were it. And (Solomon reflected) we had been given the knowledge before her and had surrendered unto God; and she was barred from it by what she was wont to worship apart from God. Verily she was from a disbelieving people. She was told: Enter the courtyard; and when she saw it she reckoned it to be a pool of water and bared her legs. He said: It is a courtyard made smooth with glass. She said: O my Lord, verily I have done wrong unto my soul, and I surrender with Solomon unto God, the Lord of the Worlds.*

The gist of what this exceedingly elliptical narration tells us is that Solomon puts Bilqīs—for so the queen is named—to two tests. She fails in both, but her failure dissolves altogether her resistance to the truth. This in itself would require no comment. It is true that the mistakes in question are, on the surface, totally innocent. Moreover, as regards the throne, she appears to see at least partially through the disguise, since otherwise her answer would have been simply no. None the less it is easily imaginable that the consciousness of being mistaken might well have a profound effect upon the soul, out of all proportion to the nature of the error. But the apparent simplicity of the facts is belied by the gravity of the Qur'ān's comments on them, and the depth of the conclusions that are drawn. We are obliged to suspect that it is not merely a question of error as such, but that the particular nature of the error is all important. In both cases it is a question of failure to penetrate through a disguise. What Solomon says about his purpose in disguising the throne could be glossed: We shall see if she penetrates to the truth of things or if she is one of those who stop short at the 'scum' of illusion. This gloss could be applied also to the other disguise, that of the courtyard. The 'scum' in this case is the illusion that water is present when in fact it is absent. But what is the knowledge which Solomon was given *before her* and of which the condition is that he had *surrendered unto God?* It could not simply be what the words literally suggest, his knowledge that the throne was in fact that of Sheba, and that the courtyard was in fact paved with glass. Such knowledge was no more credit to him than the lack of it was a discredit to her. But we are given a key in the reason why *she was barred from it*, namely her worship of false gods. It was because she took illusion to be reality that she had taken reality to be illusion, that is, she had taken identity to be a mere deceptive likeness. Having demonstrated this last error—for although the Qur'ān does not say so we must assume that Solomon tells her that the throne is in fact hers and that what she had thought to be no more than a vague resemblance is indeed identity—he proceeds to demonstrate the opposite error which is its cause, that is, her worship of false gods, her imagining divinity to be present when in fact it was absent. Here lies undoubtedly what might be called the allegorical meaning of the above-quoted verses. We must remember that when this passage was revealed, the Prophet was undergoing great difficulties for the very reason that the chief men of Mecca were blinded to the presence of truth in his message by their erroneous belief that the truth was present elsewhere, in their own worship of false gods. There are many other passages in the Qur'ān which likewise recount a historical incident which is, in one way or another, analogous to the situation in early seventh century Arabia. Solomon here stands for the Prophet, and Bilqīs sums up in herself the erring leaders of the clans of Quraysh who would not surrender to the One True God because of their involvement with a plurality of false gods. But this allegorical admonition to the chieftains of Mecca and the example of repentance which it holds out to them leaves room for a deeper interpretation that throws light on some of the details which the allegory does not account for.

The Supreme Throne is below its Tenant, but by inverse analogy every earthly throne may be said to transcend the king who sits on it, as is to be seen figured in the Seal of Solomon, if we take the apex of a triangle to be the tenant and its base the throne. Significant of the throne's transcendence is its oneness and its permanence: kings come and go, but their throne remains, ideally, forever unchanged. The question of the throne of Sheba is not that part of the Quranic narrative which is directly relevant to our theme, but it cannot be set on one side, and it serves to bring out a point of general importance, namely that a symbol which represents the transcendent may be said to open out virtually onto the Absolute Transcendent.[14] The higher of *the two seas* is strictly speaking no more than the uppermost part of the created universe; but these Waters of Life, seen from below, are merged with the Treasuries of Water, that is, with the Infinite Beatitude. Now since there is a certain analogy between the pairs Heaven-earth (*the two seas*) and throne-king, the throne may be said to signify not merely the mandate of Heaven but also the Source of that mandate, the Divine King, and thus ultimately the Supreme Self.

In considering Solomon's first test it must not be forgotten that Bilqīs is a queen. Her first lapse has thus to be defined, in all accuracy, as that of a queen failing to recognize her own throne, and seen in this light it takes on a more serious aspect. Moreover, like the lapses of Moses and Joshua with regard to the miracle of the quickening of the dried fish, the incident of the throne has a general application, for every man is by definition king of the earth and thereby the possessor of a throne which is his mandate from

14. This is an altogether universal principle of the highest practical significance. In Hinduism for example Shiva and Vishnu may be invoked as Absolute, though their hierarchic station is at the level of the higher of the two seas.

Heaven. Even in later times men are still conscious of being kings inasmuch as they have powers of intelligence and of will which incomparably surpass those of other creatures; but the majority are more or less in a state of vagueness and uncertainty about their throne, and more or less forgetful that although it, that is, the mandate, is always veiled from them or 'disguised', it is always one and the same. In other words, they are no longer kings except by virtuality; in actuality they are usurpers, since veritable kingship implies an as it were organic connection between king and throne. For the perfect king that mandate, not his human subjectivity, is his true ego, one with the Divine Self. The failure to recognize the throne is thus a violation of the Gnostic precept *Know Thyself*, whereas fulfillment of this principle is *the knowledge* which Solomon *had been given*, and of which the condition is surrender (*islām*) in its highest sense, that is, effacement of the human ego before the Supreme Subject.

The precise words with which Bilqīs answers the question that is put to her are subtly significant in this respect—subtly because there is here a disguise which is in a sense analogous to that of the throne. It is permissible to say for example, that in such a sentence as 'when asked the colour of snow, the blind man said it was black', the word 'white' is disguisedly present, because it is forced into the mind. So also when the queen is asked, Is thy throne like this? And when she wrongly answers: It is as if it were it, the right answer is forced into our minds, namely 'it is it'; and these words, *huwa huwa* (literally 'he is he', for *'arsh*, throne, is masculine) constitute the Arabic formula for expressing identity and above all, liturgically,[15] the Supreme Identity.

As Solomon's second test which serves to demonstrate why she could not recognize her throne, the meaning remains much the same as in the allegorical interpretation. There, however, what seems to be present but is in fact absent is Truth as Object, whereas here it is rather a question of Truth in the sense of Subjective Reality. In either case we are reminded of the already quoted verse which likens the works of the disbelievers to *a mirage in the desert which the thirsty man accounteth to be water;* and it will be understood from this and the other examples given of the symbolism of water why Solomon's strategy is so powerfully successful: when she lifts up her robes to avoid wetting them and steps onto the glass pavement of the court, the sudden contact of her foot with the opposite of what it had expected is a directly sensed experience of error, enough in itself to produce a profound 'alchemical' effect upon the soul; but this effect is aggravated beyond all measure by her consciousness that the error is, precisely, about water. Thus her whole outlook, already shaken by her first mistake, is transformed in a moment from heresy to orthodoxy by the shock of discovering 'water' to be absent where she had believed it to be present; and in her saying *I surrender with Solomon*, these last two words are an indication that her surrender is to

---

15. See the poem quoted above on p. 57 and also *A Sufi Saint of the Twentieth Century*, p. 114, note 2.

be understood in the same highest sense as his surrender, namely the effacement of the self before the Self, which is the condition of his Gnosis.

Were there no relation between the two worlds, no inter-connection
at all, then all upwards progress would be inconceivable from one
to another. Therefore, the divine mercy gave to the World Visible a
correspondence with the World of the Realm Supernal, and for this
reason there is not a single thing in this world of sense that is not a
symbol of something in yonder one.

Al-Ghazali (d. 1111)

Sacred Waters: Thomas Merton's Thirst for Contemplation

Jonathan Montaldo

There is intoxication in the waters of contemplation, whose mystery fascinated and delighted the first Cistercians and whose image found its way into the names of so many of those valley monasteries that stood in forests, on the bands of clean streams, among rocks alive with springs.

These are the waters which the world does not know, because it prefers the water of bitterness and contradiction. These are the waters of peace of which Christ said, 'He that shall drink of the water that I shall give him, shall not thirst for ever. But the water that I shall give him shall become in him a fountain of water, springing up into life everlasting.'

These are the Waters of Siloe, that flow in silence.

Thomas Merton, *The Waters of Siloe*

A study of the symbolic role of water in its diverse forms throughout the life and writing of the American monk and writer Thomas Merton (1915-1968) would yield fountains, streams, lakes, ponds, and an ocean of rich detail. Born under the sign of the water-bearer on January 31, Merton crossed literal, psychological and spiritual seas as his life flowed forth from France, the land of his birth, to Bangkok, Thailand, where he embarked on the final journey of his earthly embodiment upon currents of fire. In a speech in Calcutta, India shortly before his death, Merton had asserted that the real journey in life is interior. Were someone to undertake it, a sustained analysis of water imagery in his poems, essays, journals, and dreams would provide clues to the contours of Merton's secret interior voyages otherwise undetected as his heart flowed in silence toward contemplative communion with God.

What follows is the merest whetting of someone's appetite for a study of Merton's water symbolism: the beginning paragraphs from one of his most appreciated essays, "Rain and the Rhinocerous" from his collection *Raids on the Unspeakable* and two early poems from the New Directions chapbook *Thirty Poems*. The contrast between these early poems and Merton's ironic commentary that one day we humans will be sold bottled rain (we have bottled and been sold our tap water have we not?) itself speaks to the richness of Merton's imaginative appropriation of water as symbolic of the spiritual life both fertile or dried up.

Rain and the Rhinoceros (1965)

Let me say this before rain becomes a utility that they can plan and distribute for money. By "they" I mean the people who cannot understand that rain is a festival, who do not appreciate its gratuity, who think that what has no price has no value, that what cannot be sold is not real, so that the only way to make something actual is to place it on the market. The time will come when they will sell you even your rain. At the moment it is still free, and I am in it. I celebrate its gratuity and its meaninglessness.

The rain I am in is not like the rain of cities. It fills the wood with an immense and confused sound. It covers the flat roof of the cabin and its porch with insistent and controlled rhythms. And I listen, because it reminds me again and again that the whole world runs by rhythms I have not yet learned to recognize, rhythms that are not those of the engineer.

I came up here from the monastery last night, sloshing through the cornfield, said Vespers, and put some oatmeal on the Coleman stove for supper. It boiled over while I was listening to the rain and toasting a piece of bread at the log fire. The night became very dark. The rain surrounded the whole cabin with its enormous virginal myth, a whole world of meaning, of secrecy, of silence, of rumor. Think of it: all that speech pouring down, selling nothing, judging nobody, drenching the thick mulch of dead leaves, soaking the trees, filling the gullies and crannies of the wood with water, washing out the places where men have stripped the hillside! What a thing it is to sit absolutely alone, in the forest, at night, cherished by this wonderful, unintelligible, perfectly innocent speech, the most comforting speech in the world, the talk that rain makes by itself all over the ridges, and the talk of the watercourses everywhere in the hollows!

Nobody started it, nobody is going to stop it. It will talk as long as it wants, this rain. As long as it talks I am going to listen.

But I am also going to sleep, because here in this wilderness I have learned how to sleep again. Here I am not alien. The trees I know, the night I know, the rain I know. I close my eyes and instantly sink into the whole rainy world of which I am a part, and the world goes on with me in it, for I am not alien to it. I am alien to the noises of cities, of people, to the greed of machinery that does not sleep, the hum of power that eats up the night. Where rain, sunlight and darkness are contemned, I cannot sleep. I do not trust anything that has been fabricated to replace the climate of woods or prairies. I can have no confidence in places where the air is first fouled and then cleansed, where the water is first made deadly and then made safe with other poisons. There is nothing in the world of buildings that is not fabricated, and if a tree gets in among the apartment houses by mistake it is taught to grow chemically. It is given a precise reason for existing. They put a sign on it saying it is for health, beauty, perspective; that it is for peace, prosperity; that it was planted by the mayor's daughter. All of this is mystification. The city itself lives on its own myth. Instead of waking up and silently existing, the city people prefer a stubborn and fabricated dream; they do not care to be a part of the night, or to be merely of the world. They have constructed a world outside the world, against the world, a world of mechanical fictions which contemn nature and seek only to use it up, thus preventing it from renewing itself and man.

Of course the festival of rain cannot be stopped, even in the city. The woman from the delicatessen scampers along the sidewalk with a newspaper over her head. The streets, suddenly washed, become transparent and alive, and the noise of traffic becomes a splashing of fountains. One would think that urban man in a rainstorm would <u>have</u> to take account of nature in its wetness and freshness, its baptism and renewal. But the rain brings no renewal to the city, only to tomorrow's weather, and the glint of windows in tall buildings will then have nothing to do with the new sky. All "reality" will remain somewhere inside those walls, counting itself and selling itself with fantastically complex determination. Meanwhile the obsessed citizens plunge through the rain bearing the load of their obsessions, slightly more vulnerable than before, but still only barely aware of external realities. They do not see that the streets shine beautifully, that they themselves are walking on stars and water, that they are running in skies to catch a bus or taxi, to shelter somewhere in the press of irritated humans, the faces of advertisements and the dim, cretinous sound of unidentified music. But they must know that there is wetness abroad. Perhaps they even <u>feel</u> it, I cannot say. Their complaints are mechanical and without spirit.

Naturally no one can believe the things they say about the rain. It all implies one basic lie: <u>only the city is real</u>. That weather, not being planned, not being fabricated, is an impertinence, a wen [pimple] on the visage of progress. (Just a simple little operation, and the whole mess may become relatively tolerable. Let business <u>make</u> the rain. This will give it meaning.)

Song

When rain, (sings light) rain has devoured my house
And wind wades through my trees,
The cedars fawn upon the storm with their huge paws.
Silence is louder than a cyclone
In the rude door, my shelter.
And there I eat my air alone
With pure and solitary songs.

While others sit in conference.
Their windows grieve, and soon frown
And glass begins to wrinkle with a multitude of water
Till I no longer see their speech
And they no longer know my theater.

Rivers clothe their houses
And hide their naked wisdom.
Their conversations
Go down into the deep like submarines:
Submerge them, with their pale expressions, in my storm.

But I drink rain, drink wind
Distinguish poems
Boiling up out of the cold forest:
Life to the wind my eyes full of water,
My face and mind, to take their free refreshment.

Thus I live on my own land, on my own island
And speak to God, my God, under the doorway
When rain, (sings light) rain has devoured my house
And winds wade through my trees.

The Tears Of The Blind Lions,
New York: New Directions, 1949, p. 5

In the Rain and the Sun

Watch out for this peeled doorlight!
Here, without rain, without shame
My noonday dusk made spots upon the walk:
Tall drops pelted the concrete with their jewelry
Belonging to the old world's bones.

Owning this view, in the air of a hermit's weather,
I count the fragmentary rain
In drops as blue as coal
Until I plumb the shadows full of thunder.

34

My prayers supervise the atmosphere
Till storms call all hounds home.

Out of the towers of water
Four or five mountains come walking
To see the little monks' graves.
Flying the neutral stones I dwell between cedars
And see the countries sleeping in their beds:
Lands of the watermen, where poplars bend.

Wild seas amuse the world with water:
No end to all the surfs that charm our shores
Fattening the sands with their old foam and their old
    roar.

Thus in the boom of waves' advantage
Dogs and lions come to my tame home
Won by the bells of my Cistercian jungle.
O love the livid fringes
In which their robes are drenched!

Songs of the lions and whales!
With my pen between my fingers
Making the waterworld sing!
Sweet Christ, discover diamonds
And sapphires in my verse
While I burn the sap of my pine house
For praise of the ocean sun.

I have walked upon the whole days' surf
Rinsing Thy bays with hymns.
My eyes have swept horizons clean
Of ships and rain.
Upon the lacquered swells my feet no longer run.
Sliding all over the sea I come
To the lap of a slippery harbor.

Dogs have gone back to their ghosts
And the many lions, home.
But words fling wide the windows of their houses—
Adam and Eve walk down my coast
Praising the tears of the treasurer sun:
I hang Thy rubies on these autumn trees,
On the bones of the homegoing thunder.

Tears of the Blind Lions, pp. 23-24

The Others in the Kingdom*

Cecily Jones, Sister of Loretto

(for Luke)

We go to the pond for solace
and to watch the flecks the sunlight
makes on each tiny rim of water
circling in a wreath
    of slightly corrugated gold.

Some days, though, we nearly touch
the others in the kingdom
    who patrol the pond
    or glide upon the gilded whispers of the waves
    or fly in shorthand scrawls above us.

I think of that old carp
whose "hrumpff" of a splash we heard
telling us, I guess, that Badin's his domain,
his periscopic tailfin the royal emblem
    of his rule.

Four ducks hustle down the slope
elbowing each other to reach the edge,
and near the willow tree slip into the pond.
Orange-red legs paddle swiftly
but so silently it seems
    a mechanized flotilla.
The muscovy remains aloof, a scarf of red
helmeting his head as if to cloister him.
But the mallard! Now there's a diving acrobat
upending in the pond to snatch his lunch,
totally capsized, feet together toward the sky
    in Olympian precision.

When the martins shall return this spring
we'll wheel near their multi-storey house
    beside the pond
applauding swoop and flash of purple wing
as well as mighty fin, saffron feet,
and the topknot-tousled comic coif
    of those others in the kingdom.

This poem and the next from *Hidden in the Same Mystery: Thomas Merton and Loretto*, forthcoming Fons Vitae, 2010.

Wildflowers in the Dining Room

Cecily Jones, Sister of Loretto

(for all my sisters)

I know you'll query me for names
and I'll identify the few I can:
black-eyed Susans, coreopsis, Queen Anne's lace,
bee balm. Even with my *Golden Nature Guide*
I cannot match these jewels for you.
But this I know: I have imported beauty
from beside our lake—flame-orange pennants
and creamy filigrees, those bright blue cups,
and, yes, a titled one, the wild wild rose.

The dearest treasure, though, I cannot share
unless tomorrow, very early, we go together
to the deep green water over which a tendrilled mist
will swirl in clouded drift, unless our hearts will hear
the stillness of a presence we can't name, unless we walk
the path where blackberry reeds may catch our clothes
(please pick a few for breakfast!) and the tan of grasses
will be burnished to a bronze in early morning sun.

Only the hoarsest hiccups of a frog and the plunking
of a turtle on its plunge into the lake may stun the silence
of this hour. We'll see spun filaments of silver making webs
from weed to weed, nameless blooms that skirt the water's edge,
and the scarlet tinge of tangled grape and stunted oak.
We'll pause a while beneath the paper sycamore
to listen to Earth's secrets there beside the lake.

No conveyance have I found to transport mystery,
no delivery of wonder. So if you cannot go with me
in awe at early light, I offer you these slight bouquets
as tokens of the wildness and samples of the wealth.

Look deep.

Rain Light*

W.S. Merwin

All day the stars watch from long ago
my mother said I am going now
when you are alone you will be all right
whether or not you know you will know
look at the old house in the dawn rain
all the flowers are forms of water
the sun reminds them through a white cloud
touches the patchwork spread on the hill
the washed colors of the afterlife
that lived there long before you were born
see how they wake without a question
even though the whole world is burning

As a lotus flower is born in water, grows in water and rises out of
water to stand above it unsoiled, so I, born in the world, raised in the
world having overcome the world, live unsoiled by the world.

The Buddha

And if all the trees in the earth were pens, and the sea, with seven
more seas to help it, (were ink), the words of God could not be exhausted. Lo! Allah is Mighty, Wise.

Qur'ān [31:27]

---

*From an interview with W.S. Merwin by Bill Moyers, June, 2009.

The Centrality of Water in the Hopi Tradition

Alexander Price

For nearly a thousand years, the members of the Hopi Nation of Native Americans have inhabited an area of northeastern Arizona that receives an average of ten inches of rain per year (the average throughout the U.S. being thirty-four inches, with some states receiving as much as sixty inches of rain a year). The Hopis say that their ancestors chose this harsh land as their permanent residence so that their environment would serve as a powerful catalyst for their spiritual development, by forcing them to rely on their prayers and religious ceremonies to bring rain to water their crops and herds and support life in the community. In time, through their conflicts with the United States government, water would become a potent symbol of their religious faith and their right to self-governance in the land entrusted to them by the Creator.

Archaeologists suggest that the indigenous American people arrived in the continent by way of the Bering Strait sometime around or before 11,000 BCE.[1] The Native people themselves believe that they emerged directly into the North American land from the underworld at a time when no other humans occupied the planet. The Hopis locate their Place of Emergence in the basin of the Grand Canyon, about a hundred miles west of the present-day Hopi Reservation. Their oral traditions hold that their ancestors journeyed to this world to escape the corruption that had taken over the previous worlds below. Upon their arrival, they were met by the guardian spirit of the land, Maasaw, who told them that before they could settle, they had to migrate throughout the land—north, south, east and west—to claim the entire world for the Creator. He warned them not to stay too long in the comfortable areas they would find, but to remember their obligation and continue migrating until they found the place he would show to them.

They met Maasaw again, after many centuries, in the Four Corners region of the American Southwest. One Hopi spokesman relates:

> They looked around, and [said], "Why this...we came from a better place. We had nice beautiful mountains, we had a lot of rivers, we had a lot of game and all that. But this is a desolate, God-forsaken country. Why here?"
>
> The guardian spirit replied:
>
> "The reason why you are here is because this is...a most safe place, there's going to be no more things that you have to experience. No more floodings, no more earthquakes, no more fires, nothing like that is going to happen. Because now you can be so close to me, so close to spiritual being. Then you will not forget. You're going to be so humble, that you're not going to forget that I'm there." And this is the reason why he

---

1. C.f. Diamond, J. (1998). *Guns, Germs, and Steel: The Fates of Human Societies.* New York, W.W. Norton & Co.

chose it.... The severity of the intense desolate weather conditions, lack of any pristine value or mineral commodity or the elements, and finally this place was situated in the middle of the "plaza," symbolic of a center of the Universe.[2]

The Hopi religion is structured around the agricultural cycle, with seasonal ceremonies that ensure the fertility of the fields and sufficiency of rain. Their prayers are answered by the Kachinas, a genus of spirit-beings who are central to the Hopi religion. When the people misbehave or neglect their religious duties, scarcity of rain and dryness of the springs is believed to result as a just consequence of wrongdoing.

In their newsletter *Techqua Ikachi: Land and Life*, religious leaders from the Traditionalist village of Hotevilla described the Winter Solstice ceremony, Soyal:

> The Hopi Soyal ceremonial is performed and the germs of seed are planted within the mother Earth's womb. The Hopi believe the Earth is a living Mother to all life and nourishes all her living children. This planting is done with ritual and blessings in order for these seeds to form normally and perfectly.... This is also the time when plans for the coming year are made. The priests in the kivas pray for prosperity in food, health, happiness, and for protection against evil for all land and life. The Kachinas visit to bring happiness and joy for young and old. The Kachinas bring the rain of loving care upon the corn fields and deliver our messages of desire to the Rain Gods. The Creator, nature, and spirits, controllers of movement, plan both good and bad for the coming year depending upon the behavior of mankind. They say that even the wicked and the witches plan a scheme to destroy the morals of people to part them away from the Creator's divine laws in order to lead them to self destruction.[3]

It is easy to understand why rain, in such an arid desert environment, would serve as a natural metaphor for divine beneficence.

Then, about two months after Soyal:

> In Pa-mu-ya the water month (February) the Kachina, the messengers between the Hopi and the cloud spirits now come to bring food and happiness to both young and old. This part is activated by the religious groups—by the religious and spiritual leaders of every phase of the ceremonials.[4]

---

2. Quoted in Herman, RDK. 2003. *Geografia Indigena: A Project of the National Museum of the American Indian, Smithsonian Institution.* Townson University, Maryland, viewed 13 June 2009. <http://pages.towson.edu/dherman/hopi>.

3. *Techqua Ikachi: Land and Life,* 1983, no 23. All issues of *Techqua Ikachi* but one are currently (June 2009) accessible online at http://www.jnanadana.org/hopi/techqua_ikachi.html.

4. ibid.

To the Hopis, there is a literal, causal relationship between their ceremonies and the proper functioning of the natural world. If the ceremonies are not performed at the right time, by duly authorized people, not only might the rains not come, but the planet may lose its balance, the entire ecosystem may collapse and the world could be plunged into chaos. Their ceremonies, therefore, are a vital element of nature: along with the prayers and practices of religious people around the world, they say, they keep the world in balance and ensure the safety and sustenance of all creatures everywhere.

As the symbolic Center of the Universe, they consider Hopiland to be a microcosm of the world. Hopi Traditionalists (as distinguished from Progressives) interpret the neglect of religious duties and corruption of Hopi spirituality since the advent of Euro-American immigration to be a precursor of the recent climate changes. Speaking before the United Nations in 1992, Hopi spokesman Thomas Banyacya explained:

> Nature itself does not speak with a voice that we can easily understand. Neither can the animals and birds we are threatening with extinction talk to us. Who in this world can speak for nature and the spiritual energy that creates and flows through all life? In every continent are human beings who are like you but who have not separated themselves from the land and from nature. It is through their voice that Nature can speak to us.... Nature, the First People and the spirit of our ancestors are giving you loud warnings. Today, December 10, 1992, you see increasing floods, more damaging hurricanes, hailstorms, climate changes and earthquakes as our prophecies said would come. Even animals and birds are warning us with strange changes in their behavior such as the beaching of whales. Why do animals act like they know about the earth's problems and most humans act like they know nothing? If we humans do not wake up to the warnings, the Great Purification will come to destroy this world just as the previous worlds were destroyed.

Hopi tradition holds that mankind inhabited three previous worlds before migrating to the present Fourth World. The versions of this story that exist in print vary widely in their details. Some suggest the story is a metaphor for reincarnation;[5] others imply that the previous Third World still exists as a spiritual "underworld" to which we return when we die.[6] The version told most often by the Hotevilla Elders is that the previous three worlds were destroyed as a consequence of human wrongdoing, serving as a warning that if we repeat the same mistakes we will suffer the same fate.

Upon emerging to this world, the Hopis say, they were given instructions by the Creator on how to fashion a magical pot that, when properly prepared, would provide a source of water for them wherever they traveled.

---

5. Courlander, H. (1971). *The Fourth World of the Hopis.* New York: Crown Publishers.

6. Beidler, P. (1995). "First death in the Fourth World: Teaching the Emergence Myth of the Hopi Indians." *American Indian Quarterly* 19:1, p. 75-89.

To make this device, a specially-trained priest would journey to the ocean, where he would perform elaborate prayers before collecting various items from the area such as sea foam, sand and underwater plant life. He would carry this back to his people in the clay pot prepared for the task, and upon his arrival would bury it in the ground, at which time a spring would bubble forth, providing a steady source of water.

The Hopis were among the last of the indigenous North American people to be affected by European immigration. Their contact with Conquistadors and Catholic missionaries began in 1540, two decades after the fall of the Aztec empire, as the Spanish continued north in search of a fabled City of Gold. But since the Hopis occupied an uninviting land and were apparently not in possession of any desirable natural resources (such as gold roads or lakes of gold), they were more or less left to themselves through the 1850s (with the notable exception of the Catholic missionary efforts).[7] At this time a wave of settlers was traveling west across America: like their predecessors, in search of free gold. Sparked partly by curiosity for the Hopis' exotic Snake Dance, ethnographers and tourists developed a keen interest in them. The Hopis soon were increasingly confronted with demands by the new U.S. government for changes in their traditional way of life—such as the mandatory attendance of children in Euro-American schools, and the establishment of a democratic Tribal Council. Internal disagreements over whether to comply or resist led to a split among the Hopis in 1906, with the dissenting party departing from their ancestral home at Old Oraibi to found the village of Hotevilla a few miles north on Third Mesa. Water would continue to play a central role in the unfolding drama of their relationship with the land and the federal government.[8]

At first the residents of Hotevilla staunchly resisted attempts to install modern utilities such as water and power lines, which they felt would make them dependent on the government, rather than the Creator, for their survival. When the government proceeded to install utilities against the residents' wishes, the people repeatedly pulled the lines out of the ground at night so that construction had to be abandoned.

To the Traditionalists, water and other natural resources are emotionally charged symbols for their God-given autonomy. In an issue of *Techqua Ikachi*, published ca. 1976, they wrote:

> The progressive faction accuses us of withholding the good things, of keeping our children from a better future, by which they mean the advantages of modern conveniences. They are enticed by gadgets run by electricity and public water for household needs. These things would be good if one could get them freely without danger of involvement in

7. For the early history of Hopi contact with the Spanish, see: Courlander, ibid.; Weber, D. J. (1992). *The Spanish Frontier in North America*. New Haven: Yale University Press.

8. Mails, T., & Evehema, D. (1995). *Hotevilla: Hopi Shrine of the Covenant; Microcosm of the World*. New York: Marlowe & Co..

obligations that will later be regretted. Certainly these things seem to promise a nice future for our children, but our knowledge as well as the clear voice of experience in the modern world teach us the danger of allowing our life to be controlled by outside interests. A person's life too easily becomes ruled by his pocketbook, and by foreign rules....[9]

A 1978 issue of *Techqua Ikachi* included the bluntly titled article, "We Told You So," in which the Traditionalist Elders related the story of the water conflict from their perspective:

Not long ago there were many natural springs running through Hopi-land. Hopis knew all their locations, so they could drink on long journeys. Hopis always had water, enough for themselves and even some springs supplied flocks of sheep and other animals. As usual, a Bahana [White Man] from a government agency was sent to the Hopi to make a proposal. This time it was to develop our humble springs. He told us enthusiastically that by his methods we could produce more water. The religious leaders shook their heads saying that it is not good, for it would disturb the great water serpents who would then stop the water from flowing. "How foolish" thought the agent, and persisted to seek other Hopis more willing to cooperate. He explained his ideas and soon he had converted enough people to allow the development of the spring to take place. Many years later we find our springs drying up and others giving less water.

Time passed and yet another agent was sent, this time with a proposal for windmills. He assured the people he would pump the water from deep drilling made inside the earth, and that they would never run out of it. The leaders once again shook their heads, "No good," they said, "drilling will pierce the great water serpents and cause them anger, thus drying up more springs." Again the agent thought "How foolish they are," and thinking very hard, an idea came to him that he would ask the Hopi stock owners, seeing that they had money tied up in their animals and would not refuse.

So the windmills went up and more springs went dry.

It was about this time when a new government was being formed, the so-called "Hopi Tribal Council." They were ready to tackle the world. The Peabody Coal Company's stripminers came and introduced themselves with a proposal to stripmine the Black Mesa.

In their youthful folly, the Puppet Council readily agreed to the proposal and the money involved. No one bothered to seek the blessings of their elders.

Deep wells were drilled and hundreds of thousands of gallons of water went into use daily to transport the coal to distant places. There were many protests by the chiefs but all in vain. The Council and Peabody Coal Co. affirmed that the drilling would not hinder any environ-

---

9. *TI*, (1976), no. 7.

ment. The chiefs shook their heads sadly and said "The mother Earth is being raped. You are destroying the sacred shrines and the great water serpents. What will they do?"[10]

In such articles, the Elders' frustration with their community and their indignation at the destruction of their culture is plain to see.

In 1983, they reproduced a letter they sent to a government representative concerning unwanted utilities in Hotevilla:

Dear Mr. Tewa, C.D.S.:

Every nation, State, City, and Village to household has its own Leadership to make decisions for the good of the people, according to their own agreed upon laws. Hotevilla has its own agreed upon laws. We feel that the proposal to bring water, electricity, sewer line and telephone into our Village without the consent of our proper leaders was an improper action. We feel our first responsibility is to uphold our Creator's Laws and that to bring water, electricity, sewer, and telephone into our Village will interfere with our ability to fulfill our spiritual duties according to the Hopi way. We challenge you to state to us what authority you have to come into our Village and change our ways of life without the consent of our leaders.

We ask you to respect our spiritual laws and our elders, who are our leaders, and not to disturb our traditional way of life which to us is sacred.

We ask you to stop your effort to destroy our Culture.

Signed by the elders and leaders of the Village.[11]

The supremacy of the European Conquerors in the New World was determined, according to anthropologist Jared Diamond, by the power of their "Guns, Germs and Steel." The Hopis pride themselves on being a gentle, humble people—the word *Hopi*, in their language, means "peaceful." They were easily overpowered, but their endurance in the face of insurmountable opposition is a testament to the power of their faith.

One by one, the Traditionalist leaders have aged and passed away: Dan Katchongva, Titus Qomayumptewa, David Monongye, Dan Evehema, Thomas Banyacya, and many other friends and supporters, known and unknown. Today, only one Hotevilla Traditionalist remains. Although he is now in his late eighties, Martin Gashweseoma still gets up every morning at 4:00 to perform the traditional prayers. He still gets his water from the spring: his is one of the last homes in Hotevilla without running water, without electricity. His battle seems truly hopeless, but he has never given up trusting that the Savior of Hopi prophecies—*Bahana*, the "True White Brother"—will appear to vanquish the oppressors and restore justice. When he passes, as the illustrious bard so memorably put it, *the rest is silence....*

---

10. *TI*, (1978), no. 14.
11. *TI*, (1983), no. 23.

Walk on Water

Hamza Yusuf-Hanson

Walk softly on the water that is this world.
Gently, with grace, glide to the shore of the unseen world
Where precious shells await.

Walk easily with those who walked before.
Follow prophetic footsteps, traces left even on water.

Lighten your load, lest you sink.
Leave the world behind, then you will walk on water.
Leave chatter to the chatterers, then your feet will be held up by water.

Abandon yourself,
Trust the Trustworthy,
Seek and be sought.
Then you can walk on water.

Do not drown in the desert of this world.
Softly walk on it, not of it, but in it.
On water you must walk.

Don't forget the Chosen One
Who long ago walked on worldly waters in Arabia,
A sea of sand, but water no less.
How he glided to the other side

Not content to walk alone, safe
While others drowned,
Like Jesus, he taught
For the last time
How to walk on water.

Come, let us
Walk on water!

The Surface of the Waters*

Whitall N. Perry

And the spirit of God moved upon the face of the waters.

Genesis I.2

Moses means 'taken from the water'. Brahmā and Vishnu both have the appellation *Nārāyana*, 'He who walks on the waters'; another name given Brahmā is *Āpava*—'He who sports on the waters'. Lakshmi is called *Jaladhijā*, 'the ocean born'. The *Qur'ān* teaches that 'His Throne was upon the water' (XI. 7).

Hindu iconography pictures Vishnu asleep on a serpent couch amidst the waters, with a golden lotus issuing from his navel, and Brahmā enthroned in the lotus. Following the same symbolism, Lakshmi, the consort or *shakti* of Vishnu, is called *Padmā*, 'The Lotus', and *Padmālaya*, 'She who dwells on a lotus'.[1] This recalls the epithet of the Buddha: *Mani padmē*—'Jewel in the lotus'. Agni is also 'churned from the lotus' or 'lotus-born' (*puskarāt*).[2]

The lotus motif is evident in the *Shrī-Yantra* designs of Hinduism, and in the Tibetan *mandalas*; and the lotus in its quality of sacred flower reposing on the water and opening to the sunlight is the perfect expression of Peace and Beatitude and the unfolding or realization of the spiritual possibilities of the being.[3]

The macrocosmic corollary of the same symbolism pertains to sacred islands at the center of the sea. The *Montsalvat* of the Grail legends is both a 'sacred island' and a 'polar mountain', like the Hindu *Mēru*. The hyperborean *Tula* is called the 'white island', like the Hindu *shvēta dvīpa*, and the Celtic *Albion* and *Avalon*. Islamic esoterism speaks of the 'green island'

1. In the same order of ideas are the names of the Virgin Mary, such as Maris Stella, Ark of the Covenant, Mirror of Justice, Queen of Peace, Living Spring, Gate of Heaven, Mystical Rose, and Untouched Lily—these two flowers having essentially the same significance in the West as the lotus in the East.

2. Cf. Coomaraswamy: *The Rg Veda as Land-Nāma-Bōk*, p. 4; 'Angel and Titan: An Essay in Vedic Ontology' (JAOS, Dec., 1935), passim. Guenon equates Agni at the center of the swastika with the Lamb in Chrisitanity at the source of the four rivers (*Le Symbolisme de la Croix*, p. 177). Agni, (whose root is the same as the Latin *Agnus*) has for vehicle a ram. In the *Rig Veda* is the passage: 'At the navel of the earth stands Agni': and following the *Satapatha Brāhmana*, 'navel means the center.' CF. *Le Roi du Monde*, ch. IX. for assimilations between the Greek *omphalos* and *umbilicus*, and the Sanskrit word *nābhi* and nave(l), in relation to Axis, Pole, and other symbols attaching to the 'Center of the World'. What matters for the purposes of exposition here is the evident correlation between the ideas of surface, center, source, and summit.

3. Cf. Schuon: *Le Stations de la Sagesse,* pp. 193-194.

*From *The Spiritual Ascent: A Compendium of the World's Wisdom*, Fons Vitae, 2007..

(*al-jazirah al-khadrah*) and the 'white mountian' (*al-jabal al-abyad*), ideas which find their equivalent in the Celtic traditions.[4] There is also the Hindu 'Island of Jewels' (*mani-dvīpa*), with the Universal Mother (*jagad-ambā*), the *Shakti-Māyā*, enthroned in a jeweled palace over the recumbent forms of *Sakala Shiva* and *Nishkala Shiva*.[5]

The ocean supporting the Cosmic Lotus and the World Mountain corresponds to the 'lower waters' or 'chaos' of possibilities comprising the states of formal manifestation; its surface is the plane of reflection for the 'Celestial Ray' (*Buddhi*) whose vibration of *Fiat Lux* operates the transition from power to act, bringing order out of chaos. The surface also represents the plane of separation (Islamic *barzakh* , or Christian 'Cloud of Unknowing') between the two seas (*Gen.*, I. 7; *Qur'ān*, XVIII. 60: XXV. 53: LV. 19), the 'upper waters' being the sum of supraformal possibilities. In the midst of the waters is the firmament (*Gen.*, I. 6), as in Hinduism the *Brahmānda* or 'World Egg', which englobes the 'Golden Embryo' (*Hiranyagarbha*— archetypal seed of the possibilities that will develop during a cycle of manifestation) is represented floating on the primordial sea (*samudra*), covered by the swan *Hamsa*, vehicle of *Brahmā*, equatable with the Divine Breath (*spiritus*).[6] The surface of the waters is thus the point of convergence between the finite and the Infinite.

'"Walking on the water" symbolizes the domination of the world of forms and change' (Guénon: *Le Roi du Monde*, p. 81). The miraculous crossing of waters may be accomplished by actually walking on the water, or by levitation, or by the waters becoming shallow enough to wade through, or by the waters parting, as did the Red Sea for the Israelites, and the sea at Pamphylia for Alexander the Great, which according to Callisthenes, 'not only opened for him, but even rose and fell in homage'.[7]

The Spirit Upon the Waters

Thy good spirit indeed *was borne over the waters,* not borne up by them, as if He rested upon them.

St Augustine

---

4. Cf. Guénon: *Le Roi du Monde*, passim.

5. Cf. Heinrich Zimmer: *Myths and Symbols in Indian Art and Civilization*, New York, Pantheon Books, Bollingen Series VI, 1946, ch. V.

6. Cf. Guénon: *Le Symbolisme de la Croix*, ch. XXIV; *Les États multiples de l'Être*, ch. XII; *L'Homme et son Devenir*, ch V. The same author has indicated the symbolism underlying the Ark in the Flood (*Le Roi du Monde,* ch. XI), whose crescent shape from below combines with its inverse prototype the celestial rainbow from above to form the two halves of a sphere situated precisely at the juncture of the two seas, and enclose (like the 'World Egg') the 'elect' or positive possibilities of formal manifestation in embryo (*Hiranyagarbha*), 'saved out' or crystallized from the preceding world cycle to be developed in the course of the future cycle.

7. William Norman Brown: *The Indian and Christian Miracles of Walking on the Water*, Chicago, Open Court, 1928, p. 41. The question of miracles is further treated in the introductory section of the chapter, *Moving at Will—The Miracle of Flight.*

The universe was formerly water, fluid. On it Prajāpati becoming wind, moved.

Taittirīya Samhitā, Creation 26

From the Light there came forth a holy Word, which took its stand upon the watery substance.

Hermes

The earth is the Lord's, and the fulness thereof; the world, and they that dwell therein. For he hath founded it upon the seas, and established it upon the floods.

Psalm xxiv. 1, 2

The Waters (representing the principle of substance) being ripe unto conception (lit. 'in their season'). Vāyu (that is, the Wind, as physical symbol of spiration, *prāna*) moved over their surface. Wherefrom came into being a lovely (*vāma*) thing (that is, the world—picture), there in the Waters Mitra-Varuna beheld-themselves-reflected (*paryapasyat*).

Pañcavimsa Brāhmana, VII. 8. 1

Surely thou art Bhāgavat who appears before me; the great Hari, whose dwelling was on the waves.... Salutation and praise to thee, O first male, the lord of creation, of preservation, of destruction! Thou art the highest object, the supreme ruler, of us thy adorers, who piously seek thee.... Let me not, O lotus-eyed, approach in vain the feet of a deity whose perfect benevolence has been extended to all.

Srimad Bhagavatam

For God's Word, who is all-accomplishing and fecund and creative, went forth, and flinging himself upon the water, which was a thing of fecund nature, made the water pregnant.

Hermes

A holy king named Satyavrāta then reigned—a servant of the Spirit which moved on the waves.

Srimad Bhagavatam

The Spirit of God, it is said, *moved over the waters*—that is to say, over that formless matter, signified by water, even as the love of the artist moves over the materials of his art.... According to the holy writers, the Spirit of the Lord signifies the Holy Ghost, Who is said to *move over the water*—that is to say, over what Augustine holds to mean formless matter.... It is the opinion...of Basil that the Spirit moved over the element of water, *fostering and quickening its nature and impressing vital power, as the hen broods over her chickens.*

St Thomas Aquinas

This vast egg, compounded of the elements, and resting on the waters, was the excellent natural abode of Vishnu in the form of Brahmā, and there Vishnu, the lord of the universe, whose essence is inscrutable, assumed a perceptible form, and even he himself abided in it in the character of Brahmā.

Its womb, vast as the mountain Meru, was composed of the mountains; and the mighty oceans were the waters that filled its cavity. In that egg were the continents and seas and mountains, the planets and divisions of the universe, the gods, demons, and mankind.

Vishnu Purāna

They (the Egyptians) do not believe that the sun rises as a new born babe (Horus) from the lotus, but they portray the rising of the sun in this manner to show darkly that his birth is a kindling from the waters.

Plutarch

And straightaway the Lord of all spoke with his own holy and creative speech, and said, 'Let the sun be'; and even as He spoke, Nature drew to herself with her own breath the fire, which is of upward-tending nature,— that fire,[8] I mean, which is unmixed and most luminous and most active and most fecund,—and raised it up aloft from the water.

Hermes

It is named the water of life, the purest and most blessed water, yet not the water of the clouds, or of any common spring, but a thick, permanent, salt, and (in a certain sense) dry water, which wets not the hand, a slimy water which springs out of the fatness of the earth. Likewise, it is a double mercury and Azoth which, being supported by the vapour or exudation of the greater and lesser heavenly and the earthly globe, cannot be consumed by fire. For itself is the universal and sparkling flame of the light of Nature, which has the heavenly Spirit in itself, with which it was animated at first by God.

The Sophic Hydrolith

The Lord sitteth upon the flood; yea, the Lord sitteth King for ever.

Psalm xxix. 10

Vishnu, with the quality of goodness and of immeasurable power, preserves created things through successive ages, until the close of the period termed a Kalpa; when the same mighty deity, invested with the quality of darkness, assumes the awful form of Rudra, and swallows up the universe. Having thus devoured all things, and converted the world into one vast ocean, the Supreme reposes upon his mighty serpent couch amidst the deep: he awakes after a season, and again, as Brahmā, becomes the author of creation.

Vishnu Purāna

Dominating the Waters

The wise man through earnestness, virtue, and purity, maketh himself an island which no flood can submerge.

Udāna

Who sinks not in the gulf without support or stay? One who is prescient, fully synthesised, he may cross the flood so hard to pass.

Samyutta-nikāya, I. 53

---

8. Equatable with Agni, as in the Introduction, supra.

The great rishi...stayed the billowy river; when Viśvāmitra led Sudās, Indra had pleasure in the Kusikas.

Rig-Veda, III. 53. 9

Yea, the wide-spread floods Indra made into fords, easy to cross, for Sudās.

Rig-Veda, VII. 33

The children of Israel walked upon dry land in the midst of the sea; and the waters were a wall unto them on their right hand, and on their left.

Exodus, XIV. 29

And the priests that bare the ark of the covenant of the Lord stood firm on dry ground in the midst of Jordan, and all the Israelites passed over on dry ground, until all the people were passed clean over Jordan.

Joshua, III. 17

And Elijah took his mantle, and wrapped it together, and smote the waters, and they were divided hither and thither, so that they two went over on dry ground.

II. Kings, II. 8

Thus saith the Lord, which maketh a way in the sea, and a path in the mighty waters.

Isaiah, XLIII. 16

Thou didst walk through the sea with thine horses, through the heap of great waters.

Habakkuk, III. 15

I would not that ye should be ignorant, how that all our fathers were under the cloud, and all passed through the sea:
    And all were baptized unto Moses in the cloud and in the sea.

I Corinthians, X. I. 2

When thou passest through the waters, I will be with thee: and through the rivers, they shall not overflow thee.

Isaiah, XLIII. 2

Now the king (Kappina), with his thousand ministers, reached the bank of the Ganges. But at this time the Ganges was full. When the king saw this, he said: 'The Ganges here is full, and swarms with savage fish. Moreover we have with us no slaves or men to make boats or rafts for us. But of this Teacher the virtues extend from the Avici Hell beneath to the Peak of Existence above. If this Teacher be the Supremely Enlightened Buddha, may not the tips of the hoofs of these horses be wetted!'

They caused the horses to spring forward on the surface of the water. Of not a single horse was so much as the tip of the hoof wetted. On a king's highway proceeding, as it were, they went to the far shore. Farther on they reached another river. There was needed no other Act of Truth. By the same Act of Truth, that river also, half a league in breadth, did they cross over. Then they reached the third river, the mighty river Candabhāgā. That river also, by the same Act of Truth, did they cross over....

Queen Anojā, surrounded by a thousand chariots, reaching the bank of the Ganges and seeing no boat or raft brought for the King, by her own intuition concluded: 'The King must have crossed by making an Act of Truth. But this Teacher was reborn not for them alone. If this Teacher be the Supremely Enlightened Buddha, may our chariots not sink into the water!'

She caused the chariots to spring forward on the surface of the water. Of the chariots, not even so much as the outer rims of the wheels were wetted. The second river also, the third river also, she crossed by the same Act of Truth.

Buddhaghosa

Their (certain Jaina sages) strength of will was so great that they could walk on water as on land.

Triṣaṣṭiśalākāpuruṣacarita, I. 857

Said Visākhā the mother of Migāra: 'Most wonderful most marvellous is the might and the power of the Tathāgata, in that though the floods are rolling on knee-deep, and though the floods are rolling on waist-deep, yet is not a single Bhikkhu wet, as to his feet or as to his robes.'

Vinaya-Pitaka, Mahāvagga, VIII. 15

I (the Buddha) can walk on water as if it were solid earth.

Samyutta-nikāya, V. 25

'Our families, from our earliest ancestors, have dwelt on the bank of this river. Now we have never heard tell that a man walked upon the water. Who then are you, and what is your magic recipe for walking upon the water without sinking?'

The miraculous man answered them, 'I am a simple and ignorant man from the south of the river. Having heard say that the Buddha was here, I was anxious to gladden myself with his wisdom and virtue. When I arrived at the southern bank, it was not the time when the river was fordable: but I asked the people who were on the bank of the river what was the depth of the water. They replied that the water would reach to my ankle, and that nothing would prevent me from crossing. I added faith to their words, and I have therefore come crossing the river. I have no extraordinary recipe.'

The Buddha praised him, saying, 'Well done! Well done! Truly, the man with faith in the absolute truths is able to cross the gulf of births and deaths. What is there extraordinary about it then that he should be able to cross a river several *li* wide.' Then the Buddha pronounced these stanzas: 'Faith (*sraddhā*) can cross the gulf....'

Fa Kiu P'i Yu King

Reverend Sir, I had recourse to the Practice of Meditation, concentrated my thoughts on the Buddha, attained the Ecstasy of Joy (*pīti*), obtained support on the surface of the water and came hither as though I were treading the earth.

Jātaka 190

If drifting in the vast ocean a man is about to be swallowed up by the Nagas, fishes, or evil beings, let his thought dwell on the power of Kwannon,[9] and the waves will not drown him.

Kwannon Sutra

I (the Buddha) crossed the flood only when I did not support myself or make any effort.

Samyutta-nikāya, I. 1

The One God (Indra) stands upon the flowing streams at will.

Atharva-Veda, III. 3, 4

(Yasoda)[10] walked on water without breaking through just as on land.

Mahāvastu

And in the fourth watch of the night Jesus went unto them, walking on the sea.

St Matthew, XIV. 25

If ye knew God as He ought to be known, ye would walk on the seas, and the mountains would move at your call.

Muhammad

Our inner journey is above the sky.
The body travels on its dusty way;
The spirit walks, like Jesus, on the sea.

Rūmī, *Flight* 944

He is conceived in water and born in air; when he has become red in color, he walks over the water.

Michael Maier, *Pilg.* 378, *M. M.* 998

By conquering the current called *Udāna*[11] the Yogi does not sink in the water, or in swamps, he can walk on thorns, and can die at will.

Pantanjali

A man after fourteen years' penance in a solitary forest obtained at last the power of walking on water. Overjoyed at this, he went to his Guru and said, 'Master, master, I have acquired the power of walking on water.' The master rebukingly replied, 'Fie, O child! is this the result of thy fourteen years' labours? Verily thou hast obtained only that which is worth a penny; for what thou hast accomplished after fourteen years' arduous labour ordinary men do by paying a penny to the boatman.'

Sri Ramakrishna

One day (Hasan of Basra) saw Rābi'a (al-'Adawiyya) near the riverside. Hasan cast his prayer-mat on to the surface of the water and said, 'O Rābi'a, come and let us pray two *rak'as* together.' Rābi'a said, 'O Hasan, was it

---

9. A Bodhisattva (skr. *Avalokiteśvara*) whose name is much invoked in Japan.

10. A variant of the name of Yasa, the Buddha's sixth convert.

11. One of the five *vāyus* or modalities of *prāna* ('breath') having to do with expiration.

necessary to offer yourself in the bazaar of this world to the people of the next? This is necessary for people of your kind, because of your weakness.' Then Rābi‘a threw her prayer-mat into the air and flew up on to it and said, 'O Hasan, come up here that people may see us.' But that station was not for Hasan and he was silent. Rābi‘a, wishing to gain his heart said, 'O Hasan, that which you did, a fish can do just the same, and this which I did, a fly can do. The real work lies beyond both of these and it is necessary to occupy ourselves with the real work.'

'Attār

It was the custom for Sidi ‘Abdur Rahmān when the sea was calm to float on the waters off Algiers, seated on his prayer carpet. One day on a beach he came upon a poor shepherd who played a small flute (*qashbūt*), and who was so absorbed in his melody that he did not even hear the Shaykh's salām. He had promised to play for three days in a row if God would grant him the child he had long sought to have, and filled with gratitude and joy in seeing his wish accorded, he had undertaken to play for forty days. Now Sidi ‘Abdur Rahmān did not like the flute, which certain traditions would have to be the instrument of Iblis (the devil), who solaces his eternal anguish by wailing through its reeds.

He declared that this way of thanking God was absurd.[12] 'The Lord does not accept such homage. I am going to teach thee something which will reconcile thee to Him.' And he taught the shepherd the *Fātihah*, together with the rites of prayer. Then he launched his rug once more and floated out to sea.

The shepherd tried to recite the formula he had just learned. But he got confused; he had forgotten a line. Heeding nothing but his zeal, he ran after the saint to have his help in recalling the words; and thus he walked on the sea. The saint, the sage, had need of a carpet to stay miraculously afloat on the waves, and here was this ignorant man walking on them barefoot. Sidi ‘Abdur Rahmān understood the lesson and spoke to the uneducated shepherd, this man of good will, in quoting the first hadith from the *sahīh* of al-Bukhāri:

'Continue, O my brother, to play for Him. *Innamā 'l-a‘māl bi-n nīyāt.* Verily the act is in the intention.'

Sufic Tradition

Supra-normal powers are encouragements which God gives as a sort of incentive for new progress and an intense *sādhanā* (ascesis).

Swami Sivananda

He who has attained the Tao can go into water without becoming wet, jump into fire without being burned, walk upon reality as if it were a void and

---

12. The story typifies a certain Islamic attitude towards music, where it is classic first to reject (rationally) for its potential abuses an art form which is subsequently accepted (spiritually) for its essentially divine qualities.

travel on a void as if it were reality. He can be at home wherever he is and be alone in whatever surroundings. That is natural with him.

T'u Lung

The Plane of Reflection

Have not the disbelievers seen that the heavens and the earth were of one piece?[13] Then We parted them asunder, and from the water We made every living thing.

Qur'ān, XXI. 30

That which is above the heavens is the masculine, and the water which is beneath the earth is the feminine.

Book of Enoch, LIV. 8, 9

But it requires profound study to become acquainted with all the secrets of our sea, and with its ebb and flow.... The whole knowledge of our Art consists in the discovery of this our sea; any Alchemist who is ignorant of it, is simply wasting his money. Our sea is derived from the mountain.

Philalethes, Supra Introd.

And we send down pure water from the sky
That therewith We may quicken a dead land.

Qur'ān, XXV. 48-49

The name of Moses...means, taken from the water, and so shall we be taken out of instability, rescued from the storm of the world flow.

Eckhart

Our air, like the air of the firmament, divides the water; and as the waters under the firmament are visible to us mortals, while we are unable to see the waters above the firmament, so in 'our work' we see the extracentral mineral waters, but are unable to see those which, though hidden within, nevertheless have a real existence. They exist but do not appear until it please the Artist.

Philalethes

The true earth is pure and situated in the pure heaven.... But we who live in these hollows are deceived into the notion that we are dwelling above on the surface of the earth, which is just as if a creature who was at the bottom of the sea were to fancy that he was on the surface of the water, and that the sea was the heaven.... If any man could arrive at the exterior limit, or take the wings of a bird and come to the top, then like a fish who puts his head out of the water and sees this world, he would see a world beyond; and, if the nature of man could sustain the sight, he would acknowledge that this other world was the place of the true heaven and the true light and the true earth.

Plato (Phaedo, 109)

---

13. That such an observation should have passed as evident at the time the Qur'ān was revealed shows to what extent the vision of modern man has atrophied.

The Feminine and Masculine Waters in the Teachings of the Baal Shem Tov

Translated and Annotated by Rabbi Dr. Menachem Kallus

* * *

Preface Note by Rabbi Dr. Aubrey L. Glazer

Water as spiritual quest and mystical apperception in Jewish Mysticism

Water overflows with contradictions. Water can hold the stillness of silence while moving *to and fro*, gliding through the air or fluttering like angel wings. That movement of ingression and egression speaks to the nature of existence. All the more so, that movement embodies what every mystic's soul is in search of—a way to authentically express the undulating rhythms of connection and disconnection, of faithfulness and faithlessness by return- ing and retreating from total immersion in the pool of divinity. Returning to water can be in drops and drops—like the ritual washing of hands before and after breaking bread [*netilat yadayim, mayyim akhronim*]; and returning to water can be a total immersion—like the ritual bath of *mikveh* that leads to complete rebirthing. Humanity's yearning to return to its primordial union with divinity is embodied in ways Jewish mysticism navigates the tributaries of rivers, seas and oceans of limitless water.

Since the appearance of water [Hebrew, *mayyim*; Aramaic, *mayyin*] at the pivotal moment of the Second Day amidst Six of World Construction (Genesis 1:6-7), the necessary separation of water to make space for the firmament of being always leaves its residual pain. That pain is already ex- pressed early on in rabbinic *gnosis*, when Rabbi Berekiah teaches that "the lower waters did not part from the upper waters without weeping." (*Genesis Rabbah* 5:4). It is this radical amazement which Rabbi Berekiah displays in his *midrashic koan* that knows how to hold the whole earth is at once "filled with waters within waters" while still being "gathered to one place" (*Genesis Rabbah* 5:2). It is that pain of being pulled apart from primordial unity that leaves its scar on every created being, starting with the substance and symbol of water itself. That feeling of separation always yearning for reunion—so primal for every seeker of mystical union— is what leads us to always seek an immersion of self into other, a dissolution of masculine into feminine—all captured in the rhythm of water.

What the following excerpts from *Pillar of Prayer* by the renowned 18th century mystic, known simply as the Besht, o.b.m. (or R. Israel Ba'al Shem Tov, of blessed memory)—from the forthcoming volume in Fons Vitae's new series, *Spiritual Affinities: Judaism and Islam* (projected publication, 2011)—exemplify is how remarkably nuanced the mystical symbol of water becomes in articulating the pathways of the contemplative life in Judaism. Building on allusions in the Medieval Zohar texts, the Besht, o.b.m. distinguishes between Grace's flow that is at once active-creative conscious-ness (i.e. 'masculine' water or *mayyin dukrin*) as well as effortless arousals and acted-upon consciousness (i.e. 'feminine' water or *mayyin nukbin*). The mystic's soul is always yearning to swim upstream, mitigating Judgement so as to bring more flow of Divine Compassion into the world. When the mystic embodies more compassion and deeper humility, then the perfect hu-man manifestation of pure consciousness no longer remains a reflection in the water but gives way to the reality of that water itself.

* * *

148.13 Understanding, and the Dichotomies of Opinion

"... So that water be divided from water" [Gen.. 1:6]. I heard an explanation from my teacher [the Besht] of the Talmudic dictum [BT Eruvin fol. 13b, Hagiga 3b]: 'Even though these forbid and those permit, these and those are the words of the Living God'—which would seem to permit the truth of two opposites with reference to one issue. How can this be? This matter may be resolved when we consider that the three pathways of manifestation—Grace, Judgement, and Compassion proceed from the Six Days of World Construction, as is written [Psalm 89:2] 'The world shall be constructed through Grace', as one of the six directions of space. And these six directions are called: worthy, disqualified, permitted, forbidden, impure, and pure, be-cause within the realm of dimensionality the opposites are manifested. But above the six directions, all things are totally unified, and the dichotomies of worthy, disqualified, permitted, etc. do not exist. In this way, the realm of Understanding surpasses the Six Days of World Construction, and is called 'the Living God'. This is the meaning of 'although ... these and those are the words of the Living God', because Understanding serves to unite all things. However, when the matter descends, to be within the Six Days of World Construction, there arises the need to adjudicate between judgement and compassion, and between the good and evil inclinations, and reward and retribution, because within the world the opposites are actually manifested. And the words of the wise are gracious.

1.22 The Human Being as Intermediary, Uniting Worlds, Souls, and Divinity

What we may discern in the totality of all, when all return to the Divine Uni-ty, are vessels [that express the Divine Unity]. This is the realm of 'Worlds' emanated by the One Unique Master. He illuminates them by giving them life, for there is no place void of His Presence ... This is the aspect of Divin-ity, for 'The entire world is filled with His Glory' [Isa. 6:3]; because the light of the Infinite extends even to the point of the lowest depths. Now there is an intermediate level between the Divine Light and the vessels or 'worlds' containing It. This is the level of 'Souls', as well as the level of the Torah. These serve to bind together Divinity and the vessels, delivering the Divine Effluence to the manifested realm. Thus nothing exists—neither object nor even word—wherein one aspect of each of the three levels does not inhere;

each manifesting according to its level of purity. These levels [of inherence] are called in the Lurianic Writings, gestation, suckling-nurture, and mature intelligence; or, *Shekhinah*, souls, and angels.

1.24 The Unification practices of the AR"I and the Besht

Take heed and know, that the roots of these three levels are as follows: the 'worlds' are the Divine vessels, out of which come the angels; the Souls are the essence of the 'Masculine and Feminine Waters', and Divinity refers to the Transcendent Spirit, the Primordial Light contained in every word. These are the components of what is referred to in the Unification [*Yichu-dim*] Practices of the AR"I and the Besht.

20. Preparation for Prayer, and the Importance of Pacing Oneself

I heard from my teacher [the Besht], of blessed memory, that one needs to fortify oneself before prayer, so that one would have the presence of mind to pray—at the very least, without being distracted; and preferably, with conscious adhesion to the Divine Presence [*Devekut*]. This [fortification] can be achieved by reciting the Songs of Praise [*Pesuqei d'Zimrah*], or by studying Torah and entering prayer in the [mental] context of Torah study, which enhances mental acuity. But there are those, who if they were to be excessive in their reciting of the Songs of Praise or in their Torah study before prayer, they wouldn't be able to sustain their power of concentration. This is why it is said: [B.T. Menachot fol. 109] "Whether one does much or little, what is important is that one intend in one's heart, for the sake of Heaven"—so that one have proper intention during prayer. Therefore both are equal, and the Taz's question is thereby answered.

20.1 Two Types of Awakening—
Purity of Intent is more Important than Proficiency

"If a woman sprouts seed and a male-child is born ...": [Leviticus 12:1] Our sages have declared [B.T. Nidda fol. 38b]: "If a woman gives seed first, then a male is born; if the male gives seed first, then a female is born." To understand this in a metaphorical way, it should be pointed out that there are two types of arousal. In one case the person is first aroused in a self-originated sense to return to God or to do the good thing. Then the person is helped from Above, in accordance with the principle: "One who comes to be purified is helped" [B.T. Yoma fol. 35b]. The second type of awakening occurs when the person does not take to heart to return to God on one's own accord, or to do good, unless first aroused from Above—whereby the person is moved to return to God. The difference between them—as I heard from my teacher [the Besht]—is implied in the secret [metaphorical] meaning of 'if a woman gives seed first, then a male is born'. The designation 'male' refers to [the response of] Divine Compassion—so too, if the arousal is from below, meaning that the "Feminine Waters" are activated, then the "Masculine Waters" proceed from Above—yielding compassion. But the opposite implies judgement [from Above].

20.2 Effort Versus Passivity,
and the means of Rectifying Previous Passivity

I heard from my teacher [the Besht] of blessed memory, that one needs to empower oneself before prayer—and thereby, the question of the Taz is answered. Thus, when a person devises a ruse so as to arouse oneself in prayer, such an act is called 'masculine', or the active-creative consciousness of Grace. Whereas this is not the case when a person needs arousal from on-High, such as when one is spontaneously aroused to weeping, or other such effortless arousals. These are called 'feminine' or passive, acted-upon consciousness. In such a case 'one's prayer is regarded as transgression [see Psalm 109:7]! The way to rectify this, is to arouse a sense of dread upon becoming aware of not having been aroused due to one's own efforts, and having to be aroused from above. So that one 'weep' over the unintentional earlier weeping. Thereby one transforms the Feminine Waters to Masculine Waters, and becomes 'male'.

44. True Love and Awe distinguished from: 1. Self-Perceptions due to Metabolic Predisposition; 2. Self-Induced Emotions

...Observe how it is that Awe befalls you; [I refer here] not [to] the fear and awe that you arouse within yourself—for this is considered as 'the rising of Feminine Waters'. The true Awe, however, is experienced as being seized by a shuddered-trembling; and out of the awe of sudden realization, one loses orientation momentarily, and does not know where one is. Its result is experienced as one's awareness becoming purified, and at times tears well up of themselves. But when it is not like this, although it appears that s/he loves the Creator, it is nothing. Because [Psalm 118:20 and see Zohar 1:11b] "This is the gateway to God"—Awe is the gateway to Love, and if one does not enter through the Gate of Awe, it is impossible that one be in a true state of Love. And we know that [Prov. 31:23 and Zohar 1:103b] "Her Husband is known in the Gates"—when the person is 'within the gate' within fear—then the blessed holy One unites with one, because [BT Qedushim 2b] 'the way of the man is to pursue the woman'; and the blessed holy One is called 'the Man' who seeks out one who had Divine Awe—who is called 'the woman'—as in [Prov 31:30] "The woman in awe of God; she shall be praised"—and thereby, one is regarded as 'with God'—[Deut. 32:9] "For a portion of God is His Nation".

And one who does not know the likeness of this, isn't even 'a servant' [of God] and is certainly not on the level of those upon whom the Awe dawns; and does not render the service worthy of a Jew at all! Such a one serves the blessed Name only out of having been trained in this way; but imagines oneself as actually serving the blessed Name, and serving Him with joy. But this is merely the joy of excitation. Therefore, return to God with all your heart and with all your effort.

80. The Importance of Self-Arousal, and the Text of Prayer as the Soul's Procession through the Worlds

I heard from my teacher [the Besht] regarding the Morning Prayer, that it should be as though 'I awaken the dawn' [Tur Orah Hayim1], and not that the dawn awakens me. This is to say, that the person must take the initiative and exert effort in one's gradual ascent, even in the section of prayer corresponding to the World of Action, which is the lowest world, the place where the realm of the obscurations (*kelipot*) is most prevalent; until one arrives to the prayer of '*Barukh she'Amar*'. Then one may apply greater concentration, from '*Baruh she'Amar*' until '*Yishtabah*', which corresponds to the World of Formation, where the obscurations are diminished. Then, from '*Yishtabah*' until the Silent Prayer [*Amidah*] one should further increase concentration—and during the Silent Prayer, the 'embracing' and the true Union take place. Therefore [at that time] one should entirely divest oneself of physicality, as is written in Orah Hayim [section 98]. In this way, one arouses the 'Feminine Waters' and thereby, the 'Masculine Waters' are awakened. This is not the case if the arousal comes to the person without the person making the effort. Such a circumstance indicates unworthiness and tribulation—'His prayer shall be a transgression'! [Ps.109:7]. One rectifies this, when one becomes aware that this is what happened, by feeling a deep sense of remorse and dread and then, praying from the depth of one's heart.

80.1 The Practice of Contemplative Ascent

It is written [Psalm 43:3] "Send Your light and Your truth, and they shall guide me"—Have in mind at all times that the Divine Presence-*Shekhinah*, whose Dignity fills all the land is guiding your thought, from below to above with great power, and that the very firmaments split apart by means of your thought, as though they are opening before you. Enter into the World of *Yetzirah* [Formation-emotion] and after, to *Beriah* [Creation-conceptuality], and then, to the world of *Atzilut* [Emanation-direct unified Presence]. Then descend in your thought, and ascend again, so that you ascend and descend many times. And bear in mind that the descent is for the sake of a later ascent, so that you may rise even higher.

This may be likened to one who wants to toss a stone. The lower one places one's hand prior to tossing the stone, the higher it will rise once released. And when you ascends in thought into the spiritual aspect of the World of *Assiah* [Action], or *Yetzirah* [Formation], bear in mind that you are speaking [the words of prayer] within that world. Contemplate in your *Kavvanah*-intention that the Tetragrammaton is present before you, manifesting within Ten *Sefirot*, whose greatness is boundless. As you proceed in ascent, imagine and intend that you are coming close to the Blessed Name in exalted places, as the Zohar states: [2:82a] 'The legs of the King are not the same as the head of the King'. And so throughout the day, even when it is not the time of prayer, elevate yourself in thought, at all times.

You need great strength for this, so as to be able to cleave above, in your consciousness. Therefore, strengthen yourself with all of your powers. At first, although you may have the ability to rise to great height, do not rise above the [spiritual] World of Action. Rather, repair within that realm and then go on to the World of Formation, and then to the World of Creation, and then to Emanation. Let this great principle into your hands.

109. The Vicissitudes of Life in the Life of Prayer

'God has delivered Me into the hands of one through whom I cannot rise' [Lament. 1:14]: I have received [instruction] from my teachers and from holy books, [to the effect] that each day one's intention in prayer needs to be different. This is as the Talmud states [B.T. Berachot fol. 29b] "If one is able to innovate in prayer, then it is not considered 'a fixed task'". A proof that this must necessarily be the case, comes from the understanding that the purpose of prayer is to purify holy sparks from broken vessels. This is achieved by the mystical raising of Feminine Waters to *Malchut* so that She unite with Her Husband [*Tiferet*—Divine Harmony]. And the means of raising the Feminine Waters are enacted by raising the sparks that are contained in the actual thoughts that occur to the person during prayer. The wise person who has the clarity of [self-]perception knows how to 'sift out' the inner-meaning from one's extraneous thoughts. These constitute the holy sparks that entered into obscurations and thus became extraneous thoughts.

For example, if thoughts of sexual desire occur to the person, s/he should recognize them as fallen expressions of the Divine Attribute of *Hesed*-kindness, as it is written [Lev. 20:17] 'if a man shall take his sister ... it is [a disgraceful] *Hesed*', and the person should understand that if s/he has a desire for this [it is] due to a holy spark within it, so that the person may cleave to the root-meaning of this pleasure, where there is pleasure without measure. And so too with regard to idolatry, Heaven-forefend which corresponds to fallen 'harmony'; or destructive anger which is fallen 'strength-judgement'-the left side. However, dwelling on these is dangerous, and the intelligent one will be silent. Now we may observe that no two days contain the same thoughts; so too with regard to prayer it can be innovated upon each and every day, based on the person's self-observation vis-a-vis one's distracting thoughts; and then it may be regarded as genuine prayer.

To do this practice properly, one needs to cultivate the presence of broad and calm awareness and great concentration and that one's mouth and heart and thoughts should be of one consent, as is known. Whereas if one prays in a set-way, just as one did yesterday and the day before, and one's tongue is 'used to the words' and one bows down at '*Modim*' automatically, and one's heart is not abiding with one's actual presence, it is as the *Tosafot* stated [BT Rosh haShanah fol. 16b, '*vilyun*', quoting the Jerusalem Talmud: "one ought to thank one's head for bowing at *Modim*".

It seems to me that there are ten phrases used to express prayer, [Midrash, Devarim Rabba 2:1]—outcry, shout, groan-wail, exultation, chance-meeting-sensitive-vulnerability, a restrained request, a calling to, falling abjectness, hopeful-beseeching, seeking-favor—and these correspond to the Ten Attributes in *Malchut* which is called Prayer, and Its lowest aspect is 'the *Malchut* of *Malchut*'. One prays in accordance with the unique energy of the day—for each day one is required to repair and activate one spark of the aspects of these Ten Attributes of *Malchut*, so that at the end of one's days one would have rectified unto the last attribute; in order that one would be able to fully return to *Malchut* which is called Prayer—each person in the context of the integrity of his or her nature, and individual pathway. This is so on the individual level, just as is the case with regard to the [final] generation of the 'Footheels of the Mashiach' when there will be a repair of the entire world even to its lowest levels—its 'heels'. Thereupon, all of the sparks of *Malchut* corresponding to all aspects of the world will rise, and then death itself will be swallowed in eternity and Mashiach will arrive. The process [of cosmic repair] works in this way for each individual—that one's means of expression cultivated throughout one's life becomes a coherent whole.

Accordingly, a person needs to know that prayer is not merely for one's own self, but primarily for the sake of on high—for the *Shekhina* [Divine Presence]. And as the AR''I stated, if a person intends one's prayer for personal benefit, the *Shekhina* laments, saying 'God has delivered Me into the hands of one through whom I cannot rise' [Lament. ibid.]; but if one intends one's prayer for the sake of the *Shekhina*, one is answered immediately, as stated in Tiqunei *haZohar* [#18 fol. 55a] 'If the *Shekhina* is present, they open the gates immediately'. So too, one's request becomes incorporated in the attribute of Understanding, the Mother of all life. And all souls being portions of the *Shekhina*, the person praying thus is also answered.

But if one intends—in intending for the *Shekhina*—that s/he be answered, this creates a dividing-barrier. May the blessed Name illuminate us so that we serve Him with truth and simplicity. And the sign by which one knows that one is being answered is indicated in the verse [Psalm 10:17] "You will prepare their heart—Your ears shall listen". If one is aided to the extent that one is able to enter into the depth of prayer, then certainly, 'Your ears shall listen'—for if it were not a time of Divine favor, so that one is able to enter into the chamber of the King and be answered, one would not have been able to concentrate [to such an extent]. Thus the very fact that one can enter to the Presence of the King, implies that certainly one's request will be fulfilled—because there is no impediment to the fulfillment of one's request, since the blessed Name is the epitome of compassion and kindness.

Now there are those who enter to the Presence of the King whose request is not fulfilled. This may be likened to a king whose queen fell out of favor, and in the course of time she was chased away from his presence and traveled far away. Then it happened that the king had business that brought him to her environs, and when she became apprised of this, she manipulated her way to get to see him. She came before him and beseeched him, telling him how bitter is her lot on account of her having to depart from the king, and she recounted to him all that befell her from the day she was forced to depart. Her words of imploring and her intention to reestablish peace between them were successful, so that the King was won over and her request was fulfilled.

But if she would come to him with bitter complaint on account of feeling betrayed by him, then if she were to meet the king, who is himself in a pained state anyway, and she by her complaints is only adding to his pain, then her words would not be heard. Unless she finds him in a state of magnanimity so that her words 'register' with him, so that he would agree that she was right for leaving, and that it is not fitting to the honor of the king [that he ignore her] then she is answered—at a 'favorable time'—even though her manner of expression was querulous. This is why [sometimes] the *Shekhina* is called 'dissension'. Enough, for those who understand.

* * *

And God spoke to Moshe face to face [Exod. 33:11]—It is written [Prov.27:20] "As in water face answers to face, so the heart of one person to the other". In the name of the Baal Shem Tov, his soul in the arcane heights: When a person stands near water, his shadow looms large on the water. And when the person bends over to the water, the shadow [which becomes a reflection] becomes smaller—and the more the person bends over and moves closer to the water, the smaller the reflection becomes; so that if the person places her face on the water then the reflection in the water will precisely correspond to the face. So too it is with the heart of one person to the other. If the person considers himself great, with self-importance, then his companion will consider himself in the same way. And if he regards himself humbly before his friend so too will his friend be humble towards him. And when they can no longer decrease their image of self-importance, they will indeed be with each other as equals. This is the meaning of the verse "And God spoke to Moshe face to face just as a person would speak to his friend"—i.e. corresponding to the degree of genuine humbleness that the person manifests towards her friend so too will the friend react in kind, so that they become equal and really face each other. This was the case with Moshe, who humbled himself before the blessed Creator, so too did the Creator humble Himself so-to-speak vis-a-vis Moshe, and conversed with him face to face. So it was, that the 'face' of God became like a reflection of the face of Moshe. This is a level that no one but Moshe was able to attain, because Moshe was the perfect human manifestation of pure consciousness. *Or HaKhochma VaYakhel; Ki Tissa # 15*

The River of Life Flowing from God

Then the angel showed me the pure river of the water of life, as clear as crystal, flowing from the throne of God and of the Lamb down the middle of the great street of the city. On each side of the river stood the tree of life, bearing twelve kinds of fruit, yielding its fruit every month. And the leaves of the tree are for the healing of the nations. No longer will there be any curse. The throne of God and of the Lamb will be in the city, and his servants will serve him. They will see his face, and his name will be on their foreheads. There will be no more night. They will not need the light of a lamp or the light of a lamp or the light of the sun, for the Lord God will give them light. And they will reign forever and ever.

Revelation 22:1-7

"Shells upon the Shore"*

Henry David Thoreau

Water indeed *reflects heaven* because my mind does—such is its serenity—its transparence—& stillnesss.... Standing on distant hills you see the *heavens reflected* the evening sky in some low lake or river in the valley—as perfectly as in any mirror they could be—Does it not prove how intimate heaven is with earth?

...great crystals on the surface of the earth, Lakes of Light. If they were permanently congealed, and small enough to be clutched, they would, perchance, be carried off by slaves, like precious stones, to adorn the heads of emperors; but being liquid, and ample, and secured to us and our successors forever, we disregard them. They are too pure to have a market value; they contain no muck.

From the primitive word Ver, signifying water...is derived the word verite; for as water, by reason of its transparency and limpidness, is the mirror of bodies—of physical êtres, representing them in a manner as faithful and clear, as the water does a physical body.

And I forgot to say that after I reach the road by Potters barns—or further by potters Brook—I saw the moon sudden and reflected full from a pool—A puddle from which you may see the moon reflected—& the earth dissolved under your feet.

The magical moon with attendant stars suddenly looking up with mild lustre from a window in the dark earth.

13 June 1851, *Journal 3*

All the world reposes in beauty to him who preserves equipoise in his life, and moves serenely on his path without secret violence; as he who sails down a stream, he has only to steer, keeping his bark in the middle, and carry it round the falls. The ripples curled away in our wake, like ringlets from the head of a child, while we steadily held on our course.

A Week, 317

Life in us is like the water in a river.

Walden, 332

My nature may be as still as this water—but it is not so pure & its reflections are not so distinct.

What a singular element is this water!

20 January 1859, *Journal* XI

Having read the preceding essays on water symbolism, we invite the reader to read with 'new eyes' which perceive the 'meanings behind the forms', and thus practice the art and science of 'reading the Book of Nature.' -Editors

How perfectly new and fresh the world is seen to be, when we behold a myriad sparkles of brilliant white sunlight on a rippled stream! So remote from dust and decay, more bright than the flash of an eye.

24 May 1860, *Journal* XIII

A lake is the landscape's most beautiful and expressive feature. It is earth's eye; looking into which the beholder measures the depth of his own nature.

Walden, 186

What I have observed of the pond is no less true in ethics. It is the law of average. Such a rule of the two diameters not only guides us toward the sun in the system and the heart of man, but draw lines through the length and breadth of the aggregate of a man's particular daily behaviors and waves of life into his coves and inlets and where they intersect will be the height or depth of his character. Perhaps we need only to know how his shores trend and his adjacent country or circumstances, to infer his depth and concealed bottom.

Walden, 291-92

What unanimity between the water & the sky—one only a little denser element than the other. The grossest part of heaven—Think of a mirror on so large a scale! Standing on distant hills you see the heavens reflected the evening sky in some low lake or river in the valley—as perfectly as in any mirror they could be—Does it not prove how intimate heaven is with earth?

31 August 1851, *Journal* 4

A field of water betrays the spirit that is in the air. It is continually receiving new life and motion from above. It is intermediate in its nature between land and sky. On land only the grass and trees wave, but the water itself is ripple by the wind. I see where the breeze dashes across it by the streaks or flashes of light. It is remarkable that we can look down on its surface. We shall, perhaps, look down thus on the surface of air at length, and mark where a still subtler spirit sweeps over it.

Walden, 188-89

The water or lake from however distant a point seen is always the center of the landscape.

13 October 1852, *Journal* 5

How dead would the globe seem, especially at this season, if it were not for these water surfaces! We are slow to realize water—the beauty and magic of it. It is interestingly strange to us forever. Immortal water, alive even in the superficies, restlessly heaving now and tossing me and my boat, and sparkling with life!

8 May 1854, *Journal* VI

To-day it was the Purple Sea, and epithet which I should not before have accepted. There were distinct patches of the color of a purple grape with the bloom rubbed off. But first and last the sea is of all colors. Well writes Gilpin concerning "the brilliant hues which are continually playing on the surface of a quiet ocean," and this was not too turbulent at a distance from the shore. "Beautiful," says he, "no doubt in a high degree are those glimmering tints which often invest the tops of mountains but they are mere coruscations compared with these marine colors, which are continually varying and shifting into each other in all the vivid splendor of the rainbow, through the space often of several leagues."

Cape Cod, 93-94

❖

...The essence of my teachings is this:
See with original purity
Embrace with original simplicity
Reduce what you have
Decrease what you want

Tao Te Ching, from Verse 19

❖

Humility

In order for the Ocean to pour in, you must go below sea-level, instead of standing on the hillock of your self.

Source unknown

❖

We come to this learning by analogies.

Plotinus

The Role and Significance of Water in the Islamic Garden

Emma Clark

Water is present in most gardening traditions, from the Japanese and Chinese to the medieval Christian, the Italian Renaissance, and—the main focus here—the Islamic, all emphasising one aspect or another. Why is it that we are so drawn to water? The answer is very profound and lies beyond the practical requirements of irrigation, ablutions and drinking, beyond the aesthetic and sensuous delights of beholding a still, reflecting pool or feeling the water flowing through one's fingers in channels and fountains. All these pleasures attract us when walking around a garden[1]; but why is it that it is always near water where we end up sitting? Its beauty and mystery draw us like an invisible magnet. It seems that near water we discover a profound feeling of rest and calm, a sense of identification where the eye, the heart and the soul are fully engaged—we feel truly and completely at home.

There is no doubt that this total repose occurs because, whether we are conscious of it or not, water is symbolic of the soul. The soul recognises itself when 'it beholds water—finding animation in its play, refreshment in its rest, and purity in its clarity,'[2] It is written in the Qur'an 'We made every living thing of water' (XXI: 3), and human beings consist largely of water (approximately 70%)—so profoundly, we are connected to the Divine by this element. If we spend time contemplating water in a garden it is as if the hardness of one's worldly soul gradually melts into the essence of the water itself. One departs from it, refreshed and renewed, although with sadness since inevitably the worldly soul reasserts itself.

* * *

"The spirit of the garden-paradises of Europe hides in the flowers, the grass, the trees, but the soul of the Eastern garden lies in none of these; it is centred on the running water which alone makes its other beauties possible."[3]

There is no doubt that water is the supreme element in the Islamic garden, both on a practical and symbolic level. The immediate and obvious reason is that Islam is a religion born into a baking-hot desert climate where water was already, long before the advent of Islam, considered sacred and a blessing from Heaven. 'And of His signs is that thou seest the earth humble: then, when We send down water upon it, it quivers and swells. Surely He who

---

1. Or indeed a non-domestic landscape, in a wood or fields, we are still drawn by the sound of a stream, the glimpse of a lake, and, on altogether more majestic a scale, the sound of waves breaking on the sea-shore.
2. Titus Burckhardt, 'The Symbolism of Water', included in this volume, from *Mirror of the Intellect,* Cambridge, England, Quinta Essentia, 1987
3. Constance Villiers-Stuart, *Gardens of the Great Mughals*, London, 1913, p. 68

quickens it is He who quickens the dead' (XIX:22-5). The effect that even a tiny amount of water has on the desert is vivdly conveyed by Muhammad Asad's following observation:

> We had stopped for our noon prayer. As I washed my hands, face and feet from a water-skin, a few drops spilled over a dried-up tuft of grass at my feet, a miserable little plant, yellow and withered and lifeless under the harsh rays of the sun. But as the water trickled over it, a shiver went through the shrivelled blades, and I saw how they slowly, tremblingly, unfolded. A few more drops, and the little blades moved and curled and then straightened themselves slowly, hesitatingly, trembling.... I held my breath as I poured more water over the grass tuft. It moved more quickly, more violently, as if some hidden force were pushing it out of its dream of death. Its blades—what a delight to behold!—contracted and expanded like the arms of a starfish, seemingly overwhelmed by a shy but irrepressible delirium, a real little orgy of sensual joy: and thus life re-entered victoriously what a moment ago had been as dead, entered it visibly, passionately, overpowering and beyond in its majesty.[4]

As is well known, the Qur'an describes Paradise for the faithful and righteous as a beautiful garden with flowing water and shade-giving trees. The phrase 'Gardens underneath which rivers flow' (*Jannat tajri min tahtiha al-anhar*) is the one used most often to describe these *Jannat al-firdaws*, the gardens of Paradise. But the concept of the Paradise garden with water and shade as the two key elements pre-dates all three monotheistic religions, Judaism, Christianity and Islam, by centuries, going right back to the Sumerian period (4,000 B.C.) in Mesopotamia where the Paradise garden for the gods was described as having a fountain and shade-giving tree. So the idea of that Paradise is a garden of green shade and running water, central to Muslim belief, was not an innovation: it was a confirmation and renewal of what the Arabs knew already—that there is no life on earth without water and that this precious element can never be taken for granted. To them water was to be revered as a gift and a mercy from God, Martin Lings going so far as to say 'In the Qur'an the ideas of Mercy and water—in particular rain—are in a sense inseparable.'[5]

The quintessential Islamic garden is the four-fold design or *chahar-bagh* (from the Persian meaning 'four gardens') with a fountain in the centre and four channels of water flowing from it towards the four directions of space. This plan arose from a profound 'marriage' between the optimum irrigation system perfected in ancient Persia and the descriptions in the Qur'an and

---

4. Muhammad Asad, was a German Jew who converted to Islam in the 1920s and wrote about his travels and experiences in his book, *The Road to Mecca* (rev. ed. Louisville, KY: Fons Vitae, 2001).
5. See Martin Lings' essay in this volume, 'The Quranic Symbolism of Water', (from *Symbol and Archetype, A Study of the Meaning of Existence*, Quinta Essentia, 1991; Fons Vitae, 2006).

hadith of the four gardens of Paradise. Importantly, the number four encompasses a timeless and universal sacred symbolism.[6] It represents everything associated with the Earth—for example, the four cardinal directions, the four elements and the four seasons, while the circle is the great symbol of Heaven. In the Qur'an (XLVII:15) four rivers, one of water, one of milk, one of honey and one of wine are mentioned, and the Prophet Muhammad speaks of these four same rivers in a *hadith*, flowing from the centre towards the four directions of space. This echoes the Book of Genesis (II:10) in which it is written 'And a river went out of Eden to water the garden and from thence it was parted into four heads'.[7]

The four gardens of Paradise are most fully described in Chapter 55 of the Qur'an, *Surat al-Rahman*, the Chapter of the All-Merciful. Here there is a fountain in each garden, as well as a specific tree: four gardens, four rivers, four fountains, four trees. The central fountain in the Islamic garden on earth is the main source of water flowing through the garden, and sometimes (The Court of Lions at the Alhambra for example) there are also four smaller fountains, one on each of the four sides of the garden, with water flowing from them towards the centre: not only do these fountains represent the fountains in Paradise but the central one is also a reflection of the Source of all life, echoing the principle fundamental to Islam, 'from God do we come and unto Him do we return' (*inna lillahi wa inna ilahi raji'un*).[8] The fountain in the centre of an Islamic garden is often a circular basin set within a square base, the place where, in symbolic terms, Heaven and earth meet. This fountain, as with the fountains in the courtyard of a mosque, is used for ablutions and for drinking as well as symbolising the ever-flowing waters of the spirit which continually replenish and purify the soul—just as spring water is constantly purified at its source. So the Islamic garden on earth, with its ever-flowing waters, is created as both a symbol of the Heavenly gardens as well for as giving the faithful a foretaste of them whilst on earth.

There are many references to water throughout the Qur'an—it is, along with all the wonders of nature such as 'night and the day', the 'sun and the moon', one of the 'signs' of God, and the Qur'an is constantly reminding us whence water comes and not to take it for granted: 'Hast thou not seen how that God sends down out of heaven water?' (XXV: 25) 'We sent down out of Heaven water and caused to grow in it of every generous kind' (XXXI: 10). When the Virgin Mary (*Sayyidatna* Maryam) gave birth to the infant Jesus beneath a palm-tree, she was comforted in her distress by dates to eat from

---

6. There is no separation between the sacred and the profane in traditional Islam, as with all traditional societies—life and prayer and art are all inextricably linked, the practical and the spiritual go hand-in-hand.

7. Indeed, the gardens of Paradise in the Qur'an are referred to as *Jannat al-'Adn* (XVIII:31), literally 'gardens of Eden' indicating their primordial purity.

8. This four-fold plan is found—with many inventive variations—across the Islamic world, often with paths taking the place of the water-channels, for example at the gardens of the al-Batha Palace in Fes and the gardens of Alcazar in Cordoba.

the palm and a voice saying, 'Thy Lord has set below thee a rivulet' so that she could drink (XIX: 22-5). This association between sustenance from the Almighty in the form of running water—this time in the form of a 'rivulet', emphasises again the link between water and mercy, and by extension the importance of running water in channels or rills in an Islamic garden.

The lack of division between practical daily life and spiritual needs is summed up most powerfully by the dual role of water, which is both life-giving and cleansing in the obvious senses, as well as being spiritually rejuvenating and purifying. Martin Lings makes the observation that after a bather emerges from 'a lake or river or sea' the purifying effect of water upon the soul is momentarily visible upon the face of the bather 'however quickly it may be effaced by the resumption of ordinary life'.[9] In Christian baptism, the blessed water symbolically 'washes away sins' and purifies the soul. There is a similar attitude in Islam. Not only are Muslims required to make careful ablutions before their five daily prayers but these ablutions are symbolically a cleansing of the soul as well as the body, a returning to a state of purity in preparation for the ritual prayer (*salat*). 'Cleanliness is, indeed, next to Godliness' could well be an Islamic saying.[10] It is important to note that the ritual ablutions (*wudu*) of a Muslim must be carried out with running water, not still water in a basin, since running water remains uncontaminated, constantly renewing itself.[11]

This brings us back to our central theme of water symbolising the soul, about which Titus Burckhardt has written so beautifully.[12] The fluidity of water and its constantly purifying aspect—the closer to the source it is, whether it be a spring, melted snow or rain, the purer it is—is a reflection of the soul's ability to purify and renew itself. In spiritual terms this purification of the soul can only take place through the constant and sincere remembrance of God through prayer and meditation. As mentioned in the Introduction, proximity to water can open up our souls to Divine grace thereby aiding us in this remembrance. And the Islamic garden, with its multitude of ways of channelling water—trickling gently in narrow rills, cascading down small waterfalls or carved stone slabs (*chadors*, from the Persian, literally 'shawl' of water), spraying from fountains or remaining still and calm in pools—creates an harmonious environment in which the constant interplay between

---

9. See essay 'The Quranic Symbolism of Water', op.cit. It is interesting too, that regular immersion in cold water has been prescribed to people suffering from depression, for its uplifting and healing benefits.

10. John Wesley (1703-91) from his sermon no. xciii, *On Dress*. Ironically, when the Catholics gradually re-conquered Spain from the Muslims, they actively discouraged their Christian flock from washing too much since in their eyes water and washing had become associated with the Muslims who were linked with lust and lasciviousness!

11. Similarly for the Hindus, whosoever bathes in the river Ganges is cleansed in body and soul—despite its evident pollution.

12. Ibid

movement and stillness both soothes and mirrors the soul. The soul, changing as it does from one moment to the next—from alert activity to rest and renewal and many variations in between, finds itself completely at home in such surroundings, and is loath to leave.

St. Paul wrote that the spiritual person will always look beyond the visible to the invisible: 'We look not at the things which are seen but at the things which are not seen, for the things which are seen are temporal; but the things which are not seen are eternal';[13] one of the principal roles of water in an Islamic garden is to remind us of this. One moment the reflection in a still pool is crystal clear; then in a second, a breath of wind shatters the image, a telling reminder that this world is but an illusion, an ephemeral reflection of the eternal Heavenly realm. In Sufi poetry, such as that of Jalal ud-din Rumi, there is also an emphasis on the invisible and the 'garden within'—the visible object we perceive with the eye is as fleeting as a reflection in water:

> The real orchards and verdure are in the very essence of the soul: the reflection thereof upon that which is without is as the reflection in running water.[14]

Our own view of water is largely determined by the climate in which we were brought up. Water does not mean the same to inhabitants of temperate climates as to the inhabitants of many Islamic countries with unforgiving heat and inhospitable terrain. Indeed, so precious is water in such climates that the Bedouin nomads of Arabia have developed a whole vocabulary of special terms to indicate the intricate movements that water makes—not because there is so much water (like the Inuit and their words for snow) but because it is so rare and cherished. Running water in a hot climate also possesses health-giving and healing properties. The air that surrounds clean running water is always clearer and cooler, especially in an enclosed space, and this is extremely pleasant and invigorating in high temperatures. Also, the sound of water in fountains, when carefully controlled to be gentle and melodious rather than loud and gushing, has a beautifully soothing and restorative effect.

Hassan Fathy, the great Egyptian reviver of traditional Islamic architecture, suggested that the fountain in a hot country was equivalent in importance to the open fire (in a fireplace) in a cold country—in terms of both practical use and symbolic significance. There is much to be said for this analogy as it brings home both the practical necessity and the intense symbolic significance of the fountain and of the fire alike. Just as the fountain is a living grace as it were at the heart of the courtyard house, the garden or mosque, so the fire—to those who live in a cold climate—brings not only

---

13. St. Paul's Letter to the Corinthians, IV:8
14. Quoted in the author's book *The Art of the Islamic Garden*, The Crowood Press 2004, p. 91

much needed warmth but also essential cheer and homeliness, the 'life and soul' of the house in fact.[15]

The human soul has much to withstand in the modern world, and is often very agitated and in need of balm and renewal. The presence of water in a garden, as well as mirroring the soul's fluctuations, acts as a soothing balm, helping to put troubles into perspective and reminding us that the trials of life, like life itself, are as transient as a reflection in water. The apparently endlessly flowing water in the courtyard and gardens of the Alhambra and Generalife, in Spain are some of the most evocative representations of the Islamic Gardens of Paradise anywhere in the world. The sound of water not only muffles the voices of other people but has the miraculous effect of silencing one's own thoughts and giving us a taste of the peace of Paradise. Peace, salaam, is the only word spoken in the Quranic gardens of Paradise, that same peace which Jesus Christ referred to as the 'peace which passeth all understanding', when one's heart and soul are still and silent, allowing the world to pass on by.

The River Watering Eden

A river watering the garden flowed from Eden; from there it was separated into four headwaters. The name of the first is Pishon; it winds though the entire land of Havilah, where there is gold. The gold of that land is good; aromatic resin and onyx are also there. The name of the second river is Gihon; it winds through the entire land of Cush. The name of the third river is Tigris; it runs along the east side of Asshur. And the fourth river is the Euphrates.

Genesis 2:10-14

---

15. Central heating, for all its advantages, is severely lacking in this respect—the symbol is gone and with it, a whole cosmological understanding, bringing home Martin Lings' words 'Symbolism is the most important thing in existence; and it is at the same time the sole explanation of existence.' Preface to *Symbol and Archetype*, op. Cit.
It is worth noting also the etymological link between 'heart' and 'hearth'.

Take Me To The River:
The Koan of Kindness

Dharma Talk by Bonnie Myotai Treace, Sensei

A student's voice sings out, *"Take me to the river... take me to the ground... I want to be delivered...I want to be found..."* She has a beautiful voice, plaintive, and when she sings it is from a soulful, ancient place that seems to change the plain afternoon air into the suddenly liminal.

The student voice: so haunting, full of hollows around the vowels, earnestly asking for birth, for water, to be brought to earth. Our school is called BOWS, the Bodies of Water School, and Kate is singing her intention. I play her song over and over here in our hermitage. The day is bright. Outside the two waterfalls are swollen from days of rain, and their sound is more intense than usual. Light flickers through the leaves, motioning with the mild breeze. What is it to ask for water, to sing for it from the bottom of one's feet? There's an old koan that seems part of the day:

> Someone asked, *"I've heard how the teachings say that 'the great sea doesn't harbor a corpse.' What is the sea?"*
>
> Master Caoshan said, *"It includes the whole universe."*
>
> The questioner asked, *"Then why doesn't it harbor a corpse?"*
>
> The master said, *"It doesn't let one whose breath has been cut off stay."*
>
> The questioner asked, *"Well, since it includes the whole universe why doesn't it let one whose breath has been cut off stay?"*
>
> The master said, *"In the whole universe there is no virtue. If the breath is cut off, there is virtue."*
>
> The questioner asked, *"Is there anything more?"*
>
> The master said, *"You can say there is, or there isn't, but what are you going to do about the dragon king who holds the sword?"*

This is often a poignant koan, most likely because on one level it is designed to help loosen the habitual need for self-belonging— and our corollary anxiety over exclusion and abandonment, of being "outside." When it is engaged with sincerely, it opens up the vulnerability of position, both interpersonally and in terms of the nature of things. And then, with that radical quality of love that koans of genuine clarity always offer, it invites a new possibility: a confidence beyond all false posturing, a reminder that the "dragon king's" capacity to cut through duality, the "is" and "is not," (as well as "can" and "can not") has rested squarely and easily in one's own hands from the beginning of time.

Master Caoshan (Jap., Sozan), is a familiar character to many Zen students as the successor to Master Dongshan (Jap., Tozan), instrumental along with him in the forming of the Soto School. Beyond that Caoshan is a figure largely shrouded in mystery. We hear about his arrival at Dongshan's monastery and his departure years later, but there are scant references to what happened in between other than that he received Dharma Transmission. Later in his life he went on to develop a teaching style characterized by wandering, never staying at any monastery for more than one seasonal training period. It is reported that he did not like public speaking. His lineage did not continue beyond a few generations, yet his contribution through the formation of the school and his role in shaping Dongshan's subtle and profound teaching style into an enduring treasure, give him a place in the history of Zen that is quite rare and quietly powerful.

In the present koan a student asks, "I have heard that the teachings say that 'the great sea does not harbor a corpse.'" We will need to explore what the sea is and what the corpse is before we can proceed effectively into the workings of the koan.

The sea is often used in Zen to indicate that which does not exclude anything, the container of all stillness and movement— thusness, or the vastness of the unbound. It is said, "all streams return to the great sea," meaning all Buddhist teachings are aimed at awakening. All things are within one reality. Buddhist teachings are said to be like an ocean in that they become deeper the further you go into them, and also in that they have a uniform flavor: the taste of liberation. The "oceanic reflection" or "ocean seal" refers to the calm mind reflecting all things, a great sea of thusness.

In the 13th Century the great poet master Dogen in his *Mountains and Rivers Sutra,* wrote, "Water is neither strong nor weak, wet nor dry, cold nor hot, being nor non-being, delusion nor enlightenment. Solidified, it is harder than diamond: who could break it? Melted, it is softer than milk: who could break it? This being the case, we cannot doubt the many virtues realized by water. We should then study that time when the waters of the ten directions are seen in the ten directions. This is not a study only of the time when humans and gods see water. There is a study of water seeing water. Water practices and verifies water; hence there is a study of water speaking water." Here water becomes a tremendous language for teaching: Harder than diamond, softer than milk... harder than diamond expressing the unchanging suchness of all things. Just this moment! Softer than milk, likewise, referring to the conditioned suchness of things. With these two phrases—harder than diamond, softer than milk—Dogen takes up water qualities to reveal the absolute and the conditioned aspects of reality

The great sea: how great can it be if it does not offer harbor to each and every thing? The student came across this line in the Nirvana Sutra, and it drove him down the road, into deep study, expressing in some sense his primal affair. To be driven in this way is to have in place a certain quality of heart-mind: a quality that recognizes depth and calling, rather than rejecting superficial contradiction.

This long-ago student, and the tone in Kate's voice today, perhaps not so different; the river song in the hermitage continues into a refrain that begs the same question: *"Open up these lost songs... open up my light... teach me to be kind... teach me tonight... "* If nothing is excluded, why is a corpse not harbored? What is "a corpse"? Is it someone who has died the great death, the death of the ego, the death of separation? Or is it the dead weight of self-absorption, of self-centered, self-possessing delusion that precludes all real kindness? What is that weight, that lifeless thing that never finds its true harbor, or any real rest or relief from itself? How, indeed, do we become kind? How, indeed, do we become our real selves?

Buddhism teaches that as we draw the skin bag around the idea of self, we live in a bubble of delusion, not letting the fresh water of reality flow in or flow out as experience. Always, that line between "us" and "it," maintains distance. When we operate at that distance, our attempts at kindness have a pre-meditated quality, strained with yearning or hopelessness. For this and so many reasons, this koan is a great gift, like a ladle of water from that hidden spring we sense belongs to us.

Caoshan's, "It .... includes the whole universe...." is reminiscent of the way many Zen students initially try to present their first koan, Muji. "It's everything!" we say. "It's the whole universe!" But with such an answer we've just gone in a circle; nothing has really opened up. Remaining is the question: what is the entire universe? What is it that contains everything? Unless the questioning becomes increasingly acute, the process becomes muted and remains immature, never advancing beyond the kind of thinking that dulls the mind, and depresses the sensitive heart. So much more is possible.

I heard someone recently explaining that the reason many of us feel we have a lousy life is that we ask lousy questions: "Why can't I do it? What's wrong with me?" (Or "Why have we so fouled the world? What's wrong with us?") Of course, the mind creates answers: "I'm inadequate; I'm a pig; I'm being punished by an unjust universe." ("We're idiots. We'll never get out of this mess...") It is possible to ask a different quality of question: "How can I step fully into the koan? Not later, but right now? What would it be like to enjoy the process?" Even this kind of questioning can get in the way at times, but occasionally it's grand medicine. "How can I step fully into the challenges that come my way and not fight with time? What if things as they are were not a mistake and I was perfectly positioned?"

In terms of the koan at hand, the questioner does go forward, deepening the ocean by walking into it: *"Well, since it includes the whole universe why doesn't it let one whose breath has been cut off stay?"*

The master said, "In the whole universe there is no virtue. If the breath is cut off, there is virtue."

We could rephrase this: In wholeness, there is not some "thing." Intimacy allows no perspective. Where there is cutting off, however, there are things. Separation allows multiplicity of perspective. If it can be cut off, then it began. If there is being there is non-being; if there is virtue, there is evil. The koan at this point is such a shower of generosity; like the student in the story, if we don't quite see, we look for elsewhere, for "more."

A story is told about a billionaire who was asked, "What's the secret to wealth?" He said, "Gratitude. If you don't have gratitude then no matter how much you have you're poor, because you are always looking at what you don't have. If you have gratitude then you are never not wealthy." It's like the Zen story of the hermit monk living in the mountains. While he's out gathering wood and roots a robber comes and strips his cabin, "everything" is gone. As night deepens he sits at the window and looks out at the evening moon, thinking to himself, "If only I could have given the robber this perfect, white moon." He's still wealthy. And he's asking a good question: What can I give now? How can I give at this moment? What is it that doesn't exclude even our misfortune, that includes the whole universe, that is absolutely trustworthy in its completeness?

In *Sensitive Chaos* Theodore Schwenk draws a picture of birds in migration. The depiction offers a beautiful window into who we are, what relationships might be actually expressing even as we're blithely constructing our stories:

> *Each bird lies on a wave which is made in the air by the leader who initiates it. The beats of their wings follow the ups and downs of the wave and simply make visible what, as a vibrating aerial form, surrounds and bears them all in the arrow formation. ...A bird does not need much strength, for it is as though the movement of the wave of air were to raise and lower its wings for it. If one of the birds has an excess of energy it will do more than simply allow itself to be carried along. With the beating of its wings it will strengthen the whole wave, will infuse the aerial form with energy from which all will benefit. ... Indeed, even the leading bird itself draws energy from this field.... Thus it comes about that during a long flight over many hundreds of miles each single bird elastically connected with the whole flight beats its wings exactly as many times as all the others in the formation. The entire process is an aerial form, an organic whole moving through the air. The bird is a creature of the air. It is born out of the air and entrusts itself to it. It cannot possibly be abandoned by the sky.*

It cannot possibly be abandoned by the sky. Sky and sea and self: can we be abandoned? Can we secure one another? The student asks: "What is kindness?" The student asks, "Why not let one whose breath has been cut off stay?" Caoshan is not oblivious to the truth implicit in the flock of birds. So, where are we to find the compassionate wisdom at work in his teaching? "Drag this student out by his toes! Out with the dead meat!"

The teacher may seem to be explaining, but what he's doing is something altogether more unnerving. This is where "never abandoned by the sky" and "the great sea doesn't harbor a corpse" is resolved. It's where the paradox of our absolute uniqueness and our complete, inextricable connectedness is realized.

The Nirvana Sutra line contradicts what is often construed as the basic truth of Buddhism: the unity of all life. The stickiness of our mind can make it very difficult to trust the vitality of the teaching here, but just as is required in studying Dogen, one's point of view is asked to shift, to flow, if not word by word, at least line by line, to a new perspective. In the whole universe there is no virtue. What point of view is that? *No eye, ear, nose, tongue, body, mind*—in complete intimacy, where would you stand to know virtue or its lack? And then Caoshan shifts. "When breath can be cut off, there is virtue." Be alive, not later, but now. There is no other one. There is no reason to delay or defer. You and the great sea, the journey to the river and the river itself: bring it *all home.*

In another koan Caoshan is asked, "What sort of understanding should one be equipped with to satisfactorily cope with the cross-examinations of others?" Caoshan says, "Don't use words and phrases." The student says, "Then what are you going to cross-examine about?" Caoshan says, "Even the sword and axe can't pierce it through." The student says, "What a fine cross-examination. But aren't there people who don't agree?" Caoshan says, "There are." The student says, "Who are they?" Caoshan says, "Me." It always comes to this. We might say there is nothing to prove, or perhaps better: everything, absolutely everything, is owed to life.

The old koan asks which is true? The universe of no separation and no exclusion, or the universe in which the breath can be cut off, in which we are inevitably distinct and distant? The student says, "Please, isn't there something more?" How do we not, subtly or overtly, fall into the stasis of this in how we live? This is at the heart of Kate's intention-song, her imploring into the daylight for real ground, asking so earnestly for the walk we each make to the river. It is *the* good question. In water language, it is the tongue beginning to taste the inarguable, "water speaks water" (or, "water verifies water") — the moment when everything comes home, and no one can say different. What is kindness when the world, nothing but water itself, suffers such thirst? Indeed, what is kindness when one of six humans have no water suitable to drink? There is no mistake in the water, you are not in the wrong place in it—yet even as it is whole and perfect, it requires your all. It celebrates and supports your *all*. Caoshan, great teacher, leaves us with the question warm in our palm: *"You can say there is or there is not. But what are you going to do about the dragon king who holds the sword?"*

A Section of the Oconee Near Watkinsville

Coleman Barks

Before I get in
the aluminum canoe floats flat on the shine
of water. Then I ruin its poise.
Middle of the first shoal, though, I'm out,
stumbling through the ankle-breaking rocks.
Canoe free-floating downstream, without decision
or paddle. I lunge and bruise across the shallows
to get a forefinger in the rope eye on the stern.

June afternoon light. June afternoon water.

I know there's a life being led in lightness,
out of my reach and discipline.
I keep trying to climb in its words,
and so unbalance us both.
The teacher's example is everywhere open,
like a boat never tied up, no one in it,
that drifts day and night, metallic dragonfly
above the sunken log.

As the Dew

Coleman Barks

I have tried to write
in praise of the dew
and what it does,
condensing nightair
into invisible eyedroppers
of cold water that wash
the hands of the grass blades.

It is that
sudden wet breakage

that we love.

Sandpipers, Again

Lisa Starr

I went back to the sandpipers today—
it's been a while.
Six of them,
or was it twenty? Never matters;
somehow we all know when a meeting has been called,
somehow we all know
exactly when the surf will start tossing back
its wild silver hair.

One time I was astonished
to find them waiting for me on the beach in Newport.
It was so quiet it was like rain
without the rain.
I wasn't planning it
my car just brought me there,
a most uncommon thing—it's not that kind of car
but there we were, alone on a beach.
It almost made me giddy,
like today,

just now.
I'd forgotten how much
I need them.
Like me they were laughing and
sputtering about the beauty.
A few of them couldn't help it
and just kept throwing their small bodies
again and again
into the wild, white water.

For Mary Kane

Lisa Starr

As I lie here
listening
to the waves
yawn
into roars

I'm sorry that you
live in a place
where the ocean
sounds
like traffic.

Water-Lines
selections from Hafiz of Shiraz*

Translated by John Slater and Jeffrey Einboden

Why die of thirst when the water of life is near?
Drink from the source, *For all things live from water.*

[Ghazal 422]

There's a lush garden of paradise in the monk's bare cell,
his secret work is a fountain of gracious power.

Hafiz! on the edge of eternal day, drink that purest water of life
whose wellspring is a speck of dust on the floor of the poor one's cell.

[Ghazal 50]

Hafiz, your words sweat the water of life...
how can the envious quibble?

[Ghazal 87]

Rare, singular Jewel—where *are* you?
Grieving you, the world wept oceans.

From the tip of each eyelash, vast floods of water—
Come, I can show you the river.

[Ghazal 153]

Eyes, be vigilant! Who knows when the next
flash-flood will come from this place of rest.

What a road! your path so broad
the boundless ocean of the sky fades like a mirage.

[Ghazal 31]

Help! hoisting the sail of loss, the boat of my patience
has been caught by the undertow in a sea of grief.

It won't be long before the ship is sunk, crushed beneath
a wave of yearning for you... in this shore-less ocean of loss.

[Ghazal 291]

What can the tears of Hafiz weigh before the boundless wealth of Love?
Compared to that terrible flood the seven seas are a drop of dew.

[Ghazal 461]

---

*From *The Tangled Braid,* forthcoming Spring, 2010, Fons Vitae.

The Sea[*]

Ananda K. Coomaraswamy

For Plato, The Divine Life is an "ever-flowing Essence" (ἀέναον οὐσίαν), Law 966E). For Meister Eckhart, who called Plato "that great priest," the Soul is "an outflowing river of the eternal Godhead" (Pfeiffer ed., p.581, cf. 394); and he says also, "while I was standing in the ground, the bottom, in the river and fountain of the Godhead, there was none to ask me where I was going or what I would be doing…And when I return into the ground, the bottom, the river and fountain of the Godhead, none will ask me whence I came or whither I went" (p. 181). In the same way Shamsi-i-Tabrīz: "None has knowledge of each who enters that he is so-and-so or so-and-so…. Whoever enters, saying 'Tis I,' I smite him on the brow."[1]

An incessant river of life implies an inexhaustible source, or *fons*—the Pythagorean "fountain, or spring, of the ever-flowing Nature" (πηγὴ ἀενάου φύσεως, Golden Verses 48). "Imagine," says Plotinus, "a fountain (πηγὴ) that has no origin beside itself; it gives itself to all the rivers, yet is never exhausted by what they take, but always remains integrally what it was… the fountain of life, the fountain of intellect, beginning of being, cause of the good, and root of the Soul" (Plotinus III.8.10 and VI.9.9). This, as Philo says in comment on Jer. 2:13, πηγὴ ζωῆς, is God, as being the elder source not only of life but of all knowledge (*De fuga et inventione* 137, 197, 198; *De Providentia* I.336); cf. John 4:10 and Rev. 14:7, 21:6. It is Jan van Ruysbroeck's "Fountain-head from which the rills flow forth. …There Grace dwells essentially; abiding as a brimming fountain, and actively flowing forth into all the powers of the soul" (Adornment of the Spiritual Marriage, ch. 35). And in the same way, Shams-i-Tabrīz: "Conceive Soul as a fountain, and these created beings as rivers. …Do not think of the water failing; for this water is without end" (Rūmī, *Dīvān*, Ode XII). Meister Eckhart speaks of the Divine Life as both "fontal and inflowing." The concept of the return of the Soul to its source, when its cycle is completed and, as Blake says, "the Eternal Man reassumes his ancient bliss," is, indeed, universal; so that, in its present sense, the Sea, as the source of all existences, is equally the symbol of their last end or entelechy. Such an end may appear at first sight to involve a loss of self-consciousness, and a kind of death; but it should not be forgotten that in any case the man of yesterday is dead, that every ascent implies a rising on "stepping stones of our dead selves," or that the content of the Now-

---

1. Rūmī, *Dīvān*, Odes XV, XXVIII; cf. *Mathnawī* VI.3644, "Whoever is not a Lover sees in the water his own image… (but) since the Lover's image has disappeared in Him, whom now should *he* behold in the water? Tell me that." Similarly in CU VIII.8, with respect to one's reflection in water.

*Ananda K. Coomaraswamy, "The Sea," *Selected Papers, Vol. I: Traditional Art and Symbolism*, ed. Roger Lipsey, Princeton, NJ: Princeton University Press, 1977. Reprinted by permission of World Wisdom, Inc.

without-duration (Skr. *kṣaṇa*, Aristotle's ἄτομος νῦν), i.e., of Eternity, is infinite compared with that of any conceivable extent of time past or future. The final goal is not a destruction, but one of liberation from all the *limitations* of individuality as it functions in time and space.

From the Buddhist point of view, life is infinitely short; we are what we are only for so long as it takes one thought or sensation to succeed another. Life, in time, "is like a dewdrop, or a bubble on the water...or as it might be a mountain torrent flowing swiftly from afar and carrying everything along with it, and there is no moment, pause, or minute in which it comes to rest... or it is like the mark made by a stick on water (A IV.137). The "individual," a process rather than an entity, ever *becoming* one thing after another and never stopping to *be* any one of its transient aspects, is like Heracleitus' river into which you can never step a second time—πάντα ῥεῖ. But over against this perpetual flux of the *Saṃsāra* there stands the concept of the silent Sea, from which the waters of the rivers are derived and into which they must return at last. In speaking of this Sea, the symbol of *nirvāṇa*, the Buddhist is thinking primarily of its still depths: "As in the mighty ocean's midmost depth no wave is born, but all is still, so in his case who's still, immovable (*ṭhito anejo*), let never monk give rise to any swell" (Sn 290). The Sea is the symbol of *nirvāṇa*, and just as Meister Eckhart can speak of the "Drowning," so the Buddhist speaks of "Immersion" (*ogadha*) as the final goal.

"The dewdrop slips into the shining sea." The reader of these concluding words of Sir Edwin Arnold's Light of Asia may very likely have thought of them as the expression of a uniquely Buddhist aspiration, and may have connected them with the altogether erroneous interpretation of *nirvāṇa* as "annihilation"; for, indeed, he may never have heard of the "annihilationist heresy" against which the Buddha so often fulminated, or may not have reflected that an annihilation of anything real, anything that *is*, is a metaphysical impossibility. Actually, however, for man to be plunged into the infinite abyss of the Godhead as his last and beatific end, and the expression of this in terms of the dewdrop or rivers that reach the sea towards which they naturally tend, so far from being an exclusively Buddhist doctrine, has been stated in almost identical words in the Brahmanical and Taoist, and Islamic and Christian traditions, wherever, in fact, *der Weg zum Selbst* has been sought.

To begin with the Buddhist formulation, we find: "Just as the great rivers, entering the mighty ocean, lose their former names and semblances, and one only speaks of 'the sea,' even so these four kinds, the warriors, priests, merchants, and workmen, when they go forth from the household into the homeless life, into the rule established by the Truth-finder, lose their former names and lineages, and are only called 'ascetics' and 'sons of the Buddha'" (A IV.202; M I.389; Ud 55.IV). The figure, no doubt, derives from and represents an adaptation of the Vedic idea of the oceanic origin and end of the Living Waters as stated, for example, in RV VII.49.1 and 2: "forth from the Sea the sleepless waters flow...their goal the Sea (*samudrārthāḥ*)." But the words as they stand are more directly an echo of several passages in the *Upaniṣads*, notably *Praśna Up.* I.5: "Even as these flowing (*syandamānāḥ*, ῥέοντες) rivers that move towards the sea, when they reach it, are come home, and one speaks only of 'the sea,' so of this 'Witness' or 'Looker-on' (*paridraṣṭṛ*)[2] these sixteen parts that move towards the Person, when they reach the Person, are come home, their name-and-shape are broken down, and one speaks only of 'the Person' (*puruṣa*).[3] He then becomes without parts, the Immortal." Similarly in CU VI.10.1 and 2: "As these rivers flow first eastward to and after backwards from the sea,[4] and when they enter into

---

2. The Witness, or Looker-on, is primarily that one of the two birds or selves that does not eat of the fruit of the Tree of Life, but only looks on (*abhi cakṣīti*, RV I.164.20, cf. Mund. Up. III.1.1 and 2 and Philo, *Heres* 126); "the Self alive and close at hand, the Lord of what hath been and shall be...who stands indwelling (*praviśya* = ἐνοικῶν) the cave (of the heart), who looked forth in the powers-of-the-soul (*bhūtebhir vyapaśyat*, KU IV.5 and 6); "the sole Seer, himself unseen" (BU III.7.23, III.8.11); "onlooker (*upadraṣṭṛ*), approver, groom, experient, High Lord and Self Supreme, these are designations of the Supreme Person in the body" (BG XIII.22).

The term *upadraṣṭṛ*, hardly to be distinguished in meaning from *paridraṣṭṛ*, has a further particular history and interest of its own, with specific reference to Agni, the Sacerdotium *in divinis* and within you, whom the gods "measured out...to keep watch" (*aupadraṣṭryāya*, JB III.261-263); Agni is the Onlooker or Watchman, Vāyu the Overhearer, Āditya the Announcer (TS III.3.5); and it is from Agni that the Buddha derives his epithet of "the Eye in the World." Krishna's relationship to Arjuna is that of Agni to Indra, Sacerdotium to Regnum, and corresponds to that of an older text in which we also find the Purohita acting as the King's charioteer, to advise him and "to see to it that he does no wrong" (*aupadraṣṭyāya ned ayam pāpam karavat* JB III.94, see in JAOS, XVIII, 1897, 21). In ourselves, this is the relationship that the Chinese call that of the Inner Priest to the Outer King; the Onlooker's functions are those of the Socratic Daimon, Immanent Spirit, Synteresis, and Conscience.

3. There are two "forms" of Brahma, temporal and timeless, with and without parts (MU VI.15). In his temporal form Prajāpati (the Progenitor), the Year, is thought of as having sixteen parts, of which fifteen are his "possessions" and the sixteenth, constant (*dhruva*) part Himself; with this sixteenth part he is entered into (*anupraviśya* = ἐποικίζων) everything that breathes here (BU I.5.14 and 15); and it is precisely with this sixteenth, left over (*pariśiṣṭa*) when the fire of life is checked by fasting ("just as there might remain from a blazing fire only a gleed no bigger than a firefly, and that blazes up again when the fast is over"), that "you now understand the Vedas" (CU VI.7.1-5). In other words, the constant sixteenth part is the "Spark," Jacob Boehme's "God in me that knows these things" and who, as St. Augustine says, both has his throne in heaven and teaches from within the heart—"And it is established, according to Augustine and the other saints, that 'Christ, having his throne in heaven, teaches from within'; nor can any truth be known in any way except through that truth. For the same one [i.e., Christ] is the source of being and understanding." (St. Bernard, *In hexaem.* I.13, Migne, *Series latina*, V.331).

4. This can be understood in two ways, either with Śaṅkara as referring to the general circulation of the waters, which are drawn up from the sea by the sun and return

the sea there is nothing but 'the Sea,' and there they know not 'I am this' or 'I am that'—just so, my friend, all these children,[5] though they have come forth from that-which-is (*sat*, τὸ ὄν), know not that 'We have come forth from That-which-is,' but here in the world become whatever they become, whether tiger, lion...or gnat," i.e., believer that they *are* this or that; whereas MU VI.22: "those who pass beyond this diversely variegated [sonorosity of rivers, bells, or falling rains] go home again into the supreme, silent, unmanifested Brahma, and reaching That are there no longer severally characterized or severally distinguished."[6]

So, again, in China, *Tao Te Ching*, 32: "Unto Tao all under heaven will come, as streams or torrents fall into a great river or sea" [see n. 9 below]; which reminds us both of Dante's "nostra pace: ella è quell mare, al qual si move" (Paradiso III.85 and 86), and of the Vedic "When shall we come to be again in Varuṇa?" (RV VII.86.2), i.e. in that Brahma "whose world is the Waters" (Kaus. Up. I.7), or that Agni who "is Varuṇa at birth" (RV III.5.4, V.3.1) and is "the single Sea, the keeper of all treasures" (RV X.5.1). In the

---

to it in the rivers; or, as seems to me more plausible, as referring to the tides that flow alternately far up such a river as the Ganges, and back again into the sea, being "river" as they ebb and flow, but only "sea" when the tide is out. In any case the reference is to the "fontal and inflowing" circulation of the Rivers of Life, cf. RV I.164.51, *samānam etad udakam uc caity ava,* and JUB I.2.7, *āpaḥ parācīr... prasṛtās syanderan...niveṣṭamānā...yanti.*

5. *Prajā,* "children," all living things regarded as the offspring of Prajāpati, and usually to be distinguished from *bhūtāni,* "beings," in the sense of the "Breaths," i.e., "faculties" or "powers of the soul" (Pythagorean ψυχῆς ἄνεμοι, Philo's τῆς ψυχῆς δυνάμεις, etc.), of which the names, vision, etc., are those of the immanent Person's acts rather than of our own (BU I.4.7, CU V.1.15, JUB I.28-29).

As regards the reference of *prajā* to all living things, whether or not human, cf. BU I.4.3 and 4: "Thence were born human beings. ...Thus, indeed, He (*puruṣa,* the Person) emanated all (*sarvam asṛjata*), down to the ants"—a context that makes it clear that *sṛṣṭi,* too often rendered by "creation," ought rather to be rendered by "emanation" or "expression." It is one and the same universal Self that quickens all things, but It is more clearly manifested in animals than in plants, and still more clearly in man than in animals (AĀ II.3.2). In Meister Eckhart's words, "God is in the least of creatures, even in a fly"; and conversely, "any flea, as it is in God [ideally], is higher than the highest of the angels as he is in himself."

For the term "emanation," often avoided for fear of a narrow "pantheistic" interpretation, cf. St. Thomas Aquinas, *Sum. Theol.* I.45.1: "*It is appropriate* to contemplate...the emanation of all being from the universal cause which is God. ...Creation, which is the emanation of all being, is out of nonbeing, which is nothing."

God is supreme identity of "Being and Nonbeing," Essence and Nature; from Nonbeing here arises Being as a first assumption, and from Being come forth all existences.

6. "He who aims at actual gnosis...will pin his faith to the One devoid of any sort of number or variety, the One wherein is lost, is blotted out, every property and all distinctions, which are there the same " (Meister Eckhart, Evans ed., II, 64).

words of Jalālu'd-Dīn Rūmī, "the final end of every torrent is the Sea. ... Opposites and likes pertain to the waves, and not to the Sea" (*Mathnawī* IV.3164 and VI.1622, cf. Philo, *Immut.* 164).

Parallels abound in Islamic contexts. Thus, Shams-i-Tabrīz: "Enter that ocean, that your drop may become a sea that is a hundred 'seas of Omān'.... When my heart beheld Love's sea, of a sudden it left me and leapt in" (Rūmī, *Dīvān*, Odes XII and VIII)—contemporary with Meister Eckhart's "Plunge in, this is the drowning." More than once his great disciple, Jalālu'd-Dīn Rūmī, asks us, "What is Love? Love is 'the Sea of Non-existence,'"[7] he says; and again, "What is Love? Thou shalt know when thou becomest Me" (*Mathnawī* III.4723, and II, Introduction). Man is like a drop of water that the wind dries up or that sinks into the earth, but "if it leaps into the Sea, which was its source, the drop is delivered... its outward form disappears, but its essence is inviolate. ...Surrender thy drop and take in exchange the Sea...of God's Grace"; "Spill thy jug[8]... for when its water falls into the river-water, therein it disappears, and it becomes 'the River'" (*Mathnawī* IV.2616 ff., and III.3912-3913)—the River, that is to say, of Plato's "ever-flowing Nature."[9]

All this pertains to the common universe of metaphysical discourse; none of these ways of speaking is foreign to specifically Christian aspiration. For God "is an infinite and indeterminate Sea of substance" (Damascene, *De fide orthodoxa* I): and deification, or theosis, man's last end, demands an "ablatio omnis alteritatis et diversistatis" (Nicholas of Cusa, *De filiatione Dei*). "All things," Meister Eckhart says, "are as little unto God as the drop is to the wild sea; and so the soul, in drinking God, is deified, losing her

---

7. I.e., of superessential Being, unlimited by any of the conditions of ex-istence (*ex alio sistens*), those of being "thus" or "otherwise." "There is no crime worse than thy ex-istence" (Rūmī, *Dīvān*, Ode XIII, commentary, p. 233): "Most specially he feeleth matter of sorrow who knows and feels that he is. All other sorrows are unto this in comparison but as game to earnest. For he may make sorrow earnestly who knows and feels not only what he is, but that he is" (*Cloud of Unknowing*, ch. 44). The Supreme Identity, indeed, is of "Being and Nonbeing" (*sadasat*), beyond both affirmation and negation; but to attain to this last end, it will not suffice to have stopped short at Being existentially.

8. For the "jug," the psycho-physical "personality," see *Mathnawī* I.2710-2715; cf. the Vedantic symbol of the jar, of which the space contained and space that contains are seen to be the same as soon as the jar is broken; and the Buddhist comparison of the body to a jar, Dh 40, *kumbhūpamam kāyam imaṃ viditvā*.

9. It will be noticed that the terms of the symbolism are not always literally the same. The eternal source may be called the Sea, or the River, while temporal existences are either waves of the Sea, or rivers that reenter it or that are tributaries of the Rivers. The eternal source is at the same time motionless and flowing, never "stagnant"; so that, as Meister Eckhart says, there is "a fountain in the godhead, which flows out upon all things in eternity and in time" (Pfeiffer ed., p. 530); as is also implied by the "enigma" of RV V.47.5, where "though the rivers flow, the Waters do not move."

name and her own powers, but not her essence" (Pfeiffer ed., p.314). And Ruysbroeck: "For as we possess God in the immersion of Love—that is, if we are lost to ourselves—God is our own and we are His own; and we sink ourselves eternally and irretrievably in our one possession, which is God. ... And this down-sinking is like a river, which without pause or turning back pours ever into the sea; since this is its proper resting place. ...And this befalls beyond Time; that is, without before or after, in an Eternal Now...the home and the beginning of all life and all becoming. And so all creatures are therein, beyond themselves, one Being and one Life with God, as in their Eternal Origin" (Jan van Ruysbroack, *The Sparkling Stone*, ch. 9, and *The Book of Supreme Truth*, ch. 10).

So, also, Angelus Silesius in *Der Cherubinische Wandersmann*, VI.172:

> If you would speak of the tiny droplet in the great sea,
> Then you would understand my soul in the great divinity;

And to the same tradition there belongs Labadie's beautiful last testament: "I surrender my soul heartily to God, giving it back like a drop of water to its source, and rest confident in Him, praying God, my origin and Ocean, that He will take me into himself and engulf me eternally in the abyss of His being."[10] When, indeed, shall we come "to be again in Varuna?"

In conclusion: we are not much concerned here with the literary history of these striking agreements; it matters little that the Indian sources are the oldest, since it can almost always be assumed that any given doctrine is older than the oldest record of it that we happen to have found. The point is, rather, that such collations as have been made above illustrate a single case of the general proposition that there are scarcely any, if any, of the fundamental doctrines of any orthodox tradition that cannot as well be supported by the authority of many or all of the other orthodox traditions, or, in other words, by the unanimous tradition of the Philosophia Perenis et Universalis.

---

10. Cited by Dean Inge, *The Philosophy of Plotinus* (London, 1918), I, 121.

A Glass of Water*

Transmitted by Gray Henry

In India long ago, a seeker approached Vishnu. He asked, "Oh my Lord, what is the meaning of life?" Vishnu's lips parted but just before he replied, he made a small request of his own. "Before we begin, could you do me the kindness of fetching me a glass of water?"

The young man crossed a wide open, cultivated field, and approached the hut of one of the farmers. When he knocked, a beautiful young maiden opened the door—probably the farmer's daughter—or one of them. As their eyes met, the young couple fell deeply and instantly in love. They waited for the return of the family, who were overjoyed that this young man and their daughter had found happiness in one another. Soon, the preparations for the wedding festivities were underway. In the years after the marriage, a daughter and later a small son brought joy into their lives.

In India, as we know, there are the annual monsoons which sometime can be very severe. One year, as the waters began to rise, the young husband held his wife's and daughter's hands on either side and the infant son he placed upon his shoulders. As they tried to escape the rising floodwaters in the field, the water rose higher and higher and began to lap against the young man's waist. Suddenly, one such wave threw him off balance, and his son began to tumble into the water. Without thinking, he let go of the hands of his wife and daughter, and they too were washed away with the tiny boy. What suffering—what grief! The waters began to recede and as he lay there, drenched and exhausted, he noticed standing before him Vishnu, who queried, "Where is my glass of water?"

One might suppose that the young man was given the answer to his question. When he went in search of the glass of water for Vishnu, he became deeply enmeshed in normative human life and suffering. As one reads this tale, it is easy to become involved with the joy and trials of this young man—and nearly to forget the quest at hand. This is a message for us all.

---

*This story, here imaginatively retold, can be found in Heinrich Robert Zimmer's *Myths and Symbols in Indian Art and Civilization*, ed. Joseph Cambell, New York: Pantheon Books, 1992. 8th edition.

The Flood in Hindu Tradition*

Ananda K. Coomaraswamy

The primary object of the present note is to present the Indian flood legend[1] as a special case of the Patriarchal Voyage (*pitṛyāna*), and at the same time in coherent and intelligible relation with other fundamental conceptions of Vedic cosmology and eschatology. Some analogies with other traditional aspects of the flood legend are incidentally noted. Whatever grounds may or may not exist for belief in an historical flood, the doctrine of *manvantaras* is, like that of *kalpas*, an essential part of Hindu tradition, and can no more be explained by any historical event than can the Vedic angels be explained by the deification of heroes. Further, the Flood legend clearly belongs to a tradition older than any existing Indian redaction or reference, older than the Vedas in their present form; these Indian redactions must be thought of as having, with the Sumerian, Semitic, and perhaps also Eddaic versions, a common source, the correspondences being ascribable not to 'influence' but to transmission by inheritance from the common source.

'Floods' are a normal and recurrent feature of the cosmic cycle, i.e. the period (*para*) of a Brahma's life, amounting to 36,000 *kalpas*, or 'days' of Angelic time. In particular, the *naimittikapralaya* at the end of every *kalpa* (close of a 'day' of Angelic time, and equivalent to the Christian 'Last Judgment'), and *prākṛitikapralaya* at the end of the lifetime of a Brahma (close of a 'day' of Supernal Time) are essentially resolutions of manifested existences into their undetermined potentiality, the Waters; and each renewed cycle of manifestation is a bringing forth on the next 'day' of forms latent as potentiality in the floods of reservoir of being. In each case the seeds, ideas, or images of the future manifestation persist during the interval or inter-Time of resolution on a higher plane of existence, unaffected by the destruction of manifested forms.

As to this, it will be understood, of course, that the chronological symbolism, inevitable from the empirical point of view, cannot be thought of as really characterizing the timeless actuality of all the possibilities of existence in the indivisible present of the Absolute, for Whom all multiplicity is mirrored in a single image. As, then, there can be no destruction of things as they are in the Self, but only of things as they are in themselves, the eternity, or rather timelessness, of ideas is a metaphysical necessity. Hence, indeed, the conception of another type of transformation, an *ātyantika pralaya*, ultimate or absolute resolution, to be accomplished by the individual, when or

---

1. [This essay appears to have been written in the mid-1940s—Ed.] For the principal texts see Adam Hohenberger, *Die indische Flutsage und das Matsyapurana* (Leipzig, 1930).

---

*The Flood, Ananda K. Coomaraswamy, "The Flood in the Hindu Tradition," *Perception of the Vedas*, ed. Vidya Nivas Misra, New Delhi: Manohar, 2000. Reprinted by permission of World Wisdom, Inc.

wherever he may be, as Realization: when, in fact, by self-naughting a man effects for himself the transformation of things as they are in themselves, and knows them only as they are in the Self, he becomes immortal—not relatively, as are the Devas, enduring merely to the end of Time—but absolutely, as independent of time and of every other contingency. It should be noted that the ideas (images, types) in question are not exactly Platonic ideas, but ideas or types of activity, the knowledge and being of the Self consisting in pure act; in the chronological symbolism their creative efficacy is expressed in terms of *adṛśya* or *apūrva karma*, 'unseen' or 'latent consequence'.

While the creation of a cosmos (Brahmāṇḍa) at the commencement of a *para*, and the recreation of resolved elements of the cosmos at the commencement of every *kalpa*, are the work of Brahmā (Prajāpati), the All-Father, the more proximate genesis and guidance of humanity in each *kalpa* and *manvantara* is brought about by a Patriarch (*pitṛ*) of angelic ancestry, and designated Manu or Manus. In each *kalpa* there are fourteen *manvantaras*, each presided over by an individual Manu as progenitor and lawgiver; so also the *ṛṣis*, and Indra and other (*karma-*) *devas*, are individual to each *manvantara*. The first Manu of the present *kalpa* was Svāyambhuva, 'child of Svayambhū'; the seventh and present Manu, Vaivasvata, 'child of the Sun'. Each Manu is a determined and conscious survivor from the previous *manvantara*, and through him the sacred tradition is preserved and transmitted. The particular Manu intended is not always stated in the texts, and in such cases it is generally to be understood that the reference is to the present (Vaivasvaata) Manu. It is not expressly stated that a flood arises at the conclusion of each *manvantara*, but this may be assumed on the analogy of 'the' flood connected with Vaivasvata Mau (ŚB, I.8.1-10), and the analogy of the greater 'flood' that marks the conclusion of a kalpa; but whereas in the latter case the principle of continuity is provided by the creative Hypostasis, floating recumbent asleep on the surface of the waters, supported by the Naga 'Eternity' (Ananta), in the case of the partial resolution or submergence of manifested forms which takes place at the close of a *manvantara*, the connecting link is provided by the voyage of a Manu in an ark or ship. It may be observed that this is essentially a voyage up and down the slope (*pravat*) of heaven rather than a voyage to and fro, and quite other than the voyage of the *devayana*, which is continuously upwards and towards a shore whence there is no return.

We are not informed of the chronological duration of the flood and Manu's voyage. From the analogy of the greater *pralayas*, a duration equal to that of the preceding *manvantara* might be inferred, but a more plausible analogy is perhaps to be found in the 'twilights' of the *yugas*, and this would suggest a relatively much shorter period of submergence. As to the depth of the flood, we have better information. In the first place it is evident that the resolution of manifested forms at the close of a *manvantara* will be less in cosmic extent than that, namely of the 'three Worlds', which takes place at the close of a *kalpa*, and this will mean necessarily that of the 'three Worlds', *svar* (the 'Olympian' heavens) at least, and perhaps also *bhuvar* (the 'atmospheric' spheres) are exempt from submergence; we know in any case that Dhruva (the Pole Star) remains unaffected throughout the *kalpa*. The earth (*bhur*) is submerged completely. Now the voyage of Manu, typically a Patriarch (*pitṛ*), is a special case of the Patriarchal Voyage (*pitryāna*), and this as we know is a voyage to and from the 'Moon', those regularly traveling by this route being the Patriarchs (usually spoken of collectively as *pitaras*), and the Prophets (*ṛsayaḥ*) 'desirous of descendants' (*prajā-kāmāḥ, Praśna Up.*, I.9). The flood, therefore, on which Manu's ship is borne upwards, must rise at least to the level of the sphere of the Moon, though it is not necessary to suppose that the Moon itself is submerged.

While it is out of the question that the flood waters should extend to the Empyrean heavens, Mahar-loka or therebeyond, there is good reason to suppose that in rising to the level of the Moon they must also touch the shores of the Olympian heavens (Indra-loka, deva-loka). For, notwithstanding that Indra- or deva-loka is regarded as a station, not of the Patriarchal, but of the Angelic Voyage, it is undeniable that Indra-loka is continually thought of as a place of reward of the worthy[2] dead, warriors in particular, who reside there enjoying the society of *apsarasas* and other pleasures until in due course the time comes for their return to human conditions. And while it is said that the latent effect of Works remains effective in the last analysis throughout a *kalpa* (*Viṣnu Purāṇa,* II.8), it would appear from the fact that the occupancy of Indra's office lasts only during the period of a *manvantara*[3] (hence a *kalpa* may as well be called a period of fourteen Indras as a period of fourteen Manus)[4] that reward in Indra-loka generally must be of the same

---

2. 'Worthy', i.e. due to receive the reward of *kāmya* Works, though not qualified by Understanding for either gradual or immediate Enfranchisement (*mukti*).

3. Those who, as individuals, are particular to a given *manvantara* are the presiding Angels (*devāḥ*), Prophets (*ṛsayaḥ*), and Manu and his descendants, i.e. kings and other men. The Angels in question cannot, of course, be thought of as any of those of the *ājānaja* ('by birth', e.g. Kāmadeva) order, but will be of the *karma* class, holding positions to which a qualification by Works has entitled them; and of these *karma-devah* or Work Angels the chief is Indra. Hence it is constantly assumed that an individual duly preparing himself here and now may become the Indra (or for that matter even the Brahmā) of a future age; and jealousy is often attributed to the Angels with respect to those who will thus succeed them in office.

There is some inconsistency of detail, though not of principle, as between *Viṣnu Purāṇa,* II.8, where it is said that the 'immortality' of the Angels means a survival without change of state until the end of the *kalpa*, and ibid., III.1, where the lifetime of an Indra and other (*karma*) Angels is restricted to the *manvantara*.

In any case, the Hindu view of the nature of angelic offices is identical with that of orthodox Christian theology, cf. St. Greogry and St. Augustine, *Angelus nomen est officii, non naturae,* for which, and the rendering of *deva* by 'Angel', see Coomaraswamy, 'On translation: *Māyā, Deva, Tapas*', 1933.

4. Cf. *Viṣnu Purāṇa,* III.1, and *Mārkaṇḍeya Purāṇa,* C.44.

duration; therefore at the commencement of any *manvantara* general descent from the Angelic World must be initiated, no less than from the Patriarchal. It is clear that the two Worlds, Indra- or deva-loka and the Moon as *piṭr-loka*, are psychologically equivalent, both being stations of the reward of *kāmya* Works; in fact, the Patriarchs are constantly spoken of as enjoying Soma in company with the Angels, and it is specifically stated in *Vālakhilya*, IV.1 that Manu drank Soma in company with Indra. One might express the situation by saying that whereas the Moon is naturally *piṭr-loka* from the (*Brāhmaṇa*) point of view, as the posthumous abode of 'those who in the village reverence a belief in sacrifice, merit, and alms-giving' (*CU*, V.10.3), Indra- or deva-loka is naturally the home of the dead from the (*Kṣatriya*) point of view of the warrior. And if Indra-loka is listed *only* as a station of the *devayāna*, this is because it represents actually a station from which there is not only the necessity of return for those who have performed Works only, but also the possibility of a passing on by way of the Sun to the Empyrean heavens in the course of *Krama mukti* and without return, in the case of those 'who understand this and in the forest truly worship' (*BU*, VI.2.15). When it is said in *ṚV*, X.14.17 that the two kings whom the dead meet on reaching 'heaven' are not Indra and Yama, but Varuna and Yama, that is Varuna in the case of the Angelic Voyage (since he who has reached the level of the heavenly waters in confronted with the possibility of future being only under heavenly conditions), and Yama in the case of the Patriarchal Voyage, it may be supposed that Indra (-loka) is omitted as being only a stage on the way to Varuna.

Now with respect to Yama, as he is the brother of Manu (Vaivasvata) at the present time, it must be understood that 'Yama' implies always the Yama of a given *manvantara*. Yama and Manu, both designated Patriarchs (*piṭr*), are contrasted in this respect, that whereas Yama, being the first man to die, was also the first to find out the way to the other world, in other words to map out the outward passage on the *pitryāna*, and thereby, as first settler, became king and ruler of all those who followed him, Manu is as once the last and only survivor of the previous *manvantara* and progenitor and lawgiver in the present. Hillebrandt's briew (*Vedische Mythologie*, I.394; II.368, etc.) of Yama as original ruler of the sphere of the Moon, perhaps at one time simply the Moon-god, his realm or paradise being specifically that of the dead, is naturally acceptable. In any case, in one way or another, Yama and the Moon are regarded as dividers out of the dead, appointing their course (*yāna*) according as they are qualified by Works or by Understanding. This 'judgment' is expressed exceptionally in *Kauṣ. Up.*, I.2 as a selection effected by the Moon itself, qua door of the heavenly world.[5] More characteristically, the dividing out is accomplished by the two dogs of Yama, Śabala and Śyāma ('Iridescent' and 'Dark'), who correspond to

5. Cf. *BU*, III.1.6 where the Moon, reached through the efficacy of the Brāhmaṇa priest, now identified with the Intellect, is in turn identified with Intellect, Brahman, 'complete release'.

the Sun and Moon, as argued by Bloomfield (*JAOS,* XV.171) with reference to *ŖV*, X.14.10; and this is supported by *Praśna Up.*, I.9 and 10 (and Śaṅkarācārya's Commentary), where the Sun, considered as a station on the *devayāna*, is not merely in a passive sense impassible by those devoid of Understanding, but actually and actively a barrier (*nirodha*) restraining those unqualified from passing on to a paradise (*amṛtam āyatanam*) whence there is no returning. Incidentally, this also enables us to establish the correspondence of the Hebraic Angel with the Flaming Sword with the Vedic Sun qua *nirodha*; the 'Flaming Sword' being the Angel's natural weapon, in virtue of his solar character. The analogy of the *pitṛyāna* with Jacob's ladder may also be noted.

While the partial Understanding which constitutes the Wayfarer's ship on the Angelic Voyage absolves him from the necessity of return to human corporeal conditions, the latent effect of Works necessitates a return course of the Patriarchal Voyage. In other words, the *pitṛyāna* is a symbolic representation of what is not called the doctrine of reincarnation, and is bound up with the notion of latent (*adṛṣṭa* or *apūrva*) causality. The purely symbolic character of the whole conception is made all the more apparent when we reflect that from the standpoint of very truth, and in the absolute Present, there can be no distinctions made of cause and effect; and that what is often spoken of as the 'destruction of *karma*', or more correctly as a destruction of the latent effects of Works, effected by Understanding and implied with *mukti*, is not really a destruction of valid causes (as though it were possible to make that which has been not to have been, or to conceive of any potentiality of being unrealized in the Self), but simply a Realization of the identity of 'cause' and 'effect'. It must be similarly understood with reference to the designation of states of being in spatial terms, for example as 'the Sun' or 'the Moon', that these are no more to be taken literally with respect to visible luminaries than are the analogous designations, of states of being as time phases, for example, those of the light or dark fortnight, cf. *Praśna Up.*, I.12. It does not appear, in fact, that the Vedic tradition really propounds any doctrine of reincarnation in the highly individual and literal Buddhist, Jaina, and modern sense, nor in any case an individual return to identical conditions,[6] such as those of any one *manvantara*, but merely a return to analogous conditions in another age, *manvantara* or *kalpa* as the case may be. Divested thus of a too literal interpretation, the Vedic (Upaniṣhadic) doctrine of 'reincarnation' bears a certain resemblance to modern conceptions of 'heredity': we too speak of the continuity of 'germ-plasm', of relatively everlasting 'genes', and the possibility that the characteristics of a remote

---

6. An exact repetition of any past experience would be inconceivable metaphysically, since any two identical experiences, regarded from the standpoint of the absolute present, in which all potentialities of being are simultaneously realized, must be one and the same experience. Metaphysics asserts the unique character of every monad, and it is precisely this uniqueness which makes the individual unknowable as he is in himself, though intelligible as he is in and of the Self.

ancestor may recur in any descendant; we know only too well that 'Man is born like a garden ready to be planted and sown', and few of us can always discard the conviction that 'a man gets what is coming to him'.

One further point of importance in this connection: while the Vedic point of view necessarily presumes an immortality, that is to say timelessness, of all potentialities of being typally subsistent in the Self (and this may be thought of from the standpoint of the Self as an eternal existence in the world picture not merely of every individual, but of every act of every individual on whatsoever plane of being), an immortality of this kind is in no way to be thought of as an immortality from the standpoint of any individual consciousness. It is clearly enough brought out that both the relative immortality of the Angels, and the absolute immortality of Realization are conditions which are altogether dependent on individual effort; or, as it is expressed from a more limited point of view in the Christian tradition, every individual must work out his own salvation. There can be no 'immortality' for the individual monad who has not, so to speak, either acquired a 'soul' by the due performance of Works, or realized the Self either partially as a Wayfarer or wholly as a Comprehensor. As to the infrahuman beings, 'the small, continually returning creatures' of whom it is said 'Be born, and die', theirs is a 'third state'; their course is ephemeral, and neither by the *devayāna* nor the *pitryāna*, though the possibility is not excluded that even an animal, under special circumstances, could develop a consciousness with survival value. And as to those beings human in form but so little *menschlich* in nature that they do not achieve even any virtuosity (*kauśalya*) in Works, their Psyche is said to be reborn in animal wombs, or alternatively to be lost. Hence (of course only from the human point of view, there being no superiority of one state over another in the eyes of the Self) the primary importance of birth in human form; for here and now it is determined whether or not the individual shall inherit Eternal Life, or at least a renewed possibility of winning Eternal Life. Furthermore, Veda is the body of Truth in which is set forth the way of life; and this Truth, eternal in the consciousness of the Self (without distinction of 'knowledge' from 'being'), is transmitted as it has been 'heard', by a succession of Prophets (*ṛṣayaḥ*) from *manvantara* to *manvantara*.[7]

While the *pitryāna* is thus manifested in the succession of *manvantaras*, the *devayāna* is primarily a course whereon the individual is removed ever farther and farther from the 'storm of the world-flow' (Meister Eckhart, Evans ed., I, 192), those who journey by the ship of Knowledge normally 'never returning' (*punar na āvartante*). The only exception to this is in the case of an *avatāra*, whose return or descent is indeed inevitable, like that of the Patriarchs, but with this difference, that in this case the necessity arises from a purely voluntary self-commitment (as is brought out so clearly in the case of the Bodhisattvas, whose appearance as a Buddha is a consequence of previous *praṇidhāna*), and with this further distinction that in such cases

---

7. In some other versions of the flood legend, the continuity of tradition is more mechanically explained.

the descent is not so much an actual embodiment or helpless subjection to human conditions, as a manifestation (*nirmāṇa*) not infringing the centering of consciousness in the higher state of being from which the *avataraṇa* takes place.[8] In the case of an *avataraṇa* of the Supreme Lord, this has to be though of as an immediate act of will or grace;[9] and here *a fortiori* the doctrine of *nirmāṇa* or that of merely partial (*aṁśa*) incarnation must be invoked.[10]

We have seen that every procedure from one state of being to another, though formally 'death again' (*punar mṛtyu*), is envisaged from the Vedic point of view as a passing from one station to another of a voyage on the sea of life. This sea can only be thought of as having a horizontal surface for so long as our attention is confined to any one and the same state of being; whenever a change of state is involved, as in the Angelic or Patriarchal Voyages, the surface of the sea of life is necessarily conceived of as a slope[11] or limiting form of a succession of degrees, leading upwards or downwards as the case may be, and as though from a valley to a height and *vice versa*. The slope, steep, or height is designated *pravat*, contrasted with *nivat*, descent or depth. *Pravat* is met with frequently in the *Ṛgveda* and *Atharvaveda.* Here it will suffice to note *AV*, VI.28.3, where it is said that Yama was the first to achieve the scarp (*pravat*), spying out the way for many; *AV*, X.10.2, where the steeps are said to be seven in number, evidently with reference to the seven planes of being, that is to say the 'three Worlds' and four Empyrean heavens, Mahar, Jamas, Tapas and Satyam; and *AV*, XVIII.4.7, where the crossing of the fords (*tīrtha*) of the great steeps is said to be by means of the sacrificial Works of the worthy. All this is consistent with the Angelic Voyage of the enlightened in the ship of Understanding, and the Patriarchal Voyage of those whose ship is Works.

The conception of the sea of life as an ocean and of its 'surface' as a slope further explains much of the terminology of the posthumous voyages, and that of a Manu. For example, the attainment of the level of any state of being, a port of call on the voyage, is thought of as a tying up in harbor: hence in *AV*, XIX.39.7, where there is an incidental allusion to the Angelic Voyage, the sky-faring vessel is provided with a golden hawser (*bandhana*), and corresponding notions are found in *ŚB*, I.8.1.6 in the injunction to Manu, *vṛkṣe nāvaṁ pratibandhīṣva tam*, 'tie up the ship to a tree'; in *Mbh.*,

---

8. For an explanation of *avataraṇa* with reference to the Vedic Apantaratamas and others, reference should be made to Śaṅkarācārya's Commentary on the *Vedānta Sūtras*, III.3.30-1. The *nirmāṇa* doctrine corresponds to the Docetic Heresy in Christianity, and has its equivalent in Manichaeism.

9. As in *BG, passim.*

10. Just as from the Christian point of view it is not supposed that the whole being of the Son was by the fact of Incarnation imprisoned in Mary's womb.

11. As general consideration of traditional symbolism would lead us to identify this 'slope' with the pitch of a spiral having for its centre the vertical axis of the universe; or as that of the phyllotaxy of the Tree of Life.

III.187.48, 'tie up the ship to the summit of Himālaya'; and III.187.50 *nau-bandhana*, 'ship-tying', denoting the summit of Himālaya, where Manu's ship made land as the Flood subsided. In the same way the conception of a slope or 'up' contrasted with a 'down' explains the constant use of the verbal prefix *ava*, 'down', whenever a descent on the sea of life is envisaged, as in *AV*, XIX.39.8, where it is said that for those (wayfarers on the *devayāna*) who 'see immortality' there is 'no gliding down', *na'avaprabhraṁśana*,[12] and *ŚB*, I.8.1.6, where the descent of Manu's ark is spoken of as *avasarpaṇa*, with the same sense of 'downward gliding'.

The general parallel with Biblical tradition is very close; the account of creation in Genesis corresponding to the creation at the commencement of the present *kalpa*, that of the Flood and Noah to that of the Flood and Manu Vaivasvata. Manu, however, is not thought of as taking with him into the ark a wife and pairs of creatures after their kind; in other words, the apparatus of the Hebraic version in this respect is more mechanical. Many is a progenitor of mankind in the sense that all men are of the seed of Manu; and as the reincarnation of the Patriarchs is not all at once, but day by day in the natural course of events, it must be understood not that they descended in Manu's ark literally, but by the *pitṛyāna* in its general connotation, their genealogy from Manu being, as it were, implicit and by seminal virtue. Their actual birth from day-to-day is somewhat obscurely described in various accounts of return on the Patriarchal Voyage as a descent of *rasa* with the rain, and a subsequent evolution.

The Eddaic Gotterdammerung and subsequent restoration of the world may also represent the original tradition of a flood at the close of a world period: in *Voluspa*, such expressions as *vepr oll válynd, ragna rok, verold steypesk, skelfr Yggdrasels, snysk jormongandr, himen n klofnar,* followed by *Sér upp koma opro sinne jorth ór aegre ipjagroena... sás á fjalle fiske veiper,* and the assembly of the Aesir calling to mind the *fornar rúnar,* all closely parallel Indian descriptions of the end of a world age and subsequent restoration. The finding of the *gollnar toflot paers í árdage átta hofpo* recalls the Berosus version of the flood legend (Isaac Preston Cory, Ancient Fragments, London, 1832, pp. 26ff.), where as history of the beginning, procedure, and conclusion of all things (a veritable *Purāṇa*!) is buried at Sippara before the submergence of the earth, and found again after the subsidence of the flood, and then again made known to mankind.

---

12. This word, divided *nāva-prabhramśana*, was at one time interpreted as equivalent to *nau-bandhana*, but this has been rightly rejected on grammatical and other grounds. The *AV* passage does not refer to the descent of Manu's ark, but is an incidental reference to a voyage upwards on the *devayāna*.

Traversing the Waters
and the Reciprocal Blessing*

Timothy Scott

As in a ship convey us o'er the flood.

Ṛg Veda, 1.97.8

The world is my sea, the sailor the spirit of God. The boat my body, the soul he who wins back his Abode.

Angelus Silesius[1]

Water, insomuch as it is flowing, represents flux, whether this be the ebb and flow of potentiality coming "in" and "out" of being, or the ever running river of time. Both are aspects of Heraclitus' river,[2] the perpetual flux of *Samsāra*. The soul, born into these waters of becoming, is as a wayfarer engaged in a journey upon these turbulent waters, a journey whose final end is the Source, the Silent Sea (*Nirvāna*). The symbolism of the "traversing of the waters" is that of the movement from one state of Being to another. Ananda Coomaraswamy observed that the traversing of the waters can be related in three different ways.[3] The voyage can be accomplished either by crossing over the waters to the other shore, by going upstream towards the source of the waters, or by going downstream towards the sea. Similarly, there are four paradigmic forms of the "boat" or "ship" motif: the ferry of the dead, the ship of the hero, the barque of the god, and the Ark of the deluge. The first three categories of boats respectively correspond to the three forms of the voyage.

The ferry of the dead crosses the River of Death, from the shore of the living to the "Farther Shore" of the dead. In the Greek tradition this is the ferry of Charon; in Egyptian mythology, the ferryboat of Afu Rā;[4] in the *Epic*

---

1. *Cherubinischer Wandersmann*, II.69, cited in W. Perry ed., *A Treasury of Traditional Wisdom*, Louisville: Fons Vitae, 2000, p. 386.
2. 'Upon those that step into the same rivers different and different waters flow' (216); 'Heraclitus somewhere says that all things are in process and nothing stays still, and likening existing things to the stream of a river he says that you would not step twice into the same river' (218)—G. S. Kirk & J. E. Raven ed., *The Presocratic Philosophers*, Cambridge: Cambridge University Press, 1962, pp. 196 & 197; see Plato, *Cratylus*, 402A.
3. A. Coomaraswamy, 'Some Pali Words' in *Selected Papers Vol.2: Metaphysics*, R. Lipsey ed., New Jersey: Princeton University Press, 1977, pp. 324-27; see also, R. Guénon, *Fundamental Symbols: The Universal Language of Sacred Science*, Cambridge: Quinta Essentia, 1995, Ch.58.
4. See Budge, *The Book of the Dead:'The Hieroglyphic Transcript and English Translation of the Papyrus of Ani'*, New Jersey: Gramercy Books, 1995, 'The

---

*From *The Symbolism of the Ark*, forthcoming Autumn 2009, Fons Vitae.

of Gilgamesh this is the ferry of Ur-shanabi.[5] There are numerous examples available, so much so that it has been said that 'All civilizations have their boat of the dead.'[6] René Guénon remarks that this crossing of the waters of death reflects the ultimate transition: 'the shore which is left behind is the world subject to change, that is, the corporeal state in particular ... and the "other shore" is *Nirvāna*, the state which is definitely set free from death.'[7] Death is to be viewed as a birth, where 'new birth necessarily presupposes death to the former state'.[8]

The ship of the hero sails upstream to the source of the river, the *Fons Vitae*, the "Well of Honey in Viśnu's highest place,"[9] the Perennial Spring of Plotinus,[10] etc. In the context of the hero's journey this source is the hidden goal or treasure, the Golden Fleece, the Grail, etc. This is the voyage of the "solar hero" entailing the passage through the symbolic Sundoor.[11] The case of going upstream is, as Guénon observes, 'perhaps the most remarkable in certain respects; for the river must then be conceived as identical with the World Axis.'[12] As such this journey is analogous with the ascension of a "ladder" or more precisely the shamanistic climbing of the "greased pole."[13] To this Guénon adds the "rope trick" in which a rope is thrown into the air and remains, or seems to remain, vertical while a man or a child climbs it until they disappear from view. As with the voyage upstream, the movement must be continuous. The hero must remain focused and always facing forwards or risks being washed back downstream to his eternal detriment; hence the allusions, in myths of every provenance, to the danger of going back on one's tracks or of looking behind. They must be 'steadfast in the face of multiplicity,' as Meister Eckhart says, so that the 'light and grace' of the Source may be revealed to them.[14] In comparison to the "greased pole" the two parallel posts of a ladder represent the complimentary movement up and down along the axis.[15] As Coomaraswamy remarks, 'the Axis of the

---

Abode of the Blessed,' passim.

5. Tablet I, Gilgamesh from Dalley ed., *Myths from Mesopotamia: Creation, The Flood, Gilgamesh, and Others*, Oxford: Oxford University Press, 1991, p. 102.

6. J. Chevalier & A. Gheerbrant, *Dictionary of Symbols*, tr. J. Buchanan-Brown, Middlesex: Penguin, 1996, p. 106.

7. Guénon, *Fundamental Symbols*, p. 234.

8. Ibid., p. 110.

9. *Ṛg Veda* 1.154.5.

10. *Enneads* 3.8.10.

11. See A. Coomaraswamy, 'The Sun Door and related Motifs' in *Selected Papers Vol.1: Traditional Art and Symbolism*, R. Lipsey ed., New Jersey: Princeton University Press, 1977, pp. 415-521.

12. Guénon, *Fundamental Symbols*, p. 233.

13. Ibid., p. 261, n.5.

14. Meister Eckhart, Pfeiffer ed., *Vol.1*, 1924, p. 147, cited in Perry, *A Treasury of Traditional Wisdom*, p. 383.

15. Guénon, *Fundamental Symbols*, p. 229.

Universe is, as it were, a ladder on which there is a perpetual going up and down.'[16]

When we consider the "descent with the current," remarks Guénon, 'the Ocean must then be considered not as an extent of water to be crossed but, on the contrary, as the very goal to be reached and therefore as representing *Nirvāna*.'[17] Here, as Nāgārjuna observes, 'There is nothing that distinguishes *samsāra* from *nirvāna*'.[18] Coomaraswamy remarks that the 'eternal source is at the same time motionless and flowing, never "stagnant"'; so that, as Meister Eckhart says, there is a 'fountain in the godhead, which flows out upon all things in eternity and in time'; as is also implied by the "enigma" of *Ṛg Veda* v.47.5, where 'though the rivers flow, the Waters do not move.'[19] Heraclitus' river, *Samsāra*, is not other than the still Sea of *Nirvāna*.

The god upon his "barque" is a symbolic manifestation of the cosmic currents, which, from one perspective, express the flux of potentiality, or primordial chaos, and, from another perspective, the stability and stillness of cosmic order. The barque of the god is the resplendent vessel upon which the god rests in stillness and peace. The god, like Aristotle's "unmoved mover,"[20] does not move; rather the cosmic currents flow around the barque. It can even be said that these currents are caused by the "non-acting activity" (the *wei wu wei* of Taoist tradition) of the god. From a terrestrial perspective, the god traverses the endless journey upon the cosmic rhythm of *Samsāra*. This is all to say that the barque of the god is none other than Divine Immanence itself.

Joseph Campbell remarks on this symbolism as applied to the gods in general and, in turn, to the individual consciousness:

> As the consciousness of the individual rests on a sea of night into which it descends in slumber and out of which it wakes, so, in the imagery of myth, the universe is precipitated out of, and reposes upon, a timelessness back into which it again dissolves. And as the mental and physical health of the individual depends on an orderly flow of vital forces into the field of waking day from the unconscious dark, so again in myth, the continuance of the cosmic order is assured only by a controlled flow of power from the source. The gods are symbolic personifications of the laws governing this flow.[21]

---

16. Coomaraswamy, 'The Inverted Tree' in *Traditional Art and Symbolism*, p. 40.
17. Guénon, *Fundamental Symbols*, p. 235.
18. *Mūlamādhymakakārikā* 25.19-20. As Mircea Eliade remarks, 'This does not mean that the world (*samsāra*) and deliverance (*nirvāna*) are "the same thing"; it means only that they are undifferentiated' (*A History of Religious Ideas Vol.2: From Gautama Buddha to the Triumph of Christianity*, Chicago: The University of Chicago Press, 1984, p. 225; see §189, p. 222 ff.).
19. See Coomaraswamy, 'The Sea' in *Traditional Art and Symbolism*, p. 410, n.9.
20. Aristotle, *On the Soul*, 3.10; see also *Physics*, 1.2; 184 b 16.
21. J. Campbell, *The Hero with a Thousand Faces*, London: Abacus, 1975, p. 225.

For the ancient Egyptians the sky was "a vast layer of water" upon which the celestial bodies traversed in boats.[22] The idea of the sun traversing the sky in a vehicle of some description is common and recalls the daily journey of Apollo, as Helios, in his fiery chariot, among others. There are several connections that exist between the boat, the chariot, and the throne. In the *Book of the Dead* it is said of Horus that Osiris has 'made him to have his throne in the Boat of Millions of Years'.[23]

The idea of a vehicle as a throne is explicit in the *Merkabah* (throne-chariot) mysticism of the Judaic tradition.[24] The "throne of glory" (Ezek.1:26, 10:1; Dan.7:9; Rev.4:2; 1En.14:18, 71:5-11; 2En.22; 3En.1:6; TLevi 5:1) is an epithet of the *Shekhinah*, the Divine Immanence. The chariot is, in turn, the dynamic expression of the "throne of glory." As Leo Schaya says, 'The "throne," in its fullness, is the first and spiritual crystallization of all creatural possibilities before they are set in motion in the midst of the cosmos. When the "throne" assumes its dynamic aspect and cosmic manifestation begins to move, it is called the divine "chariot" (*merkabah*).'[25] Elsewhere Schaya remarks on the relationship between the tabernacle and the *merkabah*: 'The tabernacle had provided the presence of God [*Shekhinah*] with no permanent habitation, for it was set up after the model of his heavenly "vehicle" (*merkabah*), in which he would lead His people through the wilderness to the fixed "centre of the world," Jerusalem.'[26] The tabernacle and the *merkabah* are *imagines mundi* in dynamic mode. The throne is an *imago mundi* emphasizing the fixed Centre, complete and Eternal, both Transcendent and Immanent.

The barque of the god perpetually traverses the waters of becoming, while at the same time causing the flow of these waters. In contrast, the Ark of the deluge presents a voyage "on" the waters rather than a "traversing." This is not a journey from one shore to another, nor is it like the tide which perpetually moves the sea. Neither is it like the voyage downstream into the Ocean whence the "barque" remains endlessly afloat on the currents of divine Harmony. Instead, as Coomaraswamy observes, the voyage of the Ark is 'essentially a voyage up and down the slope (*pravat*) of heaven rather than a voyage to and fro, and quite other than the voyage of the *devayāna*, which

---

22. Budge, *The Book of the Dead*, p. 133. Most notable are the boats of Rā, the two boats of the Sun (Mantchet and Semktet).

23. Ch.CLXXV ii.20-21. It is considering one such mention of this "Boat of Millions of Years" that the eminent Egyptologist M. Naville recognises the Herakleopolitian legend of the Flood.

24. See G. Scholem, *Major Trends in Jewish Mysticism*, New York: Schocken Books, 1995, pp. 42-3.

25. L. Schaya, *The Universal Meaning of the Kabbalah*, tr. N. Pearson, New Jersey: Allen & Unwin, 1971, p. 84.

26. L. Schaya, 'The Meaning of the Temple' in J. Needleman ed., *The Sword of Gnosis*, Baltimore: Penguin, 1974, p. 360.

is continuously upwards and towards a shore whence there is no return.'[27] The voyage of the *devayāna* ("the way of the gods") is analogous with the voyage of the hero. We might note how many solar heroes are in fact either gods (Apollo, Mithra, Horus, Krishna, etc.) or of divine-mortal birth (Hercules, Gilgamesh, Christ, etc.).[28]

In some instances a particular mythological journey may involve the shift from one to another of these boats, as seen in the move of Afu Rā from his "serpent-boat" to his "river-boat."[29] In the *Epic of Gilgamesh* we have both the ferryboat of Ur-shanabi and the Ark of Ut-napishtim.[30] In each of these forms the journey of the boat expresses a transition between states, a "death" and "rebirth."

***

The "traversing of the waters" may also be accomplished via a "bridge."[31] Like the boat, the bridge is associated with the notion of "death" and return to the Source. 'Death is a bridge' says `Abd al-`Azīz b. Sulaymān, 'whereby the lover is joined to the Beloved.'[32] The bridge is often said to be 'broad for the righteous but as thin as a blade for the impious'.[33] Campbell recalls an Eskimo shaman crossing an abyss on a bridge as narrow as a knife.[34] In the *Katha Upaniṣad* the path is a 'sharpened edge of a razor'.[35] This is the "Sword Bridge" crossed by Sir Lancelot;[36] *Chinvat*, the "Bridge of the Separator" in Zoroastrian tradition; the "narrow" and "hard" way of St. Matthew (Matt.7:14).[37] This symbolism is again found in the assimilation of a bridge to a ray of light, on which point Guénon observes the double sense of the English word "beam," which designates both a girder, in the sense of a single beam or single tree trunk as is the case with the most primitive form of bridge, and

---

27. Coomaraswamy, 'The Flood in Hindu Tradition' in *Metaphysics*, p. 400.

28. In the case of Gilgamesh 'two-thirds of him was divine and one-third mortal' (Tablet I, Gilgamesh, Dalley ed., *Myths from Mesopotamia*, p. 51), which bears comparison with the depth to which the ark of Ut-napishtim sat in the water (see p. 111).

29. See Budge, *The Book of the Dead*, p. 146.

30. See Tablet I, Gilgamesh, Dalley ed., *Myths from Mesopotamia*, p. 102. Of course Gilgamesh does not actually travel on the ark of Ut-napishtim.

31. See Guénon, *Fundamental Symbols*, § 65 'The Symbolism of the Bridge.'

32. `Abd al-`Azīz b. Sulaymān cited in Perry ed., *A Treasury of Traditional Wisdom*, p. 226.

33. Chevalier & Gheerbrant, *Dictionary of Symbols*, p. 122.

34. J. Campbell, *The Masks of God: Primitive Mythology*, Middlesex: Penguin, 1982, p. 333.

35. *Kat ha Upaniṣad* 3.14.

36. C. De Troyes, *Arthurian Romances*, Middlesex: Penguin, 1991, pp. 244-46.

37. On this symbolism see M. Eliade, 'The Bridge and the "Difficult Passage"' in *Shamanism: Archaic techniques of ecstasy*, Middlesex: Arkana, 1989, p. 482, also p. 456; see p. 455 on "sword ladders."

a luminous ray.[38] This is a bridge between the terrestrial domain and the celestial or solar domain; its narrowness indicates its treacherous nature—the "hard way"—and it is properly speaking the path of the "solar hero." This bridge both *leads to* the Sundoor and, from a deeper perspective, *is* the Sundoor.

The "sharpness" of the Sword Bridge is again found in the analogous symbolism of the "Cutting Reeds" of Navajo tradition. Here the hero's path is barred by "cutting reeds" that 'tried to catch him, waving and clashing together.' Coomaraswamy observes these as being the same, *mutatis mundis*, with the Clashing Rocks, the Symplegades, which are a form of the "Active Door" or the Sundoor.[39] As Coomaraswamy observes, this is the same symbolism as the crossing of the "Red Sea" (Ex.14:21), where this name, *yam soof*, is said to actually mean the "Reed Sea." Samuel Fohr observes two articles by Bernard F. Batto questioning this reading of *yam soof* and offering instead the translation, "Sea of the End (of the World)."[40] Fohr remarks that the reference is to the primordial chaos.[41] These three apparently contradictory readings in fact confirm each other. The Red Sea, like the "wine-dark sea" of the Ancient Greeks, expresses the "dark" or feminine nature of the colour red, associated with the idea of the womb in which life and death are transmuted the one into the other;[42] this, then, is none other than the "womb" of primordial chaos from whence order is "born"; and born, moreover, by passage through the Active Door (the Cutting Reeds; the Symplegades). This is not all, for the Ark itself, which is analogous to the womb, is variously associated, if not explicitly constructed from, reeds (Noah, Moses, Ut-napishtim); and thus passage from the unmanifest to the manifest is effected through this symbolism of "reeds." Moreover, the "reeds" "growing" in the sea of primordial chaos are said to be the very stuff of creation. Shaikh Aḥmad al-'Alawī mentions the reeds of which the cosmic mat is woven as symbols of the manifestation of Divine Qualities out of which the whole universe is woven.[43] Reynold A. Nicholson, writing about Rūmī, observes that the reed (the Persian *ney*) is none other than 'an emblem of the transporting influence of Di-

---

38. Guénon, *Fundamental Symbols*, p. 260, n.2.

39. Coomaraswamy, 'Symplegades' in *Traditional Art and Symbolism*, p. 525.

40. B. F. Batto, 'The Reed Sea: *Requiescat in Pace*': *Journal of biblical Literature*, Vol.102, 1983, pp. 27-35, and 'Red Sea or Reed Sea': *Biblical Archeology Review*, Vol.X, No.4, 1984, pp. 57-63.

41. S. Fohr, *Adam and Eve The Spiritual Symbolism of Genesis and Exodus*, London: University Press of America, 1986, p. 98, n.5.

42. Chevalier & Gheerbrant, *Dictionary of Symbols*, p. 793.

43. Shaikh Aḥmad Al-'Alawī in Lings, *A Sufi Saint of the Twentieth Century*, 1971, p. 135; see p. 148.

vine inspiration.[44] This is the Spirit (*al-Rūh*; *Ruah*) that moves upon the Water; the Spirit, which is the *Logos*, both Uncreated and created, the bridge between the manifested and the Unmanifested.

The symbolic "bridge," in the most general sense, connects the two "shores" which, as Guénon remarks, will always, from a certain level of reference, have between them a relationship corresponding to that between heaven and earth.[45] Guénon:

> The bridge, therefore, is the exact equivalent of the axial pillar that links heaven and earth even while holding them apart; and it is because of this meaning that it must be conceived of as essentially vertical like all the other symbols of the "World Axis"—for example, the axel of the "cosmic chariot" when its two wheels represent heaven and earth. This establishes also the fundamental identity of the symbolism of the bridge with that of the ladder...[46]

The symbol of the bridge is further associated with that of the "rainbow."[47] In the Scandinavian Epic poem, *Gylfaginning*, the great king High explains to Gangleri, 'Has no one ever told you that the gods built a bridge to heaven from earth called Bilfrost [or *Byfrost*]? You must have seen it, maybe it is what you call the rainbow.'[48] The rainbow is generally considered as symbolising the union of heaven and earth. However, Guénon, discussing the relationship of the bridge and the rainbow, is less happy with this assimilation or identification. On the whole, he feels, 'the rainbow seems to have been above all connected, in a general way, with the cosmic currents by which an exchange of influences between heaven and earth operates much more than with the axis along which direct communication between the different states is effected'.[49] These "cosmic currents" derive from the action of the cosmic forces: expansion and concentration, the movement of which is better portrayal by a curve than the "straight" path of a bridge. The curved form of the rainbow is more precisely compared with the spiral winding around an axis;[50] from another perspective, this spiral corresponds to the two parallel posts of the ladder. The difference here, as Guénon remarks, is that 'between the "axial" way, which leads the being directly to the principial state, and the more "peripheral" way which implies the passage through a series of

44. R. A. Nicholson, *Commentary on the Mathnawī*, Bk.ii, 323, cited in L. C. Bauman, 'Initiatic Grace in the Masterwork of Jala ud-din Rumi,' *Sacred Web* 6, 2000, p. 76, as discussing the "reed of the Spirit," a winged horse (*faras*) like *Buraq*.
45. Guénon, *Fundamental Symbols*, p. 261, n.4.
46. Ibid., p. 261.
47. See Chevalier & Gheerbrant, *Dictionary of Symbols*, p. 783; Guénon, *Fundamental Symbols*, § 66 'The Bridge and the Rainbow.'
48. *Gylfaginning* in S. Sturluson, *Edda*, London: Everyman, 1998, p. 15.
49. Guénon, *Fundamental Symbols*, pp. 263-64.
50. A circular or semicircular form such as the ouroboros or the rainbow can be considered as the plane reflection of a spiral.

hierarchic states one by one [be they the levels of the spiral or the rungs of the ladder] even though in both cases the final goal is necessarily the same.'[51]

***

The descending current, the celestial or spiritual influence, is symbolised by the analogous symbols of rain and light.[52] As Guénon observes, the symbolism of dew, closely connected to that of rain by its very nature, is likewise to be recognised here.[53] This draws attention to the common identification of biblical *manna* with dew, which in turn connects dew with light, for as Schaya remarks, 'The pure and redemptive light symbolised in the Talmud by "manna," is called *Nogah*, "brightness," in the Kabbalah.'[54] The rainbow is a bridge fashioned from the union of water and light. Pure light, colourless and a unity, refracts through the prism of water to create the spectrum of the rainbow which, through the six primary colours, gives birth to the multitude colours of creation.[55] Creation is born from the passage of light through water.

The descending current is in turn answered by the ascending current, the terrestrial or human influence. This is found in the rising smoke of the sacrifice (cf. Gen.8:21; *Gilgamesh* XI, iv), which symbolises the flow of blessings or prayers that humankind offers "up" in response to the blessing of Creation. In the language of the Kabbalah, the universe is maintained by the "living waters" which flow down from above. In turn the "children of Israel," that is humankind, must maintaining the recitation of prayer to ensure the flow of these "living waters."[56]

Rabbi Joseph Gikatilla observes that word *berakhah* (blessing) is a cognomen for the Name, *Adonay* (Lord). *Berakhah* comes from *braichah*, which means "pool." The Lord, says Rabbi Gikatilla, is 'like a pool from which a river draws its waters and carries the pool's waters to irrigate the garden and provide water to drink.'[57] It is this blessing to which we respond through the traversing of the waters of our lives and through the reciprocal blessing of our prayers, which rise like dew returning to heaven in the heat of the morning.

Macrocosm and microcosm: the living waters that flow from above are returned to God through the most precious water of our body, our

---

51. Guénon, *Fundamental Symbols*, p. 266.

52. See Guénon, *Fundamental Symbols*, § 62 'Light and Rain.'

53. Ibid., p. 246.

54. Schaya, *The Universal Meaning of the Kabbalah*, p. 94.

55. See Guénon, *Fundamental Symbols*, § 59 'The Seven Rays and the Rainbow'; also M. Lings, *Symbolism & Archetype: A Study of the Meaning of Existence*, Cambridge: Quinta Essentia, 1991, Ch.4 'The Symbolism of the Triad or Primary Colours.'

56. Rabbi J. Gikatilla see *Gates of Light (Sha'are Orah)*, tr. A. Weinstein, Walnut Creek: AltaMira, 1994, pp. 17-19.

57. Rabbi J. Gikatilla, *Gates of Light*, p. 16.

tears. 'Jesus wept' (Jn.11.35). This is the great prayer of water. Let us finish with the beautiful words of John Chryssavgis:

> Tears signify an opening of new life, a softening of the soul, a clarity of mind. They bring us to rebirth and the world to healing. They signify a true homecoming. Through tears we are able to enter the treasury of the heart.[58]

The cure for anything is salt water: sweat, tears or the sea.

Isak Dinesen

---

58. J. Chryssavgis, *In the Heart of the Desert: The Spirituality of the Desert Fathers and Mothers*, Bloomington, IN: World Wisdom, 2003, p. 51, see Ch.7 'Silence and Tears'; also M. Lings, *A Return to the Spirit: Questions and Answers*, Louisville, KY: Fons Vitae, 2005, Ch.4 'What is the Spiritual Significance of Tears and of Laughter?'

On Contemplating the Commissioned Portrait of a British Viceroy of India, Carrying the Caption "Served with Distinction, 1910-1932"

Huston Smith

Who could have dreamed, gazing on this willful face,
That India touched him more than he touched her.

Trains multiplied, of course. Huge
Baby-booms of belching smoke and whistle's wail.

English, too, improved, as Etons
—short pants, broad white collars, the works—
sprouted in unlikely places.

Even the manly sports took hold,
As yogas bowed to bat and ball.
Horses wheeled to mallet's stroke
While women watched in printed frocks.

But I have heard:

His wife declared he mellowed through the years.
Listened more, insisted less.
Was more patient when a servant slipped.

And when the time to leave rolled round,
He knelt and kissed the parched red ground.
A tear met the dust in that waterless land,
That had known so well his heavy hand.

On The Spiritual Significance of Tears by Martin Lings[*]

Gray Henry

In his final book, *A Return to the Spirit*, completed days before his death, Martin Lings draws our attention to those tears which are "spontaneous overflowings of the body" in which "the material realm is transcended". At this highest level of tears "which is indicated here by the word 'spiritual', the psychic plane is also largely surpassed."

We have all experienced being moved to tears by Beauty, a sight in Virgin Nature, a mountain peak, mists enveloping a landscape or the ocean at sunset. We have also wept before sacred art or perhaps within a sanctuary. Tears have flowed down our cheeks at the realization of a great Truth, at the recounting of a heroic feat of utter selflessness, at the marriage vows of a friend or the birth of a child. Good news that brings relief may melt the heart with tears of gratitude and joy. Music may similarly transport us. We remember these moments clearly and always.

It has been said that the presence of God in form is Beauty, the presence of God in the will is Virtue, and the presence of God in the intellect is Truth. And so, in the face of immense Truth, Goodness and Beauty, our hardened hearts melt and we all are thus regularly and mercifully carried into the Divine Presence through the medium of our tears, shed as "spontaneous overflowings of the body", transcending the world of matter.

Martin Lings points out that "it must be clearly understood that the words 'religious' and 'spiritual' are by no means synonymous. The domain of the Spirit may be said to coincide with the *Paradiso* of Dante's epic, but it lies beyond the *Purgatorio*. Without belittling the extreme importance of tears of contrition, they can and must be relegated to their own degree in the hierarchy of the faculties. The Spirit, by definition, can have no cause for repentance. Gratitude on the other hand is an essential aspect of the Spirit, and it can therefore be affirmed that although not all tears of thanksgiving are up to that level, some such tears may indeed be described as spiritual. When it is said in Christianity that he or she is blessed with *dona lacrimarum*, the gift of tears, this privilege is generally considered to be the outward sign of a venerable degree of spirituality...

"Islam is insistent that there can be no true piety without wonderment at the marvellous signs of God which surround us on all sides in this world, but which an increasing majority of people take for granted. Nonetheless there are always some who take them for what they truly are or, otherwise expressed, who are more or less conscious of the Divine Archetype in which the signs are rooted and which they manifest in this earthly plane. This con-

---

[*]Excerpts from the chapter "What is the Spiritual Significance of Tears and Laughter?" found in *A Return to the Spirit: Questions and Answers*, Fons Vitae, 2006.

sciousness is a mode of wonderment, and wherever wonderment is granted it may be accompanied by those tears which are at the level of our theme, though their absence cannot be said to diminish the escape that wonderment is in itself...

"Macrocosm and microcosm, great outer world with all that it contains and small world of each single human being. Both these worlds are made in the image of God, and they are therefore analogous; but man has fallen whereas the world he lives in remains as it was created except insofar as fallen man has desecrated it. God has however promised that 'the earth shall not be found lacking in forty men whose hearts are as the heart of the friend of God,' that is, Abraham. There are also the other messengers of God, each a model of human perfection. Moreover for the people of each particular religion the founder of that religion is still mysteriously present with them, enough to be wondered at by those who are capable of wonderment."

In the life of the Indian there was only one inevitable duty—the duty of prayer—the daily recognition of the Unseen and Eternal. His daily devotions were more necessary to him than daily food. He wakes at daybreak, puts on his moccasins and steps down to the water's edge. Here he throws handfuls of clear, cold water onto his face, or plunges in bodily. After the bath, he stands erect before the advancing dawn, facing the sun as it dances upon the horizon, and offers his unspoken orison. His mate may precede or follow him in his devotions, but never accompanies him. Each soul must meet the morning sun, the new sweet earth and the Great Silence alone!

Ohiyesa (Charles Eastman), Wahpeton Dakota
Indian Spirit, ed. M. Fitzgerald

Returning to The Primordial:
The Water Symbolism of Baptism

Graeme Castleman

All instruction is either about things or about signs; but things are learnt by means of signs.

St Augustine of Hippo,
On Christian Doctrine, Bk 1 Ch 2

O strange and inconceivable thing! we did not really die, we were not really buried, we were not really crucified and raised again; but our imitation was in a figure, and our salvation in reality. Christ was actually crucified, and actually buried, and truly rose again; and all these things He has freely bestowed upon us, that we, sharing His sufferings by imitation, might gain salvation in reality.

St Cyril of Jerusalem,
Catechetal Lectures 20.5

Introduction

Baptism is as old as the Church itself and vehicles a sacramental grace to the participant: a grace that affects a spiritual death and rebirth in Christ. The liturgical rites of baptism declare and expound the nature and workings of this grace and in doing so vehicle the saving *gnosis* that is the noetic complement of the volitive sacramental grace. As Mathis remarks:

> The rites of the Church and the greater feasts of Her liturgical year were intended to be an unfailing means, not only for transmitting the grace of the Sacraments, but also for instructing the faithful in their meaning and in the meaning of the whole Christian life.[1]

Baptism confers an initiatic grace upon the participant and at the same time the symbols of the ritual 'text' 'enlighten' the gnostic, or noetic faculties of man. The drama of death and rebirth played out in the ritual and the volitional core of the sacrament—the choice of life over death, good over evil—engage the psychic or passional aspects of man. The physical elements of the rite; candles, music, processions, incense, garments, as well as the 'physicality' of the sacramental water and oil, engage the body and its temporality, for "God fashioned man with his own hands and impressed his own form on the flesh he had fashioned, in such a way that even what was visible might bear the divine form."[2] All of these forms of communication—noetic/spiritual, psychic, somatic—and the immensity of what is communicated (the

---

1. Editor's Note in Daniélou, J., *The Bible and Liturgy* (Notre Dame, Indiana: University of Notre Dame Press, 1956). p. vii.
2. Irenaeus, *Demonstratio 11* cited in *Catechism of the Catholic Church*, (Homebush, Aust.: Society of St Paul, 1994). §704. p. 186.

baptismal grace itself), along with fastings, vigils, teachings and prayers that precede baptism are preparations for and responses to the Divine Presence so revealed.

Baptism not only vehicles sacramental grace but through its symbolism transmits a knowledge of the nature and workings of that grace in order that the Christian initiate "may know (*gignōskō* from the noun *gnōsis*) him, and the power of his resurrection, and the fellowship of his sufferings, being made conformable unto his death."[3] In doing this it addresses itself to the 'whole man', for it is the 'whole man' who is reborn and saved.[4]

The rites of baptism synthesize all modes of *gnosis* possible within their own formal terms and points of reference. Hence baptism is also called Enlightenment:

> It will be worth your while to apply your minds to what we say, and to receive our discourse on so important a subject … [as Baptism] with ready mind, since to know the power of this Sacrament is itself Enlightenment (φωτισμός).[5]

The baptismal rites address differing human temperaments, receptivities, and capacities; hence the scholastic maxim: *quidquid recipitur per modum recipientis recipitur* ("whatever is received is received according to the manner of the one receiving"). Nevertheless, the *gnosis* that is communicated is in its own formal limits a full disclosure, for the miracle of revelation is that the finite contains the infinite: *finitum capax infiniti*. The *gnosis* that is transmitted in the baptismal rites is that of the relationship between God, man and the *kosmos*, and the change in this relationship wrought by baptismal grace. It is a theological knowledge that is transmitted through a complex web of inter-related symbols.

* * *

While baptismal rites varied according to time and place there is a common stock of symbols and practices that disclose the meaning of the sacrament. There is a great deal that may be considered—the pedagogical and ritual elements of the catechumenate, the symbolism of pre-baptismal anointing with oil, the symbolism of the changing of garments and ritual nudity, the symbolism of the *sphragis* (the sealing with oil of the sign of the Cross on the forehead of the newly baptized) and the descent into Hell and cosmic

---

3. Php 3:10.
4. Christianity also addresses the 'whole man' in the corporate sense: a universal community. It is pneumatic for the *pneumatikoi*, psychic for the *psychikoi*, and corporeal for the *somatikoi*. As Theodotus remarks: "the sea is open to all, but one swims, another sails, and a third catches fish; and as the land is common, but one walks, another ploughs, another hunts,—somebody else searches the mines, and another builds a house: so also, when the Scripture is read, one is helped to faith, another to morality, and a third is freed from superstition by the knowledge of things." (Theodotus, *exerpta ex Theodoto*. 28.)
5. St Gregory Nazianzen, *orationes*. 40 (On Holy Baptism), 1.

ascent which the initiate ritually undergoes—but this essay will focus upon the symbolism of the baptismal waters in which the initiate is thrice immersed and the OT typology by which the baptismal waters are understood, especially the cosmogony, the Deluge and the Exodus.[6] All this shall be considered with an eye to the symbolic exposition of baptism—including some idiosyncratic themes—as (on the one hand) the recapitulation of the divine cosmogonic act and (on the other hand) the return to Eden and the recapitulation of the creation of man, both symbolising a return to principle and remanifestation or rebirth.

The Soteriological Drama: Creation, Fall and Re-creation

> Know ye not, that so many of us as were baptized into Jesus Christ were baptized into his death? Therefore we are buried with him by baptism into death: that like as Christ was raised up from the dead by the glory of the Father, even so we also should walk in newness of life.
>
> The Epistle of St Paul to the Romans, 6:3-4

Baptismal practices in the ancient world varied depending on location and period but shared a body of symbols and a more or less common theology of grace and salvation upon which those symbols are grounded. Man—and through him the entire *kosmos*—is created for union with God but as a consequence of the primordial sin of Adam the channels of grace that Adam denied are closed—their inaccessibility being precisely the state of original sin. The sacrament of baptism reopens these channels of grace and what had been lost in Adam is regained in Christ. It is in this sense that Gregory of Nyssa employs the Old Testament account of Jacob meeting Rachael at the well and removing the stone which covered the waters[7] as "a shadow of what should come." He explains:

> There was lying, then, upon the well the spiritual stone [ὁ λίθος ὁ νοητός—literally 'noetic stone'], Christ, concealing in the deep and in mystery the laver of regeneration which needed much time—as it were a long rope—to bring it to light. And none rolled away the stone save Israel, who is mind [νοῦς] seeing God. But he both draws up the water and

---

6. For a fuller treatment of these other aspects of baptismal symbolism and their place in the cosmogonic and primordial interpretation, see Castleman, G., "The Primordial in the Symbols and Theology of Baptism," *Eye of the Heart: A Journal of Traditional Wisdom*, no. 4 (2009).

7. Gen. 29. It is significant that this event follows from Jacob's vision of the heavenly ladder, after which he "went on his journey, and came into the land of the people of the east" (Gen. 29:1) where he met Rachel at the well. The symbolism of the east as the primordial place—which is significant to the baptismal context—will be dealt with later in this essay.

gives drink to the sheep of Rachel; that is, he reveals the hidden mystery, and gives living water to the flock of the Church.[8]

This movement from separation to union as the return to the primordial is well illustrated by the angelic guardians who—in the post-lapsarian ages—prevent access to the Garden: "So he drove out the man; and he placed at the east of the garden of Eden Cherubims, and a flaming sword which turned every way, to keep the way of the tree of life."[9] Christ overcomes this barrier: "A fiery sword barred of old the gates of Paradise; a fiery tongue which brought salvation restored the gift."[10] Thus in baptism the Christian initiate is returned to the primordial, ante-lapsarian state and confirmed in it. This requires the death of the man who is born into the post-lapsarian state of sin and the birth of the man who is freed from it and its consequences.

The symbolic elements of baptism are underpinned by the theology of sin and redemption and the initiatic power of the soteriological drama; that of the God who entered into human life and death and thus entered into an intimate fellowship with man.[11] This saving drama of Christianity presents two phases: the *theo-drama* and the *anthropo-drama* that is its consequence and participating image. The first concerns the action—or salvific economy—of the Christ who participates in humanity, died and "rose again in accordance with the Scriptures" and in doing so overcame the limitations of death and the determinations of sin. The second relates to what Christ has accomplished in this act, the soteriological power by which means his initiates participate in his victory over the fallen order. As Daniélou remarks, "Adam became Satan's prisoner"[12] but, as Küng explains, through the Christic grace, "over against all compulsion to sin... [man] now has the possibility of acting according to God's merciful commands."[13] Irenaeus:

> For as by one man's disobedience sin entered, and death obtained [a place] through sin; so also by the obedience of one man, righteousness having been introduced, shall cause life to fructify... And as the protoplast himself Adam, had his substance from untilled and as yet virgin

---

8. St Gregory of Nyssa, "*in baptismum Christi* (On the Baptism of Christ)." There is a symbolic correspondence here with the stone that covered the well of Zamzam until it was removed by the uncle of the Prophet. Lings, M., *Muhammad: his life based on the earliest sources* (Cambridge: Islamic Texts Society, 1991). p. 11.
9. Gen. 3:24.
10. St Cyril of Jerusalem, "Catechetal Lectures." 17.15.
11. "For we have not a high priest which cannot be touched with the feeling of our infirmities; but was in all points tempted like as *we are, yet* without sin. Let us therefore come boldly unto the throne of grace, that we may obtain mercy, and find grace to help in time of need." (Heb. 4:15-17.)
12. Daniélou, J., *A History of Early Christian Doctrine Before the Council of Nicaea*, 3 vols., vol. 2 (London: Darton, Longman & Todd, 1973). p. 179.
13. Küng, H., *The Church*, trans. R. & R. Ockenden (London: Search Press, 1968). p. 152.

soil ... so did He who is the Word, recapitulating Adam in Himself, rightly receive a birth... from Mary, who was as yet a virgin.[14]

In the *anthropo-drama* the initiate participates in the ordeals of Christ in such a way that he becomes identified with Him. The pattern of the initiatic rite enacts the *theo-drama* with the human initiate ritually in the place occupied by Christ. Clement of Alexandria dismisses the rites of the pagan mysteries as "murders and funerals"[15] but the same may be said of Christianity. As the "firstborn of the dead"[16] Christ makes possible for the initiate—"being made conformable unto his death"—an incorporation into the Life of the divinity: "For He was made man that we might be made God".[17] In Christ, the whole of the created order is recapitulated—re-created—and man, whose unique role in the economy of creation—what Islam identifies as man's status as *khalifah*—enables him to serve as the 'conduit' through which the whole of the *kosmos* is transfigured and redeemed, just as through man the whole of the *kosmos* 'fell': "For the earnest expectation of the creation waiteth for the manifestation of the sons of God. ... Because the creation itself also shall be delivered from the bondage of corruption into the glorious liberty of the children of God."[18] In the re-creation of man lies the re-creation of the whole *kosmos*. From the soteriological point of view, therefore, man stands at the centre of the *kosmos*. Lossky:

> ...the earth is *spiritually central* because it is the body of man, and because man, penetrating the indefiniteness of the visible to bind it again to the invisible, is the central being of creation, the being who reunites in himself the sensible and the intelligible and thus participates, richer than the angels, in all of the orders of 'earth' and of 'heaven'.[19]

The Christian Paschal drama and the corresponding initiatic engagement with it both 'unmakes' (destroys or kills) and 'remakes' (re-creates) the *kosmos*, both micro- and macro-cosmic.

The symbolism we will consider expresses both microcosmic (salvific) and macrocosmic (apocalyptic) aspects, sometimes emphasizing one, sometimes the other; both are expressed in the symbolic web of baptism and especially in its cosmogonic and primordial symbolism. Thus St Cyril of Jerusalem understands the breathing (by the Resurrected Christ) of the Holy Spirit upon the Apostles (Jn 20:22) as a recapitulation of the first breathing of the Spirit by which life was imparted to Adam.[20] The waters of Creation, of the

---

14. Irenaeus, *adversus haereses*. 3.21.10.

15. Clement of Alexandria, *cohortatio ad gentes* (Exhortation to the Gentiles). 2.

16. Col. 1:18.

17. St Athanasius, *de incarnatione verbi* (On The Incarnation of the Word). 54.3. Compare Irenaeus, *haer*. 3:19.

18. Rom. 8:19, 21. Translation based on King James Version.

19. Lossky, V., *Orthodox Theology: An Introduction*, trans. I & I Kesarcodi-Watson (Crestwood, NY: St Vladimir's Seminary Press, 1978). p. 64.

20. St Cyril of Jerusalem, *cat.* 17.12.

Flood and of the Red Sea are universally interpreted as baptismal waters. The recapitulation of primordial man by the inbreathing of the Spirit—the microcosmic—on the one hand and the connection between the cosmogonic waters—the macrocosmic—and those of baptism on the other hand lie at the heart of baptismal symbolism and theology. This death and rebirth—the end of one creation and the coming to be or *genesis* of another—is accomplished by the sacramental grace conveyed under the symbol of the water; the baptismal font being both the tomb of the old man and the womb of his rebirth.

Baptismal Waters: Creation, Deluge and Exodus

…when once the longsuffering of God waited in the days of Noah, while the ark was a preparing, wherein few, that is, eight souls were saved by water. The like figure whereunto even baptism doth also now save us… by the resurrection of Jesus Christ

First Letter of Peter 3:20-21

But now the holy day of the Passover is at hand, and ye, beloved in Christ, are to be enlightened by the Laver of regeneration.

St Cyril

The font is the tomb of the 'old man' and also the womb through which the rebirth or regeneration of the Christian initiate, the 'new man,' takes place. R.M. Jensen notes, in her study of North African baptismal fonts, a number of labial shaped fonts[21] and this makes clear the symbolism of the font as womb and baptism as rebirth. The font is the initiatic cave, the womb of Mother Church, "the mother of us all, which is the spouse of our Lord Jesus Christ."[22] The fruit of this Christic nuptial mystagogy—the initiate—is the golden or solar child in whom are united the terrestrial and celestial natures in one *hypostasis*. Tertullian acknowledges this nuptial mystery of Christ and His Church and the child it bears in his instructions to catechumens:

when you ascend from that most sacred font of your new birth, and spread your hands for the first time in the house of your mother, together

---

21. Jensen, R.M., "Womb, Tomb, and Garden: The Symbolism of the North African Baptismal Fonts" (paper presented at the American Academy of Religion Annual Meeting, 1997). Pt I. Sec. C. Accessed electronically at http://people.vanderbilt. edu/~james.p.burns/chroma/baptism/jensbapt.html. Compare the Areopagite, who describes baptism as affecting a "divine birth" and a "divine and sacred regeneration" "EH" 2. 392C, A, in Pseudo-Dionysius, *Pseudo-Dionysius: The Complete Works*, trans. C. Luibheid (New York: Paulist Press, 1987). pp. 201, 200.
22. St Cyril of Jerusalem, *cat.* 18.26. In the thirteenth century William Durandus wrote that the Church is called "sometimes a *bride*, because Christ has betrothed her to Himself… sometimes a *mother*, for daily in baptism she beareth sons to God." Durandus, W., *The Rationale Divinorum Officiorum: The Foundational Symbolism of the Early Church, its Structure, Decoration, Sacraments and Vestments. Books I, III, and IV*, trans. J.M. Neale, et al. (Louisville, KY: Fons Vitae, 2007). 1.1.4. p. 4.

with your brethren, ask from the Father, ask from the Lord, that His own specialties of grace and distributions of gifts may be supplied you.[23]

As well as symbolizing the waters of the human womb, the waters of the font symbolize the waters of the Genesis cosmogony: "...and darkness was upon the face of the deep (LXX: *abysson*). And the Spirit of God moved upon the face of the waters."[24] St Ambrose remarks:

> Consider...how ancient is the mystery [of baptism] prefigured even in the origin of the world itself. In the very beginning, when God made the heaven and the earth, "the Spirit," it is said, "moved upon the waters."[25]

St John Chrysostom explains that baptism "creates and fashions us anew not forming us again out of earth, but creating us out of another element, namely, of the nature of water. For it does not simply wipe the vessel clean, but entirely remoulds it again."[26] Baptism is in effect, cosmogonic; it is a 'second,' *creatio ex nihilo*. The 'new man' is entirely new, having no continuity with the 'old man'. As St Paul exclaims: "Therefore if any man be in Christ, he is a new creature: old things are passed away; behold, all things are become new",[27] for "we are his workmanship, created in Christ Jesus unto good works".[28] Christian baptism is more than a purificatory washing, it is a complete recapitulation of the primordial creative act itself.

The association of baptismal and cosmogonic waters is a commonplace of baptismal liturgies and commentaries on baptism from the earliest periods of the Church. Tertullian emphasizes the cosmic primordiality and pristine nature of water:

> For water is one of those things which, before all the furnishing of the world, was quiescent with God in a yet unshapen state...they were the seat of the Divine Spirit... water alone—always a perfect, gladsome, simple material substance, pure in itself—supplied a worthy vehicle to God.[29]

Further, he draws a direct link between the cosmogonic waters and those of baptism:

> ...the Spirit of God, who hovered over (the waters) from the beginning, would continue to linger over the waters of the baptized [*intinctorum*].

23. cf. Tertullian, *de baptismo* (On Baptism). 20. For the corresponding macrocosmic vision of the Church as Mother, see "The Shepherd of Hermas." 2nd vision ch 4. "'Who is it then?' say I. And he said, "It is the Church." And I said to him, "Why then is she an old woman?'"Because," said he, "she was created first of all. On this account is she old. And for her sake was the world made."'

24. Gen. 1:2.

25. St Ambrose, *de mysteriis* (Concerning the Mysteries). 3(9).

26. St John Chrysostom, *in catechumenos* (Instruction of Catechumens). 1.3.

27. 2Cor 5:17. See also Gal 6:15.

28. Eph 2:10.

29. Tertullian, *de baptismo*. 3.

...All waters, ...in virtue of the pristine privilege of their origin, do, after invocation of God, attain the sacramental power of sanctification... [30]

St Cyril of Jerusalem likewise employs this symbolism of the cosmogonic waters, noting that all things unfold from them.[31] Water is present and effective in all the divine acts in the created order, being the first created thing, the created first principle (*archē*) from which all else unfolds.[32] The heavens and the earth are from the waters, and, according to Tertullian "... the work of fashioning man himself [was] also achieved with the aid of waters.... Suitable material is found in the earth, yet not apt for the purpose unless it be moist and juicy...."[33]

Tertullian declares that the "waters were in some way the regulating powers by which the disposition of the world thenceforward was constituted by God"[34] and this points to a significance beyond that of one of the traditional quaternary of elements. These waters are prior to that imposition of formal qualities by which fire, air, earth and water may be distinguished, indeed prior to even the division of the upper and lower waters, a division that 'creates a space,' so to speak, in which the unfolding of form may take place. The cosmogonic waters are the non-formal created principle or *archē* of the four manifest formal elements and of all manifestation. It is the *materia prima*, the formless matter (ἀμόρφου ὕλης) of Wisdom 11:17, the 'earth' which was "without form and void (Heb. *tohu wabohu*)"[35] which is "the mixture [we might otherwise say 'potential'] of still undifferentiated elements":[36] that *materia* from which all else sprung and in which the waters of baptism symbolically participate.[37] This explains Tertullian's insistence upon the

---

30. Tertullian, *de baptismo*. 4.

31. St Cyril of Jerusalem, "cat." 3.5.

32. See *recognitiones Clementinas* (Clementine Recognitions). 6.8: "...water was made at first by the Only-begotten; ... when you have come to the Father you will learn that this is His will, that you be born anew by means of waters, which were first created." Compare *homiliae Clementinae* (Clementine Homilies). 11.24: "... water makes all things, and water receives the production of its movement from spirit, ... being born again by the first-born water, you may be constituted heir of the parents who have begotten you to incorruption."

33. Tertullian, *de baptismo*. 3. This is a reference to Gen 2:6-7. "But there went up a mist from the earth, and watered the whole face of the ground. And the LORD God formed man...".

34. Tertullian, *de baptismo*. 3.

35. See Castleman, G., "Cosmogony and Salvation: The Christian Rejection of Uncreated Matter," *Sophia: The Journal of Traditional Studies* 9, no. 2 (2003/04). Esp. pp. 117-18. For Christianity, the *materia prima* remains a valid concept, with a Scriptural basis, but only when considered as the first stage of the hierarchic unfolding of the 'six days' and not as a second uncreated principle alongside (we might say *outside of*) God.

36. Lossky, *Orthodox Theology*. p. 65.

37. Lossky, *Orthodox Theology*. p. 65.

presence of the waters in the dust or earth from which Adam was made and also the qualification he makes when identifying the waters of baptism and those of the cosmogony: one is baptized "...not with those [cosmogonic] waters, of course, except in so far as the *genus* indeed is one, but the *species* very many. But what is an attribute to the *genus* reappears likewise in the *species*."[38] By *'genus'* and *'species'* Tertullian indicates the distinction between principle and manifestation, universal and particular.

Just as the first creation—*from* the Father, *through* the Son and *in* the Holy Spirit—arises from the water, just so *through* the salvific work of Christ (sent *from* the Father) and *in* the Holy Spirit (whom the initiate receives in baptism) the second creation is achieved. "Never", Tertullian observes, "is Christ without water":

> ...He is Himself baptized in water [Mt 3.13-17]; inaugurates in water the first rudimentary displays of His power, when invited to the nuptials [Jn 2:1-11]; invites the thirsty, when He makes a discourse, to His own sempiternal water [Jn 7:37-8]; approves, when teaching concerning love, among works of charity, the cup of water offered to a poor (child) [Mt 10:42]; recruits His strength at a well [Jn 4:6]; walks over the water [Mt 14:25]; willingly crosses the sea [Mk 4:36]; ministers water to His disciples [Jn 13:1-12]. Onward even to the passion does the witness of baptism last: while He is being surrendered to the cross, water intervenes; witness Pilate's hands [Mt 27:24]: when He is wounded, forth from His side bursts water [Jn 19:34]...[39]

The close association between the cosmogonic waters and the waters of baptism, and the function of water in the divine economy, is for Tertullian the reason why water has a universal symbolic significance: it is implicit in the nature of water itself[40] and confirmed in the actions of the Incarnate God. Answering his own rhetorical question "How foolish and impossible it is to be formed anew by water. In what respect, pray, has this material substance merited an office of so high dignity?"[41] Tertullian's answer is in part that "...the mere nature of water, in that it is the appropriate material for washing away",[42] establishes its symbolism. "Water was the first to produce that which had life, that it might be no wonder in baptism if waters know how to give life."[43]

---

38. Tertullian, *de baptismo.* 4.

39. Tertullian, *de baptismo.* 9. See also 19: "...when, withal, the Lord's passion, in which we are baptized, was completed. ... when the Lord was about to celebrate the last Passover, He said to the disciples who were sent to make preparation, 'Ye will meet a man bearing water.' He points out the place for celebrating the Passover by the sign of water."

40. Compare Nasr: a symbol proper "is an aspect of the ontological reality of things..." Nasr, S.H., *Sufi Essays* (London: Allen & Unwin, 1972). p. 88.

41. Tertullian, *de baptismo.* 3.

42. Tertullian, *de baptismo.* 5.

43. Tertullian, *de baptismo.* 3.

* * *

We will now turn to two further instructive and commonplace examples of Old Testament types of baptism; the Exodus from Egypt and the Deluge. While there are a great many Old Testament types of baptism, these two are the most significant: not merely because they are the most common[44] but because they both employ—and thereby reinforce—the symbolism of the cosmogonic waters, describing a return to the primordial *abysson* when those waters which would be separated out into the upper and lower waters were still one.

The waters of the Deluge purged the world of wickedness, bringing death but also a 'new creation', the seed of the new age preserved in the family of Noah and the animals of the ark. The book of Genesis explains that "all the fountains of the great deep [were] broken up, and the windows of heaven were opened. And the rain was upon the earth forty days and forty nights."[45] Thus the sinful generation is destroyed "with the earth."[46] That the earth is also destroyed here is significant; the ark is returned to the state prior to the emergence of the earth from the waters. Here we are again in the presence of the cosmogonic waters. The waters of the Deluge are those of the upper and lower waters of the Genesis cosmogony coming together again from above and below. Thus the seed of regeneration, the ark, is returned to the state of primordial potentiality before the division of the waters and the emergence of form.[47]

The seven days in which Noah gathers in the animals to the ark reverse the unfolding of the seven days of creation. It is a return to the first created principle, a 'winding back' of time, so to speak until the ark went "upon the face of the waters (LXX: ἐπάνω τοῦ ὕδατος)"[48] just as the Spirit moved "upon the face of the waters (LXX: ἐπάνω τοῦ ὕδατος)"[49] in the first cosmogonic 'moment.' The days of the cosmogony represents an unfolding of the principle in an hierarchic *order* (the literal meaning of the Greek '*kosmos*') symbolized by a temporal succession. This unfolding, the actualizing of the principle, is *folded back* into the ark and is returned to the archetypal state from which the new order may unfold. This unfolding or regeneration is further symbolized by the forty days and nights of rain which refer to the forty weeks of human gestation and this alerts us that the symbolism of rebirth in

---

44. See for example St Augustine, *de catechizandis rudibus* (On the Catechising of the Uninstructed). Ch 20 (34); but it is a patristic commonplace and examples could be multiplied almost indefinitely.

45. Gen 7:11.

46. Gen 6:13.

47. Compare Fohr, S., *Adam & Eve: The Spiritual Symbolism of Genesis and Exodus*, 4th ed. (Hillsdale: Sophia Perennis, 2005). p. 115: "In the flood narrative, the two [waters, upper and lower], as it were, come together once again, the heavenly waters serving to spiritually regenerate the world."

48. Gen 7:18.

49. Gen 1:2.

this *mythos* is not only cosmic but microcosmic; hence its applicability to baptism. As Fohr notes, the ark "is at once the seed or egg of the regenerated world and the regenerated person."[50] After the waters receded, God commanded Noah:

> Go forth of the ark.... Bring forth with thee every living thing that is with thee, of all flesh, both of fowl, and of cattle, and of every creeping thing that creepeth upon the earth; that they may breed abundantly in the earth, and be fruitful, and multiply upon the earth.[51]

This also recalls the cosmogony, specifically the description of the fifth and sixth days of creation on which the animals were created,[52] and repeats the blessing to 'be fruitful and multiply.'

The ark that floats upon the cosmogonic waters of potentiality returns to manifestation, actualizing the potential it contains as it is grounded upon the summit of Mt. Ararat. The mountain is an axial symbol and as the waters recede so the earth reemerges from the summit of the peak outward—a horizontal extension from centre to circumference. The peak of Ararat and the ark that is grounded upon it are the *omphalos*, the centre or navel of the world from which the new order unfolds. The folding back into the ark employs the symbolic numbers seven and then forty: seven days in which the animals are gathered in (a 'reverse' of the seven days of creation) and forty days of rain. The unfolding from the ark back out into manifestation employs the same symbolic numbers but in reverse order. First, from the grounding of the ark on Ararat to the sending out of the raven, forty days pass. Then the sending out of the birds, the raven and then the dove three times, occur at intervals of seven days. Hence, there is here a movement from manifestation to principle and thence to remanifestation. The sending out of the birds four times invokes manifestation by its numerical symbolism. Guénon: "the quaternary is always and everywhere considered as the number of universal manifestation. In this respect, it therefore marks the very starting point of cosmology."[53] St Ambrose identifies the Baptist's vision of "the Spirit de-

---

50. Fohr, *Adam & Eve*. p. 115.

51. Gen 8:16-17.

52. Gen 1:20-25. The only discrepancy between the cosmogonic and Deluge accounts is the creation of those creatures which "fill the waters in the seas" which are omitted for obvious narrative reasons that do not affect the central symbolic theme.

53. Guénon, R., *Fundamental Symbols: The Universal Language of Sacred Science*, trans. A. Moore Jr. (Bartlow: Quinta Essentia, 1995). §16. p. 75. Within the patristic tradition see, for example, Irenaeus, who argues that the New Testament canon should include only four Gospels because of the nature of quaternary symbolism: "For, since there are four zones of the world in which we live, and four principal winds, while the Church is scattered throughout all the world, and the "pillar and ground" of the Church is the Gospel and the spirit of life; it is fitting that she should have four pillars [ie. The Gospels], breathing out immortality on every side, and vivifying men afresh." (Irenaeus, *haer*. 3.11.8.) Note here also the theme of Church as the agent of renewal or rebirth.

scending from heaven like a dove"[54] upon the Christ as an indication that the Deluge is to be understood as an historical prefiguration of the sacrament.[55] This symbolic link between the dove and the Holy Spirit also serves to return us to the cosmogony myth. The spirit 'hovers' [*rachaph*] over the cosmogonic waters,[56] and the Hebrew recalls the movement of a bird:[57] The Holy Spirit symbolized by the dove in Christ's baptism recalls the dove sent out from the ark and also the work of the Spirit in the cosmogony.

The enfolding back to principle becomes an unfolding into manifestation and the opening of the ark marks the beginning of the new creation. This is further signaled by a calendric *motif*: "...in the first month, the first day of the month, the waters were dried up from off the earth: and Noah removed the covering of the ark".[58] We also encounter this use of calendric symbolism to mark the new beginning in the account of the Exodus—to which we now turn—and in the Christian assimilation of the Paschal lamb to Christ.

* * *

The waters of the Red Sea, through which Moses led the Hebrews out of bondage in Egypt, also prefigure the waters of baptism.[59] By this passage through the sea, according to St Paul: "were all baptized unto Moses in the cloud and in the sea."[60] Cyril explains this symbolic link to the catechumens:

> ...for Israel deliverance from Pharaoh was through the sea, and for the world deliverance from sins by the washing of water with the word of God. Where a covenant is made with any, there is water also. [61]

The old man who dies in the waters is symbolized by the armed hosts of Pharaoh while the Hebrews casting off their bondage are the new man who emerges from the waters into freedom and this freedom is a new beginning. God commands of the month in which the Hebrews are released "This month shall be unto you the beginning of months: it shall be the first month of the year to you...."[62] This recalls the calendric symbolism already mentioned in relation to the Deluge; in both instances, the re-beginning of the calendar marks the beginning of the new creation. Christianity builds upon these calendric correspondences. While the Christian liturgical year begins

---

54. Jn 1.32.
55. St Ambrose, *de mys.* 4(24).
56. Gen 1:2.
57. "As an eagle stirreth up her nest, fluttereth [*rachaph*] over her young, spreadeth abroad her wings, taketh them, beareth them on her wings: So the LORD alone did lead him [Jacob]..." (Deut. 32:11-12.)
58. Gen 8:13.
59. St Augustine, *cat. rud.* Ch 20 (34)
60. 1 Cor 10:1-2.
61. St Cyril of Jerusalem, *cat.* 3.5. Compare Tertullian, *de baptismo.* 9, quoted above.
62. Ex 12:2

in Advent (or in September in the Eastern Orthodox tradition), residual elements of the Jewish new year remain, as all lights in the church are extinguished with Christ's death and new fire kindled with His Resurrection on Easter morn. The paschal candle of the previous year is removed and a new one blessed, put in its place and lit from the new fire. Christ is the Passover Lamb of Exodus 12, both slain on the fourteenth day of Nisan. The blood of the Passover Lamb which protects the Hebrews from the death of the first-born, the final plague upon Egypt that leads to the Hebrews' release, is the blood of Christ. This Scriptural correspondence is marked in part by the role of hyssop in both stories. Hyssop is used to mark the lintels with the blood of the lamb[63] and appears also in John's crucifixion account.[64] Likewise, with the Resurrection on Easter Day "we have clean escaped from Egypt and from Pharaoh".[65]

In relation to baptism, it is important for this symbolism that we understand that the Egyptians and the Hebrews are the sinful and the righteous aspects of the one man who enters the baptismal waters. It is in this light that we may understand that, after Pharaoh had relented and let the Hebrews go, God hardened "Pharaoh's heart, that he shall follow after..."[66] and be destroyed by the waters:

> ...the tyrant was pursuing that ancient people even to the sea; and here the daring and shameless spirit, the author of evil, was following thee even to the very streams of salvation. The tyrant of old was drowned in the sea; and this present one disappears in the water of salvation.[67]

In order that the new man may be born, first the old man must die: "And the Egyptians were urgent upon the people, that they might send them out of the land in haste; for they said, 'We be all dead men.'"[68] Tertullian makes the same association and Gregory of Nyssa concurs:

> For even now, whensoever the people is in the water of regeneration, fleeing from Egypt, from the burden of sin, it is set free and saved; but

---

63. Ex 12:22.
64. Jn 19:29-30. "...and they filled a sponge with vinegar, and put it upon hyssop, and put it to his mouth. When Jesus therefore had received the vinegar, he said, It is finished: and he bowed his head, and gave up the ghost." Symbolically, the New Testament use of hyssop at the crucifixion identifies the salvific function of Christ's sacrifice. It is used in the ritual cleansing of leprosy (Lev. 14, where it is likewise dipped in the blood of the sacrifice), of one who has had contact with unclean things (Num 19:16) and, most importantly for our context, the purgation from sin (Ps 51). In short, hyssop is related to sacrifice, purification and protection, all of which are themes of baptism.
65. St Gregory Nazianzen, *or.* 1.3.
66. Ex 14.4.
67. St Cyril of Jerusalem, *cat.* 19.2.
68. Ex 12:33.

the devil… is choked with grief, and perishes, deeming the salvation of men to be his own misfortune.[69]

This symbolic reading can also be found—cast in a dualistic context—in the Gnostic *Pistis Sophia*, where "they are Egypt, because they are matter."[70]

The inspiration of Pharaoh towards watery death is the inspiration of conversion that leads man to baptism, which is the death of the old man "by which", St Augustine explains, "the faithful pass into the new life, while their sins are done away with like enemies, and perish."[71] And St Ambrose instructs:

> …observe that even then holy baptism was prefigured in that passage of the Hebrews, wherein the Egyptian perished, the Hebrew escaped. For what else are we daily taught in this sacrament but that guilt is swallowed up and error done away, but that virtue and innocence remain unharmed?[72]

Thus Pharaoh and his hosts represent the lower, infernal, tendencies, those which impel man towards separateness and death and which must be conquered in order that one may walk the spiritual way.[73] They are the 'sinful generation' that is destroyed in the Deluge. Through the waters the Hebrews enter into freedom and "the devil, their old tyrant, they leave quite behind, overwhelmed in the water."[74] Fohr notes that the 'Red Sea' of the Exodus *mythos*, '*yam sup*' is better translated as "'Sea of the End (of the world)' and the reference is to the primordial chaos"[75] and this links these two symbolisms—the crossing of the Red Sea and the cosmogony—together, making of the former a symbol of rebirth or re-creation. The Hebrews return to the primordial abyss of the cosmogonic waters but they do not remain there, just as the waters of the Deluge do not endure perpetually. The forty years—again a reference to the period of gestation—in the desert (in one of its aspects a symbol of the non-manifested) culminate with the crossing of the Jordan (the place of Christ's baptism) where the waters again part (before the ark of the covenant) to allow the passage of the Chosen Ones into the Promised

---

69. St Gregory of Nyssa, *bapt. Chr.*

70. *Pistis Sophia: A Gnostic Gospel,* trans. G.R.S. Mead (Blauvelt, NY: Spiritual Science Library, 1984). 1.18 p.22. Although orthodox Christianity would deny the identification of matter with evil which is present here.

71. St Augustine, *cat. rud.* Ch 20 (34)

72. St Ambrose, *de mys.* 3(12).

73. On this theme see Fohr, *Adam & Eve.* Ch 12, pp. 165-180.

74. Tertullian, *de baptismo.* 9.

75. Fohr, *Adam & Eve.* p. 169. n. 5. Fohr cites here two articles by B.H. Batto: 'The Reed Sea: *Requiescat in Pace*', *Journal of Biblical Literature*, v. 102 (1983), pp. 27-35 and 'Red Sea or Reed Sea', *Biblical Archeology Review*, v. 10 no. 4 (July/August 1984), pp. 57-63, in which doubt is cast upon the reading 'Reed Sea'.

Land.[76] As with the Deluge *mythos*, the process of return to principle is reversed in the process of remanifestation.[77]

To return to the *mythos* of the Deluge, St. Ambrose (who baptized St Augustine) draws the raven and the dove within the scope of baptismal symbolism:

> The water, then, is that in which the flesh is dipped, that all carnal sin may be washed away. All wickedness is there buried. The wood is that on which the Lord Jesus was fastened when He suffered for us. The dove is that in the form of which the Holy Spirit descended, as you have read in the New Testament, Who inspires in you peace of soul and tranquility of mind. The raven is the figure of sin, which goes forth and does not return, if, in you, too, inwardly and outwardly righteousness be preserved.[78]

Here the symbolic meaning of the raven and that of the hosts of Pharaoh and the forty years in the desert in the Exodus *mythos* coincide. Symbolically the two stories are identical in the interpretative framework of Christian baptism.

* * *

Augustine notes that both of these Old Testament types, the Exodus and the Deluge, it is not the power of water alone that is at work but also what he calls "the sacrament of the wood."[79] The waters of the Red Sea gave safe passage to the Hebrews when "Moses smote with his rod, in order that that miracle might be effected."[80] Likewise, it is the wood of the ark that bears Noah and his family upon the waters and brings them safely to the new covenant. This wood is the wood of the Cross. "For what is water without the cross of Christ? A common element, without any sacramental effect."[81] By the wood of the ark, the new human race—Noah and his family—are borne safely over the waters, which otherwise destroy the sinful generations. The announcement of the new world in which this new race would live takes the form of the branch carried by the dove.

> On each occasion life comes by means of wood. For in the time of Noah the preservation of life was by an ark of wood. In the time of Moses the sea, on beholding the emblematical rod, was abashed at him who smote

---

76. Jos 3.

77. The years in the wilderness are the length of time required for the idolaters—who worshipped the Golden Calf—to pass away, leaving only the righteous behind. This is another symbol of the death of sin wrought in baptism, analogous to the death of Pharaoh's host and the destruction of the 'sinful generations' by the Deluge.

78. St Ambrose, *de mys.* 3 (11) *cf.* St Cyril of Jerusalem, *cat.* 17.10.

79. St Augustine, *cat. rud.* Ch 20 (34).

80. St Augustine, *cat. rud.* Ch 20 (34).

81. St Ambrose, *de mys.* 4(20). See also St Cyril of Jerusalem, *cat.* 3.3.

it; is then Moses' rod mighty, and is the Cross of the Saviour powerless? … The wood in Moses' case sweetened the water…[82]

This last point, the wood making the water sweet, is a reference to the spring at Marah.[83] St Ambrose elaborates on the efficacy of the wood—which prefigures the Cross—in his baptismal reading of Marah. He writes:

> Marah was a fountain of most bitter water: Moses cast wood into it and it became sweet. For water without the preaching of the Cross of the Lord is of no avail for future salvation… As, then, Moses… cast wood into that fountain, so, too, the priest utters over this font the proclamation of the Lord's cross, and the water is made sweet for the purpose of grace.[84]

Ambrose does not discuss it but the passage from Exodus notes that from the Red Sea to the well of Marah was a journey of three days. This is surely a type of the three days which Christ spent in the tomb: three days between the 'death' in the Red Sea and the sweetening of the bitter waters in the 'resurrection' at Marah. The priest blesses the waters of the font with the sign of the cross—symbolically touching them with the wood of the Cross[85]—and makes the bitterness sweet: "…it is not of the waters but of grace that a man is cleansed";[86] "…water does not cleanse without the Spirit."[87] This again recalls the cosmogonic waters over which the Spirit hovered as well as the creation of man, into whose body of dust (and, according to Tertullian, of water) God 'blows' His spirit. Despite its natural qualities which make it the perfect material symbol for the sacrament, the Fathers are clear that it is not merely by the agency of the water that one is spiritually cleansed. This is not a 'natural' salvation, nor a magical charm or poultice but one wrought by divine grace, inseparable from the sacramental orders of the Church. Thus we might say that the qualities of the waters are such that, while not efficacious in their own right, are the perfect receptacle for and vehicle of the baptismal grace. "Quiescent with God in a yet unshapen state".[88] The water is pure potentiality, pure receptivity; it is capable of receiving or responding to the divine Spirit but is not itself that Spirit.

Old Testament types of baptism can be multiplied almost indefinitely, as St Gregory of Nyssa remarks: "the discourse would extend to an infinite

---

82. St Cyril of Jerusalem, *cat.* 13.20.
83. Ex 15.22 ff.
84. St Ambrose, *de mys.* 3(14) Compare Tertullian, *de baptismo.* 9. "Again, water is restored from its defect of 'bitterness' to its native grace of 'sweetness' by the tree of Moses. That tree was Christ, restoring, to wit, of Himself, the veins of sometime envenomed and bitter nature into the all-salutary waters of baptism."
85. In some Christian traditions an actual cross or crucifix is used to sign and bless the waters of the font.
86. St Ambrose, *de mys.* 3(17)
87. St Ambrose, *de mys.* 4(19)
88. Tertullian, *de baptismo.* 3.

length if one should seek to select every passage in detail, and set them forth in a single book."[89] Nevertheless, these types which we have considered are enough to indicate the fundamental meaning attributed to the waters of baptism. They are waters of death and of new life. Each of our Old Testament types indicate a return to the primordial waters before the primal division of the upper and lower waters and the establishment of the heavens and the earth: an unmaking of the old order, the return to principle, and the going out into the a new beginning. The old man is unmade—that is, dies—and the new man is born.

* * *

The old man dies in the waters of baptism, and here the rite may be considered as both a 'drowning' and a corpse-washing.[90] From these same waters the new man is born and here the fontal waters take the symbolism of the waters of the womb and the cosmogony. The old man is immersed and, dying, is left behind and the new man, the new creation emerges, reborn into eternal life. At "the self-same moment ye were both dying and being born; and that Water of salvation was at once your grave and your mother."[91] Baptism is a death that liberates one from death. Baptized man has vanquished sin because, having already died in Christ, sin (and death) has no hold over the initiate, as St Gregory of Nyssa explains:

> Now if we have been conformed to His death, sin henceforth in us is surely a corpse, pierced through by the javelin of Baptism... Flee therefore from us, ill-omened one! for it is a corpse thou seekest to despoil, one long ago joined to thee...[92]

Christ liberates man from the bonds of sin and enables the supreme act of self-determination which is the 'Amen' to God—the same Amen by which the Blessed Virgin consented to give birth to the Christ—by which the initiate accepts the radical freedom of rebirth. Salvation requires re-creation.

This last point serves to link the primordial cosmogonic symbolism that we have explored with a complementary Edenic symbolism that is equally present in baptismal symbolism. While our primary focus in this study is upon the symbolism of water, a few remarks on Edenic symbolism in baptism—which also has a component of water symbolism—will not be out of

---

89. St Gregory of Nyssa, *bapt. Chr.*
90. This corpse washing motif is also found in the pre- and post-baptismal anointings with oil, which correspond to the anointing of the corpse in preparation for its entombment. See Mk 16:1, Lk 23:56, Jn 19:39-40. Also significant here is the episode of the woman anointing Christ (Mk 14:3-8) with spikenard, and the Johannine parallel where Mary anoints his feet (Jn 12:3-7.) Christ explains: "She is come aforehand to anoint my body to the burying." (Mk 14:8) and "Against the day of my burying hath she kept this." (Jn 12:7)
91. St Cyril of Jerusalem, *cat.* 20.4.
92. St Gregory of Nyssa, *bapt. Chr.*

place, for it is in the Edenic *mythos* that the need for salvation which baptism makes available is contextualized.[93]

Streams of Living Water: the Return to Eden

> In Paradise was the Fall, and in a Garden was our Salvation. From the Tree came sin, and until the Tree sin lasted. "In the evening, when the Lord walked in the Garden, they hid themselves"; and in the evening the robber is brought by the Lord into Paradise.

St Cyril of Jerusalem,
Catechetal Lectures 13.19

Narratively of a different order, the Edenic *mythos* anagogically plays out this same cosmogonic movement from potentiality or formlessness to actuality or formality and this anagogic relationship is signalled by Genesis 2.6, 10: "…there rose a fountain (πηγή) out of the earth, and watered the whole face of the earth. … And a river proceeds out of Eden to water the garden."[94] What is considered macrocosmically in the cosmogony is present microcosmically in Eden and the creation of man. In accord with this Edenic order of symbolism the baptismal oil is, according to the *Clementine Recognitions*, the essence of the Tree of Life. Man was removed from the presence of the Tree by his expulsion from Eden. Baptism returns man to his former proximity to the Tree, which is also the Cross of Christ: "Adam by the Tree [of the Knowledge of Good and Evil] fell away; thou by the Tree [of Life] art brought into Paradise."[95]

'Natural,' post-Edenic man, as St Augustine asserts, is born into the disequilibrium of original sin which affects not only the external conditions of the *kosmos* in which he finds himself but also his psychic, interior disposition. This disequilibrium predisposes him to compound and confirm the primordial sin. Baptism 'unmakes' the Adamic decision to sin and returns the initiate to the Edenic state which Theophilus of Antioch describes as a state of potentiality:

> Neither… immortal nor yet mortal did He make him [man], but… capable of both so that if he should incline to the things of immortality, keeping the commandment of God, he should receive as reward from Him immortality, and should become God; but if, on the other hand, he

---

93. Again, for a more comprehensive consideration of the order of Edenic symbolism, see Castleman, "The Primordial in Baptism."

94. Lxx. The Vulgate gives '*fons*', which the Douay version rightly translates as 'spring' while the AV gives 'mist' for the Hebrew ''*ed*'. While both are references to water (and we have already considered the use Tertullian makes of this and its connection to the cosmogonic waters), the Lxx and Vulgate are to be preferred here as the stronger indicators of this symbolic relationship: synonyms, they both emphasis water's function as *archē*, source, or principle and furthermore indicates the perpetual presence of the principle in its manifestation.

95. St Cyril of Jerusalem, *cat.* 13.31.

should turn to the things of death, disobeying God, he should himself be the cause of death to himself.[96]

The choice of sin and separation determines the conditions of human existence such as they are, bound to mortality and death. Baptized man returns to the state of Adamic potentiality and is no longer bound by the consequences of the primordial choice; the gates of Eden are once more opened and man may again enter in, as Gregory of Nyssa remarks: "No longer … shall the flaming sword encircle Paradise around, and make the entrance inaccessible to those that draw near".[97] Jensen notes the prevalence of garden motifs in the symbolic ornamentation of fonts—trees ("palms, fig, and apples, and olives"), flowers, birds—as well as a number of fontal pavements showing "harts drinking from streams of living water".[98] It is this symbolic connection with Eden that underpins the instructions of the *Didache*—the earliest extant document on Christian practices—to baptize in "living water." The one who enters the font enters into the Garden of Eden and the Presence of the Tree of Life and the rivers of Paradise that flow from it.

St Ambrose describes a baptism ritual in which foot-washing—a ritual participation in Christ's actions on Holy Thursday—plays a part.[99] For Ambrose, the baptismal immersion remits personal sin but does not remove the stain of original sin. That, he says, is the role of the *pedilavium*.

> Peter was clean, but he must wash his feet, for he had sin by succession from the first man, when the serpent overthrew him and persuaded him to sin. His feet were therefore washed, that hereditary sins might be done away…[100]

Idiosyncratic it may be[101] but the symbolism underlying it is significant as it points once more to the restoration of Edenic purity. Amongst the curses that accompany the expulsion from Eden and which delineate the nature of the fallen state is the following addressed to the serpent: "I will put enmity between thee and the woman, and between thy seed and her seed; it shall bruise thy head, and thou shalt bruise his heel."[102] It is precisely original sin symbolized as a wound to the foot that is removed, according to St Ambrose, by the *pedilavium*. Again, what is indicated here is the undoing of the lapsarian determinations and the return to Edenic purity.

---

96. Theophilus of Antioch, *Ad Autolycum* (To Autolycus). 2.27.

97. St Gregory of Nyssa, *bapt. Chr.*

98. Jensen, "Womb, Tomb, and Garden". Pt I. Sec. D.

99. Jn 13.

100. St Ambrose, *de mys.* 7(31-32)

101. In *de sacramentiis* 3.1.4 Ambrose acknowledges and defends this idiosyncrasy of the Milanese Church against its critics.

102. Gen 3:15. This is one aspect of the changed relationship between man and the *kosmos* he inhabits (one might also say the *kosmos* he is). The curses upon Adam and upon Eve reveal other aspects of this changed relationship as well as a change in the relationship between man and woman, and between human persons in general.

The baptismal waters effect a dissolution of the form determined by the Fall and a return to the state of pure potentiality that Theophilus of Antioch ascribes to Adam (and we have already considered in relation to the cosmogonic waters, the waters of the Deluge and those of the Red Sea and the desert of the Exodus *mythos*). With this dissolution of form comes the dissolution of the bonds of death and separation by which this form is held. The Areopagite writes: "...it is quite appropriate to hide the initiate completely in the water as an image of this death and this burial where form is dissolved."[103] It is the "death and dissolution" of what is opposed to God.[104] The initiate is stripped of the "rough garment of... [his] offences",[105]—the manifestation of his determination to sin—and returned to the state symbolized by unabashed Edenic nudity, which is his primordial integrity: "O wondrous thing! [In baptism] ye were naked in the sight of all, and were not ashamed; for truly ye bore the likeness of the first-formed Adam, who was naked in the garden, and was not ashamed."[106] St Gregory of Nyssa: "No longer shall Adam be confounded when called by Thee, nor hide himself, convicted by his conscience, cowering in the thicket of Paradise."[107] Theodore of Mospuestia uses judicial imagery to the same purpose. He explains that:

> ...we must run with all diligence to the judge and show and establish the title which we possess: that we did not belong to Satan from the beginning... but to God who created us... and made us in His own image.[108]

In overcoming the Devil and escaping his dominion, the Christian initiate returns to his original, divine, 'owner' under whose auspices he now dwells. The baptized is free because he has returned to the Edenic state, prior to the bondage of sin and death, and to his rightful owner: "We have rightly reverted to our Lord to whom we belonged before the wickedness of Satan, and we are, as we were in the beginning, in the image of God."[109] Whatever claim Satan—the adversary and 'prosecutor'—has over us, God has a prior and overriding claim. Reacknowledging that claim is the return to the Edenic origin and the restoring of the divine image in which man was made but which is disfigured by sin.

Here the symbolism of light, and solar symbolism in particular, is significant. The neophyte faces to the west and renounces Satan, and then turns to the east and accepts Christ. The neophyte turns away from the darkness of sin, death, and ignorance, and turns to the "light which enlightens ev-

---

103. EH 2.7 404B p. 208.
104. EH 2.5 401B p. 206.
105. St Cyril of Jerusalem, *cat.* 1.1. That is, the 'coats of skins' of Genesis 3:21.
106. St Cyril of Jerusalem, *cat.* 20.2.
107. St Gregory of Nyssa, *bapt. Chr.*
108. Theodore of Mospuestia, *Commentary of Theodore of Mopsuestia on the Lord's Prayer and on the Sacraments of Baptism and the Eucharist (Liber ad Baptizandos part 2)*, trans. A. Mingana, 7 vols., vol. 6, Woodbrooke Studies (Cambridge: W. Heffer and Sons, 1933). Ch 2. p. 28.
109. Theodore of Mospuestia, *Liber ad Baptizandos pt. 2*. Ch 2. p. 30.

ery man".[110] More significant for our purposes, however, is the fact that the turning from west to east is a turning towards Eden, which is symbolically 'eastward' because it dwells 'in the light' and 'at the beginning,' as St Cyril explains to his neophytes:

> When therefore thou renouncest Satan, utterly breaking all thy covenant with him, that ancient league with hell, there is opened to thee the paradise of God, which He planted towards the East... and a symbol of this was thy turning from West to East, the place of lights...[111]

The initiate has returned 'to the beginning.' in both cosmogonic and Edenic aspects. The Christic recapitulation of primordial man makes available to the Christian initiate a return to Eden that is sacramentally achieved through baptism.

* * *

The regeneration of baptism is not only the return to the Edenic potential but also the *remaking* of the primordial decision. Its pattern is that of the alchemical *solve et coagula*; the dissolution and return to principle—the death of the old manifestation—is followed by a reformation or remanifestation—the regeneration of baptism—in a higher state: manifestation perfected. As the Areopagite explains, "order descends upon disorder within him. Form takes over from formlessness. Light shines through all his life."[112] Having shed the 'garments of sin' and returned to Adamic nudity, the initiate is dressed in white robes "as a sign that you were putting off the covering of sins, and putting on the chaste veil of innocence".[113] This redetermination does not, as it did for Adam, involve leaving Eden. The Christian initiate is, rather, confirmed in Eden. The Christian life into which one is baptized is life "as it was in the beginning" and the initiate is called to live perpetually

---

110. Patristic sources for this practise are commonplace. Typical of these is St Cyril of Jerusalem: "First ye entered into the vestibule of the Baptistery, and there facing towards the West ye listened to the command to stretch forth your hand, and as in the presence of Satan ye renounced him." (St Cyril of Jerusalem, *cat.* 19.2). Lactantius: "...the east is assigned to God, because He Himself is the fountain of light, and the enlightener of all things, and because He makes us rise to eternal life. But the west is ascribed to that disturbed and depraved mind, because it conceals the light, because it always brings on darkness, and because it makes men die and perish in their sins." (Lactantius, *Divine Institutes.* 2.10): "therefore, looking with a symbolical meaning towards the West, ye renounce that dark and gloomy potentate." (St Cyril of Jerusalem, "cat." 19.4.) This turning from west to east—symbolizing the renunciation of Satan and acceptance of Christ—is still practiced in the Orthodox Church.
111. St Cyril of Jerusalem, *cat.* 19.9.
112. EH 2.8. 404B p. 208
113. St Ambrose, *de mys.* 7 (34).

in this primordial state.[114] This primordial state is both the beginning and the *telos* (end and perfection) of the created order.

The man born of baptism is not Adam, he is greater than Adam because he has achieved what Adam did not. He has returned to the first created principle and re-emerged into manifestation, experienced not as the dualism of 'original sin' but as a dyadic unity that transcends both its terms, terrestrial and celestial. This transcendence of dualism is what Moses and the Hebrews accomplish in the crossing of the Red Sea; as Fohr notes, the walls of water through which they pass "symbolize the dualistic view of reality. ... The Egyptians, who can be said to represent a person tied to the lower tendencies and hence immersed in dualism, do not make it through."[115] This dualistic state is also that through which the ark brings its inhabitants safely to the primordial unity.

Manifestation is no longer seen through the illusory, separative mode (the knowledge of Good and Evil) but rather its unitive mode (the Tree of Life or the primordial, undivided, waters). Indeed, the seeming polarity between these two 'trees' or poles of manifestation evaporates; 'either-or' paradigms become meaningless. Adam chooses the Tree of Good and Evil and thus imposes upon himself the separative either-or conditions whereby he is deprived of the Tree of Life; the Christian initiate, by comparison, participates in the 'both-and'[116] paradigm of Christ's Incarnate Person. By his rebirth from the united upper and lower waters of the cosmogony he is, so to speak, amphibian: earthly and heavenly, transcending the boundaries between the two just as Christ "in His burial... made peace between heaven and earth, bringing sinners unto God".[117] These two—earth and heaven—interpenetrate in what the Latin theologians would call the *communicatio idiomatum* and the Greeks *perichoresis*. Thus "...the spirit is corporeally washed in the waters, and the flesh is in the same spiritually cleansed."[118]

Here the Edenic and the cosmogonic symbolisms converge as two aspects of the same symbolism from microcosmic and macrocosmic perspec-

---

114. Christ's determinations on the indissolubility of the marriage covenant carry the same force of a return to the primordial state, hence Matthew's Gospel: "Have ye not read, that he which made them at the beginning made them male and female, And said, For this cause shall a man leave father and mother, and shall cleave to his wife: and they twain shall be one flesh? Wherefore they are no more twain, but one flesh. What therefore God hath joined together, let not man put asunder. They say unto him, Why did Moses then command to give a writing of divorcement, and to put her away? He saith unto them, Moses because of the hardness of your hearts suffered you to put away your wives: but from the beginning it was not so." (Mt 19:4-8.)

115. Fohr, *Adam & Eve*. p. 170.

116. "For the Son of God, Jesus Christ... was not yea and nay, but in him was yea." (2Cor 1:19.)

117. St Cyril of Jerusalem, *cat.* 14.3.

118. Tertullian, *de baptismo.* 4.

tives respectively. The return to Eden and the return to the cosmogonic waters both symbolically indicate a return to the primordial potentiality and its reactualization. In baptism man returns to the created first principle—the waters called 'abyss' in the Septuagint—of which the heavens and the earth are formed. From thence the initiate is remade and in himself remakes the *kosmos*. The microcosm and the macrocosm are linked together; what is true of one is true of the other, as Guénon observes: "...the being reintegrated into the center of the human state... dominates the conditions of existence in this world of which it has become master".[119] Fohr notes in relation to the Hebrews having passed out of Egypt through the waters and passed beyond dualism, "they symbolize a person who has reached the Terrestrial Paradise",[120] the perfection and end (*telos*) of the created order. It is the end of this fallen *kosmos* and the beginning of the new, perfected *kosmos*. It is the return to the first day, the primordial day, the Edenic state, not lost as it was in Adam but regained and made eternal, which is the entry into Heavenly Jerusalem of St John's apocalyptic vision:

> And I saw a new heaven and a new earth: for the first heaven and the first earth were passed away; and there was no more sea. And I John saw the holy city, new Jerusalem, coming down from God out of heaven, prepared as a bride adorned for her husband."[121]

The relationship between the Heavenly Jerusalem and the Garden of Eden is signaled by the position of the Tree of Life in both.[122] Here heaven and earth come together; the upper and lower waters, once parted, are rejoined; the 'Red Sea', the 'sea of the end of the world,' is crossed and man has entered into the new creation.

This eternal kingdom, the new creation, the Edenic state regained and made eternal, is known as the eighth day—the *ogdoad* or octave. It is the first cosmogonic day recapitulated and perfected in Christ. Victorinus explains that the eighth day is the day of "future judgment, which will pass beyond the order of the sevenfold arrangement"[123] that symbolizes the separative conditions of this age and temporal succession. "The "totality of time," ex-

---

119. Guénon, R., "The Secret Language of Dante and the 'Fedeli d'Amore'-II," in *Insights into Christian Esoterism*, ed. S.D. Fohr (Ghent, NY: Sophia Perennis, 2001). p. 52.

120. Fohr, *Adam & Eve*. p. 170.

121. Rev 21:1-2. It is tempting here to read the phrase "and there was no more sea" as symbolising the fullness of the actualized state. Potential (the sea) is no more, the *kosmos*, like God, is pure *act*: there is nothing unrealized in it (evil being not a thing but a privation, a lack of the realization of the fullness of man's potential to be united to God). I know, however, of no Patristic source for this reading. The sea is also understood symbolically as the dwelling place of the monster that must be vanquished, the 'great dragon of the sea,' and this must also inform the symbolism at work in this phrase.

122. Rev 22:1-2, 14.

123. Victorinus, *On the Creation of the World*.

plains St Gregory of Nyssa, is measured "through the circle of seven days...
[but] once time... comes to a close, the octave succeeds it."[124] It is, as St
Basil describes, a

> day without evening, without succession and without end... [called] ...
> the eighth day, because it is outside this time of weeks. Thus whether
> you call it day, or whether you call it eternity, you express the same
> idea.[125]

Entry into the eighth day requires the destruction of the sevenfold cycle,
which destruction Victorinus understands to be symbolized by the Lord's
breaking of the Sabbath as well as the holy Sabbath breakers of the Old
Testament, such as Joshua and Isaiah. Thus in the *Epistle of Barnabas* it is
written that the Lord says:

> Your present Sabbaths are not acceptable to Me, but... I shall make
> a beginning of the eighth day, that is, a beginning of another world.
> Wherefore, also, we keep the eighth day with joyfulness, the day also on
> which Jesus rose again from the dead.[126]

Thus Christians observe as holy not the seventh day, that of the Jewish Sabbath, but the eighth day, "as signifying the resurrection".[127] "Accordingly the
eighth day, which is the first day of the week, represents to us that original
life, not taken away, but made eternal."[128] The eighth day is the creation
begun again, its potentialities fully actualized: "and there was no more sea."
Hence it is the new creation in Christ, in whom was fully realized the supreme human potential. For the musical octave the eighth note repeats the
first, only at a 'higher' level; just so the eighth day, the apocalyptic octave.

Conclusion

> Great is the Baptism that lies before you: a ransom to captives; a
> remission of offences; a death of sin; a new-birth of the soul; a gar-
> ment of light; a holy indissoluble seal; the delight of Paradise; a
> welcome into the kingdom; the gift of adoption!

> St Cyril of Jerusalem, Procatechesis 16

Drawing upon a wide arrange of sources from across the ancient Christian
world, and despite variations in the particulars of the baptismal rites and
symbols, we nevertheless find a consistent emphasis upon baptism as the
return to the Primordial. Baptism is the unmaking of the fallen manifestation
by the return to the Principle beyond form and the re-creation of the human
hypostasis in the fullness of the potential denied by Adam. In both these
symbolic orders water plays a central role.

---

124. St Gregory of Nyssa, *Homilia in Ps. 6* (On the Sixth Psalm, Concerning the
Octave), tr. R. McCambly, http://www.sage.edu/faculty/salomd/nyssa/octave.html.
125. St Basil, *In Hexaemeron.* 2.8
126. *Epistle of Barnabas.* 15.
127. St Augustine, *Epistle 55.* 13 (23).
128. St Augustine, *Ep. 55.* 9 (17).

The mysteries of baptism are of a cosmological order, as demonstrated by the cosmogonic and Edenic symbolism that permeates the rites. The reintegration of the human *hypostasis*, and by analogy the *kosmos*, is the precondition of salvation. The baptismal grace sacramentally confers this integrity and its symbols expound the nature of the creation and the way whereby it enters into a proper relationship with the Absolute. It is, according to the Christian vision, the state conferred by baptism—and this state alone—that enables man to enter into the mystery of the divine Person Himself at the Eucharistic feast.[129] Thus the 'robe without blemish' of the newly baptized is the wedding garment of the soul, which it assumes as befitting the wedding banquet that it is about to enter as bride of Christ.

> He has commanded us... to invite you to the supper of the heavenly King, which the Father hath prepared for the marriage of His Son, and that we should give you wedding garments, that is, the grace of baptism; ... as a spotless robe with which he is to enter to the supper of the King...[130]

In his baptismal perfection, man is prepared for the Eucharistic feast. It is in this state of primordial harmony that he approaches the altar and the sacrament of the Body and Blood of Christ.[131] St Cyril makes the relation between these two sacraments clear: "Begin at once to wash your robes in repentance, that when called to the bride-chamber ye may be found clean."[132] Baptism is the preparation for the wedding feast of the Eucharist, in which man and God are united. The movement that is begun at the font is fulfilled at the altar. The kosmic perfection of baptized man reaches its metacosmic perfection in union with the Trinitarian Godhead and the sacramental *theosis* by which 'we are made by grace what Christ is by nature' in participation in the Eucharistic Presence.

> Creation and salvation—the two terms of manifestation—both begin in water and indeed end there, for as from the pierced side of the Christ "came there out blood and water",[133] so the Eucharistic 'cup of salvation' contains not only wine but water also; "never is Christ without water."

---

129. Bearing in mind, of course, that "the Spirit bloweth where it listeth."
130. *Clem. recogn.* 4.35.
131. Mt 22:11-13: "And when the king came in to see the guests, he saw there a man which had not on a wedding garment: And he saith unto him, Friend, how camest thou in hither not having a wedding garment? And he was speechless. Then said the king to the servants, Bind him hand and foot, and take him away, and cast him into outer darkness; there shall be weeping and gnashing of teeth."
132. St Cyril of Jerusalem, *cat.* 3.2. The nuptial symbolism follows that of Isa 61.10: "I will greatly rejoice in the LORD... for he hath clothed me with the garments of salvation, he hath covered me with the robe of righteousness, as a bridegroom decketh himself with ornaments, and as a bride adorneth herself with her jewels."
133. Jn 19:34.

Excerpts From The Gospel
of Shrī Rāmakrishna

Shrī Rāmakrishna Paramahansa

Shrī Rāmakrishna Paramahansa (1836-1886) was born in a Bengali village. As a young man, he went to Calcutta but refused to acquire a modern secular education. At the age of 30, he became a priest in the temple at Dakshineshwar, where he remained for most of his life. He is reputed to have obtained the vision of God by following the paths laid down in the Scriptures. He had direct experience of Christianity and Islam, and was the first spiritual authority in modern times explicitly to teach the transcendent unity of all the revealed and orthodox religions. His instruction on the sacramental nature of invocatory prayer is summed up in his saying: "God and His Name are one." His teachings are enshrined in The Gospel of Shri Ramakrishna, a comprehensive record by Mahrendranath Gupta of his talks, over many years, with his disciples and intimates.

* * *

God is formless, and God is possessed of form too. And He is also that which transcends both form and formlessness. He alone knows what all He is. For the sake of those that love the Lord, He manifests Himself in various ways and in various forms. Verily He is not bound by any limitation as to the forms of manifestation, or their negation. God has form, and again, He is formless.

* * *

The water and its bubble are one. The bubble has its birth in the water, floats on it, and ultimately is resolved into it. So also the individual ego (Jivatman) and the supreme Spirit (Paramatman) are one and the same. The difference is in degree; the one is dependent, the other independent.

* * *

God is to man as magnet is to iron. Why does He not then attract man? As iron deeply imbedded in mud is not moved by the attraction of the magnet, so the soul deeply imbedded in Maya feels not the attraction of the Lord. But as when the mud is washed away with water, the iron is free to move, so the soul when by constant tears of prayer and repentance washes away the mud of Maya that makes it cling to the earth, it is soon attracted by the Lord.

* * *

If God is omnipresent, why do we not see Him? Observing from the bank of a pool thickly covered with scum and weeds, you will not see the water in it. If you desire to see the water, remove the scum from the surface of the pond. With eyes covered with the film of Maya, you complain that you cannot see God. If you wish to see Him, remove the film of Maya from your eyes.

The magnetic needle always points to the north, and hence it is that the sailing vessel does not lose her direction. So long as the heart of man is directed towards God, he cannot be lost in the ocean of worldliness.

* * *

A disciple asked his teacher, 'Sir, please tell me how I can see God'. 'Come with me,' said the guru, 'and I shall show you.' He took the disciple to a lake, and both of them got into the water. Suddenly the teacher pressed the disciple's head under the water. After a few moments he released him and the disciple raised his head and stood up. The guru asked him, 'How did you feel?' The disciple said, 'Oh! I thought I should die; I was panting for breath.' The teacher said, 'When you feel like that for God, then you will know you haven't long to wait for His vision.'

* * *

Who is the best devotee of God? It is he who sees, after the realization of Brahman that God alone has become all living beings, the universe, and the twenty-four cosmic principles. One must discriminate at first, saying, 'Not this, not this', and reach the roof. After that one realizes that the steps are made of the same materials as the roof, namely, brick, lime, and brick-dust. The devotee realizes that it is Brahman alone that has become all these—the living beings, the universe, and so on.

* * *

One must have faith and love. Let me tell you how powerful faith is. A man was about to cross the sea from Ceylon to India. Vibhishana said to him: 'Tie this thing in a corner of your wearing-cloth, and you will cross the sea safely. You will be able to walk on the water. But be sure not to examine it, or you will sink.' The man was walking easily on the water of the sea—such is the strength of faith—when, having gone part of the way, he thought, 'What is this wonderful thing Vibhishana has given me, that I can walk even on the water?' He untied the knot and found only a leaf with the name of Rama written on it. 'Oh, just this!' he thought, and instantly he sank.

* * *

There is a popular saying that Hanuman jumped over the sea through his faith in Rama's name, but Rama Himself had to build a bridge.

* * *

Ordinary souls are afraid to teach others. A piece of worthless timber may itself somehow float across the water, but it sinks even under the weight of a bird. Sages like Narada are like a heavy log of wood, which not only floats on the water but also can carry men, cows, and even elephants.

* * *

The tortoise moves about in the water. But can you guess where her thoughts are? There on the bank, where her eggs are lying. Do all your duties in the world, but keep your mind on God.

* * *

The mind is like milk. If you keep the mind in the world, which is like water, then the milk and water will get mixed. That is why people keep milk in a quiet place and let it set into curd, and then churn butter from it. Likewise, through spiritual discipline practised in solitude, churn the butter of knowledge and devotion from the milk of the mind. Then that butter can easily be kept in the water of the world. It will not get mixed with the world. The mind will float detached on the water of the world.

There is a "fountain in the Godhead, which flows out upon all things in Eternity and in Time."

Meister Eckhart

Everything passes away like a river, day and night, never resting.

The Annals of Confucius

Though the rivers flow, the Waters do not move.

Rg Veda v. 47:5

Muddy water, let stand—becomes clear.

Lao Tzu

The Eternal Source is at the same time motionless and flowing, never stagnant.

Ananda Kentish Coomaraswamy

Water as Healer

Katherine Murray

The cure for anything is salt water: sweat, tears or the sea.

Isak Dinesen

Water. Imagine the sound of the ocean waves, spreading across the smooth sand like loving hands reaching to touch your tired feet...

Remember the pattern of raindrops falling in a steady, comforting rhythm on your roof...

See the calm, still surface of a freshwater lake mirroring the deep blue heavens...

As Isak Dinesen said, salt water in its varied forms offers cure for the strains, stresses, and struggles we seem to attract in our busy workaday lives. It invites us to relax, release, and let go of what we are clinging to, whether it is a problem we are trying to solve, a heartache we are trying to hide, or a physical challenge we are trying to overcome. A simple, basic gift, water supports and sustains us. And over the course of our lives we slowly learn that if we trust it, we float.

Flowing Naturally

Continually moving, always changing, into and out of form—our lives, like water, are in constant flow. We almost catch a glimpse of the essence and then itis out of sight, coursing first within our banks and then overflowing with sweet abandon, the wild and loving essence of who we are. The flow never stops. As a beautiful expression of the One life through bodies, minds, and souls, it must move, touch, nourish, fill, satisfy, transform, and connect.

With no beginning and no end, the flow of love through our lives continues unhindered. We may create channels and dams; we may try to direct or divide it; but ultimately the water must move naturally, rising to the air and falling again, fresh, to run through our lives in a new way. We can pool it, bottle it, share it, save it for a rainy day, but ultimately it again rejoins the One, making its way to the seas, rising only to fall in beautiful silent cycles of life.

Becoming Part of the River

In our everyday world, most people and objects we encounter have clear edges we recognize and respect. We each have boundaries that mark where one of us ends and another begins. My skin seems to be the surface of my physical self, even though I know on a cellular level I am continually interacting with all the elements that comprise me—water, wind, light, and soil. Years ago I traveled to the Columbia River Gorge and was suspended in awe by the beauty I found there. Hiking down the bank to a shallow spot, I peeled off my socks and shoes and waded out into the rushing water. Standing in the water with my bare feet on the smooth stones, with the cool current pulsing at my ankles, I felt a sense of rightness—the calm of peaceful connection.

Who was river and who was woman? In that moment, there was only Life, enjoying.

Finding the Calm, Still Surface

Thoreau said, "Instead of looking into the sky, I look into the placid reflecting water for the signs and promise of the morrow." The clarity and calm of a still surface has the power to draw us back to that point in ourselves that is still, resting, at peace. When we gaze out over the beautiful reflection of a still lake, we see, feel, absorb the open space, the clear energy, the magnificent reflection of a limitless sky. In challenging moments, however, it may be difficult or impossible for many of us to travel to a point of beauty at the water's edge. What can we do for a moment's tranquility when a hike is out of the question? Drawing the calming image to mind is one possibility, but accepting water's invitation is another.

The water that runs from the tap in the kitchen, the water in the rainbarrel, the water in the bottle at the office—it is all the same water, essential to life, a gift of welcoming, spaciousness, calm, and possibility. Yes, it may be chlorinated by your local water provider, or sold for a profit by any one of a number of vendors. But no matter what its conduit, the water, the essence, invites you. Enter in. Feel the smooth coolness on your palms. Splash the liquid peace on your face and neck. Know that you are connecting with a vital source of your very own embodied life—these drops know each other. This contact with water wherever you find it reminds you that you are the calm, still surface, even now.

Water as Solace

And then the sadnesses of life come, perhaps like storms—sudden and dramatic—or more like drought, a time of dryness, brittle without joy's nourishing presence. In times of brokenness and anguish, water invites us to attend the deeper places, mixing tears with the essence of source and sustenance.

With the gift of embodiment comes the question of agency—how much of creating this daily life is up to us and how much is allowing life to arise in and through us? Sadness often comes when a creative, loving effort—sometimes a blossoming creative force—seems unfruitful or unfulfilled.

Water says, "Come. Float." I wade out into the lake, not completely trusting. I think about it. I debate myself. I sit down.

Relax. Stretch out your legs.

I do. I feel the sun on my knees and the water beneath them. I am for the moment the physical marriage of light and water. The water is cool; the sun hot. Life feels a little better. The water invites me. I float.

When I emerge from the lake, whatever drew my sadness may still be there. But my tears and my allowing—the floating, the letting go—have opened up a space of peace in me. Returning to the sadness, I remember who I am and, knowing now, I take that sweetness back into the waiting world.

The Death Throes of the River Jordan

Christiana Z. Peppard

> He said to me, 'Mortal, have you seen this?'
> Then he led me back along the bank of the river.
>
> Ezekiel 47:6

The Dead Sea is quietly heaving. Its predatory shores pursue the salty sea and press it inward, creating sandy sinkholes the size of houses. Truth be told, this is not the fault of the sea: waters always hold an elusive agency toward their own persistence. Nor is this strictly the fault of the shores, which are mere accessory to the Dead Sea's decline. It might be said that the fault lies with the Jordan River, which for centuries has fed fresh water into its hypersaline terminus, but which now flows toward the sea as a pea-green, sluggish trickle of agricultural runoff.

Environmental Status of the Jordan River

> As waters fail from a lake, and a river wastes away and dries up,
> so mortals lie down and do not rise again...
>
> Job 14:11

Historically, the Jordan River flooded its banks with seasonal cycles of precipitation in this arid region.[1] For the vast majority of its history, environmental change came slowly, due largely to overgrazing and agricultural clearing of forest.[2]

All of that changed in the 20th-century. In less than 100 years, the waters of the Jordan have been politically allocated, dammed, diverted and polluted. Augmented by regional population growth, these factors have steadily strangled the river. Since the mid-20th century, the flow of the lower Jordan River (between the Sea of Galilee and the Dead Sea) has decreased by 90%.[3] This statistic is staggering, and the consequences are everywhere evident. The contemporary Jordan River is nothing short of beleaguered.

Waters in the Bible

There are many ways that water is invoked in the Bible. Among these, "flowing water" is one of the most important classificatory categories, especially in the Hebrew Bible. "Flowing water" refers primarily to water from springs or rivers: waters that are healthy and in motion, in contrast, for example, to water drawn from stagnant wells. This concept also emerges in the New

---

1. Joshua 3:15 reports, "Now the Jordan overflows all its banks throughout the time of harvest ..." See also Sirach 24:26, "it runs over, like the Euphrates, with understanding, and like the Jordan at harvest time."

2. Daniel Hillel, *Rivers of Eden: The Struggle for Water and the Quest for Peace in the Middle East* (New York: Oxford University Press, 1994), 147.

3. Pre-20th century flows of the river are estimated at roughly 1.2 billion cubic meters per year. Only once in the past 20 years has the annual flow reached 350 million cubic meters (MCM). More frequently, it hovers closer to 100 MCM.

Testament; scholars seem to agree that the "living water" described by Jesus in the story of the Samaritan woman at the well (John 4) is playing on the known difference between flowing waters and well waters.

In addition, the Jordan River is an extremely important site in narrative accounts of events throughout the Bible.

Hebrew Bible and theological resonances

The Jordan River appears as a proper noun in at least 82 contexts in the Hebrew Bible.[4] Several are particularly worthy of our attention. The river first emerges in the Book of Genesis, where the plain of the Jordan is said to be "well watered everywhere, like the garden of the Lord"[5]—and resurfaces occasionally thereafter, often as a liminal entity to be crossed. One preeminent example is when Joshua establishes a memorial to the Israelites' crossing of the river with the Ark of the Covenant. King David also crosses the Jordan with his triumphal retinue.[6] In 2 Kings, Elijah parts the waters of the Jordan, and his mantle and spirit are passed to Elisha, who similarly parts the river and later heals Naaman on the river's banks.[7] In the book of Judges, Gideon and his people cross the Jordan.[8] And the famous Maccabees, brothers Judah and Jonathan, are also said to have traversed the river.[9]

The symbolism of the Jordan River, and especially the liberation entailed in its crossing, has been an enduring motif in literature, poetry, and the gospel music that was birthed from American slave spirituals, like "Deep River" or "Get Away, Jordan." Such cultural references to the Jordan River bear "witness to its vibrant metaphorical and literary depth for the Israelites and their genealogical and spiritual descendants."[10] We see that the significations of the Jordan River in the Hebrew Bible are more than textual relics: the Jordan River remains a living metaphor that conveys meaning.

New Testament and theological resonances

In the New Testament there are eleven explicit references to the Jordan River, the vast majority of which are in the context of the baptism of Jesus. One cluster of New Testament texts refers to the charismatic John on the banks of the Jordan, proclaiming a baptism of repentance to people who streamed in

---

4. The frequency increases when referred to simply as "the river," although not every use of the term "river" in the Hebrew Bible refers to the Jordan.

5. Genesis 13:10.

6. Joshua 3:15-17, 4:1-23; 2 Samuel 19:14-19. After wrestling with an angel and receiving the name Israel, Jacob crossed the Jabbok—a tributary of the Jordan (Gen 32:22-28).

7. 2 Kings 2:6-9 and 5:10-14.

8. Judges 7:24, 8:4

9. 1 Maccabees 5:24.

10. Jeremy Hutton, "The Transjordanian Palimpsest: The Overwritten Texts of Personal Exile and Transformation in the Deuteronomistic History," Ph.D. Dissertation (Harvard University, 2005), 8.

from Jerusalem and the Judean countryside.[11] The Gospels of Matthew and Mark also report the arrival of Jesus at the waters of the Jordan, his baptism by John, and the descent of the Spirit of God identifying him as "my Son, the Beloved."[12] The Jordan occasionally figures as a geographic referent for events in Jesus' ministry[13] or as a region ("beyond the Jordan") from which people came to witness his teachings.[14] The baptism of Jesus is one of the few events recounted in all four gospels of the New Testament.[15]

Whatever the specific nature of the revelation of Jesus' power at the Jordan, it can be stated with certainty that the resonances of baptism in the Jordan are at least two-fold. The first resonance has to do with the enduring significance of the baptism of Jesus in the Jordan River. Historically speaking, churches' celebration of Jesus' baptism preceded the celebration of Jesus' nativity (although the extent to which it was celebrated is uncertain). There is evidence for the celebration of Jesus' baptism as early as the 2nd century, whereas nativity (Christmas) did not gain prominence until the 4th century.[16] The commemoration of Jesus' baptism still occurs annually in churches worldwide, where it is celebrated most directly as the Orthodox feast of Theophany. The second resonance is the fact that contemporary baptismal rites hearken back—some more explicitly than others—to the baptisms conducted by John at the Jordan River, including the baptism of Jesus. In any event, Jesus' baptism in the Jordan was a fundamental event in the development of Christian liturgy and doctrine.[17]

The Value of the Jordan River?

The contemporary degraded environmental reality of the Jordan River stands in stark contrast to the symbolic importance of the river as transmit-

---

11. Matthew 3:5-6, Mark 1:5, John 1:28.
12. Matthew 3:13, Mark 1:9. The baptism of Jesus is also narrated in Luke 3:21-22, but the Jordan is not specified.
13. Matthew 19:1, Mark 10:1, John 10:40.
14. Matthew 4:15, 25; Mark 10:1.
15. The baptism of Jesus is mentioned retrospectively, but not narrated, in John 3:26.
16. Clement of Alexandria (2nd c.) knew of the celebration of Epiphany. For a compilation and historical analysis of the evidence for Epiphany and Nativity in early Christianity, see Hermann Usener, *Religionsgeschichtliche Untersuchungen. Erster Theil: Das Weihnachtsfest* (Bonn, 1889).
17. Kilian McDonnell, *Baptism of Jesus in the Jordan: The Trinitarian and Cosmic Order of Salvation* (Collegeville: Liturgical Press, 1996).
    There are various theories about the origin of baptism, particularly as related to Jewish rites such as *mikveh* or rituals of purification as stipulated in the Holiness codes of Leviticus. There is little consensus on precisely where baptism originated. What is clear is that scriptural references to John's baptisms in the Jordan, and his baptism of Jesus, have become central parts of Christian liturgy and theology.

ted through scripture, liturgy, and theology. How might we think ethically about this disjuncture?

(1) Survival Value

The explicit references to the Jordan in the bible do not stipulate guidelines for environmental status of the river or issues of access and distribution. Yet concerns about distribution and fair access shape the lives of many people in the region and should be part of our ethical reflections.[18]

At the end of a very long day along the Jordan River, I asked a man from Amman, "When you think about water in your country, what do you feel?"

Anger, he replied quietly. At first I did not understand him, despite his excellent English. *Anger* was simply not a concept on the map of possibilities that I had previously considered.

In Jordan, he explained, water does not flow freely. It is mostly bottled, rationed, or sold via water trucks. He receives piped water five hours per week; he can store enough for two weeks. His children bathe together once per week and otherwise wash their hands with clay. *He is not poor.* He fears a future in which people must gather water in buckets or glasses or anything they can find from the taps or the sky.

Water is a survival entity in the Rift Valley that shrouds the Jordan River—its presence or absence has physiological and existential impact in human lives.

Desalination will not provide all of the answers, he maintained, anticipating my next question. It would provide more water to the Dead Sea; it would provide some water to populous areas; but he doubts that it would solve endemic problems. The question of desalination is a contentious one in this part of the world (as it is elsewhere), as societies attempt to quench growing thirst.[19]

---

18. Elsewhere in the Bible one can find statements of obligation and hospitality to provide water to the thirsty stranger (e.g., Job 22:7 and Matthew 10:42). The mobilization of those textual resources is a project for another time.

19. In this region, the World Bank has overseen an initial proposal to build a canal from the Red Sea to the Dead Sea, termed the "Red-Dead," to rescue the declining Dead Sea and, purportedly, to alleviate fresh water shortages in the region. Those who support it seem to look to tourism on the Dead Sea as a long-term profit source, or they have become resigned to political roadblocks to rehabilitating the Jordan (the Dead Sea's sole fresh water source) and pragmatically see no other way to redress water shortages. Others are skeptical that the benefits would outweigh the costs, which are economic and environmental. As in other regions of the world, it is not clear that technology alone will solve the kinds of problems posed by scarce—and valuable—resources. To that end, Friends of the Earth Middle East has called for the World Bank to look at regional issues in water management, to consider long-term sustainability, and to be transparent and involve the public in decision-making about the project.

(2) Memory and the Shape of the River

> O God, my soul is cast down within me;
> I remember you from the land of Jordan
> and of Hermon, from Mount Mizar.
>
> Psalm 42:6

In his epic book, *Rivers of Eden,* scientist Daniel Hillel writes about spending summers of his youth in the early-20th century near the Jordan River. "The ultimate in daring," he writes,

> ...was to trek downstream, past the dam [just south of the Sea of Galilee], to where the river began its sinuous course ... In late spring, when the dam was opened, and the river was in spate and flowed full force, we would throw ourselves into the gushing current and be swept around the curve of a nearly circular meander, then grab onto the overhanging tamarisk branches ... The whirlpools were treacherous, ... so the entire deed was a rather foolhardy test of youthful courage. But we did all this with sheer delight and heady abandon, completely mindless of the river's epic past and sacred significance.[20]

I asked Dr. Hillel how this memory fits into his assessment of the current state of the river. He described seeing his old swimming site, now a completely different terrain, as nothing short of bewildering—even tragic. Yet this original memory still shapes his sense of the river.

In an era characterized by drought, uneven distribution of water resources, and environmental degradation, the memories of those individuals who have experienced a different Jordan River could form an important horizon of possibility—if only to indicate that the river can, and perhaps should, flow in a better way.

Collective memory also has a role. How do scriptures, spirituals, and rituals mediate communal memory of a once-mighty river? How has the Jordan River—whether as physical landscape or as symbolic landscape—shaped the being and becoming of our predecessors and even ourselves?

We are left with the question: *Is it enough to recognize the symbolic significance of the Jordan while ignoring its degraded environmental state?*

(3) Rhetoric vs. Reality: What makes these waters holy?

Throughout the year Christian pilgrims flock to three different sites in Israel, the West Bank, and Jordan where Jesus might have been baptized. Two sites are clustered near the Dead Sea, one each on the banks of the river in the West Bank (Qasr el-Yehud) and Jordan (Bethany-beyond-the-Jordan). What do these contemporary pilgrimages have to do with the environmental status of the river? Does it matter to liturgical practices or theologies of baptism that the Jordan River is degraded?

Some theologians have asserted that using any form of polluted water in baptism would mean that "[t]he person spiritually bathed in, blessed by, and

---

20. Hillel, *Rivers of Eden,* 4.

cleansed through such water would be distracted from appreciating its spiritual significance because of its polluted material condition"[21] and that, more broadly, "[a]buse of water in any form is an abuse of the divine, a sinful and criminal act."[22] How much more so for the pollution of the Jordan, which is the original font of Christian baptism, and a continued site of pilgrimage? How, then, do so few Christians seem to care about the current polluted and diminished state of the river in which the ministry of Jesus is said to have begun?

As noted previously, there are multiple purported baptism sites on the banks of the Jordan. The number of tourists and pilgrims at those locations both reveals and generates their continued cultural significance.[23] Indeed, after the Kingdom of Jordan recently granted the Episcopal Diocese of Jerusalem permission to build a retreat center and "medium-sized Gothic church" at their site, the Anglican Archbishop of Jerusalem noted that "[w]e stand... in a region that had witnessed a great happening in Christian life and history as recorded in the Holy Scriptures."[24] This quotation recognizes that something significant happened at the Jordan—something significant enough to draw hundreds of thousands of pilgrims, to justify a land grant from the Kingdom of Jordan to the Anglican Diocese, to build a Gothic church.

Strangely, the emphasis is not on the waters of the Jordan. Yet it is the *river's* flows that determine whether there are banks on which to commemorate Jesus' baptism. Furthermore, it is the *waters* of the Jordan—not merely its sandy banks—that confer sanctity, whether to pilgrims dipping a toe or to people purchasing its waters over the internet. It is true that waters are not as amenable to human preservation as are their shores. Yet, elsewhere, water constitutes the holy site and is the sacred substance—as is the case at Lourdes, France (the waters of which, not incidentally, can also be purchased online).

Conclusion

Do not be ashamed to confess your sins,
and do not stop the current of a river.

Sirach 4:26

---

21. John Hart, *Sacramental Commons: Christian Ecological Ethics* (Lanham: Rowman and Littlefield, 2006), 90. An important point of comparison would be the Ganga, which is widely known to be extremely polluted, yet which is nonetheless understood by many to be ritually cleansing.

22. Gary Chamberlain, *Troubled Waters: Religion, Ethics, and the Global Water Crisis* (Lanham: Rowman and Littlefield, 2008), 171.

23. According to the Episcopal Diocese of Jerusalem, approximately 400,000 people visited the Bethany baptism site in the Hashemite Kingdom of Jordan. See "Jordan's King donates land for church at baptismal river site," *Christian Century* (May 6, 2008), 18.

24. http://www.baptismsite.com/content/view/83/1/lang,english/. Accessed 23 January 2009.

The Jordan River is precariously hemmed in by flagrant demand and entrenched political contestations. Simultaneously, it is a river that has shaped the lives and religious frameworks of millions of people worldwide—most of whom have never been to the river itself. Whether the Jordan River may return to a sustainable state, or whether it will trickle into a salty myth whose vibrancy exists only in collective memory, we do not know. Its future depends on concerted human effort across boundaries both literal and figurative.

Where water is defined by its lack, there are no easy answers. The Jordan Valley is a crucible. Might living waters be forged in it once more?

The frog does not drink up the pond in which he lives.

Teton Sioux Proverb

Nothing is softer or more flexible than water, yet nothing can resist it.

Lao Tzu

My father explained this to me. "All things in this world," he said, "have souls or spirits. The sky has a spirit, the clouds have spirits; the sun and moon have spirits; so have animals, trees, grass, water, stones—everything."

Edward Goodbird, HIDATSA 1914

Pure Water. Pure Life.

D.E. Adams

EDGE OUTREACH...your global water partner
www.edgeoutreach.com

Imagine! A car battery and table salt can purify fifty-five gallons of water per minute! This device can be delivered easily into the remotest and neediest regions of our world.*

Every language in the world has a word for water. In art, literature, and religion, water is a universal metaphor in the story of human history. Water is intrinsic to us. Our thirst is a daily desire to live, physically and spiritually.

EDGE OUTREACH is a faith-based non-profit that trains individuals and organizations to provide safe drinking water to people in so-called developing countries. EDGE has year-round, hands-on training in water treatment, filtration, community water assessment, health and hygiene, sanitation and hand-pump repair. This is obviously a practical work, and for us a practical spirituality. Our mission is to empower ordinary people to do acts of mercy that reflect the love of Christ.

We are firmly convinced that helping people have clean water to drink is an extraordinary act of mercy. It is also an urgent work and every day is filled with a sense of purpose. Three and a half million people die each year from water-related diseases. This is about ten thousand people continuously suffering until death finally comes. Eighty percent of these are children under the age of five. Personally, sitting here in Louisville, Kentucky, it is disturbing to think about knowing this is happening while I am enjoying some of the best water in the world and plenty of it. Yet when I have been in a village where we are helping to provide safe water, the urgency gives us energy to meet the unknown -- and there are a lot of unknowns. The urgency also brings peace. Peace is an experience of the spirit that opens us to be selfless and generous. Taking the time to work together, we discover a relationship of mutual concern and friendship. As we are often with indigenous people of Christian faith, it is life-changing to have the God in me recognized by people whose language I cannot speak and of whose life circumstances I know so little. Still, water is life and working with them to provide safe water to the village is to join in their faith and hope for the future.

You may be wondering how EDGE OUTREACH happened. I will give you a brief history and tie it up with a favorite Old Testament vision.

---

*The New Life water purifier, through electrolysis, generates chlorine with a car battery and a mere handful of salt (this handful of salt is good whether the water being purified is 100 or 5,000 gallons). The entire apparatus can fit in a small suitcase which can be delivered to the needy. It only costs $1200 (in case you wish to donate one), and then later there is the cost of the two water tanks and the training of the indigineous people who receive this gift of life.

EDGE did not start out to be a water organization. EDGE began as a short-term missions developer, planning and leading mission experiences with partnerships locally and internationally. In June of 2001, a simultaneous mission initiative to three countries called "EDGE 2001" was ready to take off. On the night before 165 people were to be commissioned, Mark Hogg, Executive Director of EDGE, received a phone call from a stranger who said he had heard about the EDGE 2001 project and had invented a small water purifier which the team going to Kenya could take. Mark responded that it was too last minute, that they had no money for such a thing and no time to learn how it worked. The stranger said the purifier was free and he would come to Louisville that night and teach Mark to use it. Mark and a couple of high school students stayed up until 2 am learning to operate the McGuire Water Purifier.

Arriving with the team in Kenya, Mark was still uncertain about what he had gotten himself into with the purifier. But when the day of the installation of the system came, Mark's uncertainty was quickly dissipated by the unanticipated response of the community. Setting up the system and starting the process was of great interest to the people, and their desire to see it work was tangible. It was a moment when the heart of the community was touched. Standing with people whose health was at risk because the water they must drink to survive makes them sick and giving them water that would help the whole community to have better health was a holy experience. It could even be called a healing experience for all involved. Mark knew that THIS was important, and EDGE had to be part of it.

Following EDGE 2001, EDGE OUTREACH began to focus on sustainable water solutions. The manner in which we go about helping people have clean drinking water is built on working side-by-side with them to solve their water problems. EDGE does not operate from any sort of agenda to push our faith and culture on others or to be the rich Americans who bring a packaged solution and then leave. Our agenda is simply about caring for other people. We believe that when that happens, there is something wonderful, miraculous, and divine in it.

EDGE OUTREACH has become a leader in a water technology that is highly adaptable, inexpensive and sustainable by indigenous people. EDGE calls its water training program PureWater PureLife (PWPL).

Below is a brief timeline of the history of EDGE's activities since that 2001 trip:

2002   PWPL modifies chlorine generator by incorporating basic plumbing skills to develop mini-water treatment plant. Begins installing systems and teaching mission teams traveling around the world.

2003-2007 PWPL launches endeavors to install systems and develop leaders throughout Costa Rica and the Dominican Republic, resulting in over 30 mini-water treatment plants which serve tens of thousand of people. Training for missionaries, indigenous leaders and mission teams continues.

2005   EDGE hires full-time staff person for PWPL to design water purification trips and inspire involvement. Hundreds of travelers, dozens of leaders and an internship program results.

2006   PWPL hosts its 1st International Water Training conference, producing materials and a training video. As a result of this conference, people who thirst for safe water are helped in Sudan, India, Rwanda, The Dominican Republic, Costa Rica.

Winter 2007   PWPL is donated its first water-well drilling rig. Training expands.

April 2007 PWPL builds an indoor water training school in Louisville, Kentucky, offering "On Demand Training" and certification in the following:

        Working with electric pumps
        Water testing in the field
        Community water and health assessment
        Health and hygiene education
        Water filtration
        Building mini-water treatment plants
        Hand pump repair

Summer 2007   PWPL hosts visiting youth mission teams from around the U.S. to learn about water problems around the world.

October 2007   PWPL hosts its 2nd annual International Water Training conference, with 70 people from 5 different countries attending, and holds its 1st 3-day hand pump repair course.

October 2008   Completes construction of one of only two indoor, year-round hand pump repair schools in the world, in Louisville, Kentucky. 1st 3-day hand pump repair course on the indoor platform. PWPL hosts its 3rd annual International Water Training conference.

January 2009   1st disaster relief effort in Costa Rica following 6.1 magnitude earthquake. PWPL trains and works with Red Cross and Salvation Army to provide safe drinking water for disaster victims.

March 2009   PWPL hosts its first International Water Training conference in St. Louis, Missouri. Water conferences planned in other U.S. cities.

May 2009 PWPL trains leadership of Costa Rica Red Cross and Salvation Army for water response in disaster situations. Preparation and construction begins for Central America water training base in San Jose, Costa Rica. Well drilling project begins in Haiti.

September 2009   Educational Concerns for Hunger Organization (ECHO) invites EDGE to speak at their SouthEast Asia Conference in Chaing Mai, Thailand. ECHO and their partnering organizations had discussed the water problem for years, but knew of no simple and inexpensive ways to solve it. They found EDGE had the solution.

October 2009   PWPL to host its 4th annual International Water Training conference and its 2nd 3-day indoor hand pump repair course.

The history goes on. Our context is now the vision. In Ezekiel 47, we are told about the river that flows from the new Temple. At the Temple the river is just a trickle, but then we are invited to step out from the Temple and walk in the water. The farther we get from the Temple the deeper the water until it becomes so deep that we can not even swim across. We step to the shore where we can see what is happening. Where the river flows it brings healing and life.

> He took me out through the north gate and led me round by an outside path to the east gate of the court, and I saw water was trickling from the south side. With a line in his hand the man went out eastwards, and he measured off a thousand cubits and made me walk through the water; it came up to my ankles. Again he measured off a thousand cubits and made me walk through the water; it came up to my knees. He measured another thousand cubits and made me walk through the water; it came up to my waist. He measured another thousand cubits and it was a torrent I could not cross; the water had risen and was deep enough to swim in, a torrent impossible to cross. 'Take note of this, O man,' he said, and he lead me back to the bank. When I got to the bank I saw a great number of trees on each side. He said to me, 'This water flows out to the region lying east, and down to the Arabah; it will run into the sea whose waters are noxious, and they will be made fresh. When any one of the living creatures that swarm upon the earth comes where the torrent flows, it will draw life from it. Fish will be plentiful, for wherever these waters come, the sea will be made fresh, and where the torrent flows, everything will live.
>
> Ezekiel 47: 2-9

It is not the clean water we bring to people which draws me to this vision. What draws me is the relationships we are building with people all over the world. The clean water does bring better health and life to these communities, but the relationship of trust and friendship which grows in the process is like the river that flows from the temple into the noxious waters, making them fresh: *and where the torrent flows, everything will live.*

Walter Brueggemann speaks to this effect: when we become listeners with our lives to the story of God's redemption, we discover God is a player in our lives. God is With us and For us as we live to serve. We become elemental in God's redemptive work.

Got water? Help somebody who doesn't. You can.

Appendix:
The Emerging Alliance of World Religions and Ecology

Mary Evelyn Tucker and John A. Grim

Yale University Forum on Religion and Ecology
www.yale.edu/religionandecology

Introduction

This article aims to present a prismatic view of the potential and actual resources embedded in the world's religions for supporting sustainable practices toward the environment. An underlying assumption is that most religious traditions have developed attitudes of respect, reverence, and care for the natural world that brings forth life in its diverse forms. Furthermore, it is assumed that issues of social justice and environmental integrity need to be intricately linked for creating the conditions for a sustainable future.

Several qualifications regarding the various roles of religion should be mentioned at the outset. First, we do not wish to suggest here that any one religious tradition has a privileged ecological perspective. Rather, multiple perspectives may be the most helpful in identifying the contributions of the world's religions to the flourishing of life for future generations.

Second, while we assume that religions are necessary partners in the current ecological movement, they are not sufficient without the indispensable contributions of science, economics, education, and policy to the varied challenges of current environmental problems. Therefore, this is an interdisciplinary effort in which religions can play a part.

Third, we acknowledge that there is frequently a disjunction between principles and practices: ecologically sensitive ideas in religions are not always evident in environmental practices in particular civilizations. Many civilizations have overused their environments, with or without religious sanction.

Finally, we are keenly aware that religions have all too frequently contributed to tensions and conflict among ethnic groups, both historically and at present. Dogmatic rigidity, inflexible claims of truth, and misuse of institutional and communal power by religions have led to tragic consequences in various parts of the globe.

Nonetheless, while religions have often preserved traditional ways, they have also provoked social change. They can be limiting but also liberating in their outlooks. In the 20th century, for example, religious leaders and theologians helped to give birth to progressive movements such as civil rights for minorities, social justice for the poor, and liberation for women. More recently, religious groups were instrumental in launching a movement called Jubilee 2000 for debt reduction for poor nations.[1] Although the world's religions have been slow to respond to our current environmental crises, their moral authority and their institutional power may help effect a change in attitudes, practices, and public policies.

The challenge of the environmental crisis
and the role of religions in meeting it

The environmental crisis has been well documented as a plural reality in its various interconnected aspects of resource depletion and species extinction, pollution growth and climate change, population explosion and overconsumption.[2] Thus, while we are using the term "environmental crisis" in a singular form, we recognize the diverse nature of the interrelated problems. These problems have been subject to extensive analysis and scrutiny by the scientific and policy communities and, although comprehensive solutions remain elusive, there is an emerging consensus that the environmental crisis is both global in scope and local in impact. A major question we confront is: What are the appropriate boundaries for the protection and use of nature? The choices will not be easy as we begin to reassess our sense of rights and responsibilities to present and future generations, and to reevaluate appropriate needs and overextended greed regarding natural resources.

Many organizations and individuals have been calling for greater participation by various religious communities in meeting the growing environmental crisis by reorienting humans to show more respect, restraint, and responsibility toward the Earth community.[3] Consider, for example, a statement by scientists, "Preserving and Cherishing the Earth: An Appeal for Joint Commitment in Science and Religion," issued at a Global Forum meeting in Moscow in January of 1990. It suggests that the human community is committing "crimes against creation" and notes that "problems of such magnitude, and solutions demanding so broad a perspective, must be recognized from the outset as having a religious as well as a scientific dimension. Mindful of our common responsibility, we scientists—many of us long engaged in combating the environmental crisis—urgently appeal to the world religious community to commit, in word and deed, and as boldly as is required, to preserve the environment of the Earth." It goes on to declare that "the environmental crisis requires radical changes not only in public policy, but in individual behavior. The historical record makes clear that religious teaching, example, and leadership are powerfully able to influence personal conduct and commitment. As scientists, many of us have had profound experiences of awe and reverence before the universe. We understand that

---

1. The movement, which began in Britain, has had demonstrable influence on the decisions of the World Bank and other lending organizations to reduce or forgive debts in more than twenty countries. See http://www.jubilee2000uk.org

2. See, for example, IPCC 2007: http://www.ipcc.ch/ipccreports/ar4-syr.htm

3. See http://www.thomasberry.org

what is regarded as sacred is more likely to be treated with care and respect. Our planetary home should be so regarded. Efforts to safeguard and cherish the environment need to be infused with a vision of the sacred."[4]

Although the responses of religions to the global environmental crisis were slow at first, they have been steadily growing over the last 25 years.[5] Just as religions played an important role in creating sociopolitical changes in the 20th century (e.g., human and civil rights), so now religions are poised in the 21st century to contribute to the emergence of a broader environmental ethics based on diverse sensibilities regarding the sacred dimensions of the natural world.

Religion and ecology

Religion is more than simply a belief in a transcendent deity or a means to an afterlife. It is, rather, an orientation to the cosmos and our role in it. We understand religion in its broadest sense as a means whereby humans, recognizing the limitations of phenomenal reality, undertake specific practices to effect self-transformation and community cohesion within a cosmological context. Religion thus refers to those cosmological stories, symbol systems, ritual practices, ethical norms, historical processes, and institutional structures that transmit a view of the human as embedded in a world of meaning and responsibility, transformation and celebration. Religion connects humans with a divine or numinous presence, with the human community, and with the broader Earth community. It links humans to the larger matrix of mystery in which life arises, unfolds, and flourishes.

In this light nature is a revelatory context for orienting humans to abiding religious questions regarding the cosmological origins of the universe, the meaning of the emergence of life, and the responsible role of humans in relation to life processes. Religion thus situates humans in relation to both the natural and human worlds with regard to meaning and responsibility. At the same time, religion becomes a means of experiencing a sustaining creative force in the natural and human worlds and beyond. For some traditions this is a creator deity; for others it is a numinous presence in nature; for others it is the source of flourishing life.

This experience of a creative force gives rise to a human desire to enter into processes of transformation and celebration that link self, society, and cosmos. The individual is connected to the larger human community and to the macrocosm of the universe itself. The transformative impulse seeks relationality, intimacy, and communion with this numinous power. Individual and communal transformations are expressed through rituals and ceremonies of celebration. More specifically, these transformations have the

---

4. "Preserving and Cherishing the Earth: An Appeal for Joint Commitment in Science and Religion," 1990.
5. For two examples of this, see: http://rockethics.psu.edu/climate/events/ssrecc/ and http://www.oikoumene.org/en/programmes/justice-diakonia-and-responsibility-for-creation/climate-change-and-water/public-campaign-on-climate-change.html

capacity to embrace the celebration of natural seasonal cycles as well as various cultural rites of passage. Religion thus links humanity to the rhythms of nature through the use of symbols and rituals that help to establish moral relationships and patterns for social exchange.

The issues discussed here are complex and involve various peoples, cultures, worldviews, and academic disciplines. Therefore, it is important to be clear about our terms. As it is used here, the term "ecology" locates the human within the horizon of emergent, interdependent life rather than viewing humanity as the vanguard of evolution, the exclusive fabricator of technology, or a species apart from nature. "Scientific ecology" is a term used to indicate the empirical and experimental study of the relations between living and nonliving organisms within their ecosystems. While drawing on the scientific understanding of interrelationships in nature, we are introducing the term "religious ecology" to point toward a cultural awareness of kinship with and dependence on nature for the continuity of all life. Thus, religious ecology provides a basis for exploring diverse cultural responses to the varied earth processes of transformation. In addition, the study of religious ecology can give us insight into how particular environments have influenced the development of cultures. Therefore, one can distinguish religious ecology from scientific ecology just as one can distinguish religious cosmology from scientific cosmology.

This awareness of the interdependence of life in religious ecology finds expression in the religious traditions as a sacred reality that is often recognized as a creative manifestation, a pervasive sustaining presence, a vital power in the natural world, or an emptiness (*sunyata*) leading to the realization of interbeing.[6] For many religions, the natural world is understood as a source of teaching, guidance, visionary inspiration, revelation, or power. At the same time, nature is also a source of food, clothing, and shelter. Thus, religions have developed intricate systems of exchange and thanksgiving around human dependence on animals and plants, on forests and fields, on rivers and oceans. These encompass symbolic and ritual exchanges that frequently embody agricultural processes, ecological knowledge of ecosystems, or hunting practices.[7]

Methodological approaches to study of religion and ecology

There is an inevitable disjunction between the examination of historical religious traditions in all of their diversity and complexity and the application of teachings or scriptures to contemporary situations. While religions have al-

---

6. The term "interbeing" is used in the writings of the Vietnamese monk Thich Nhat Hanh.
7. See Eugene N. Anderson, *Ecologies of the Heart: Emotion, Belief, and the Environment* (New York and Oxford: Oxford University Press, 1996) and John A. Grim, ed., *Indigenous Traditions and Ecology: The Interbeing of Cosmology and Community* (Cambridge, Mass.: Center for the Study of World Religions, Harvard Divinity School, 2001).

ways been involved in meeting contemporary challenges over the centuries, it is clear that the global environmental crisis is larger and more complex than anything in recorded human history. Thus, a simple application of traditional ideas to contemporary problems is unlikely to be either possible or adequate. In order to address ecological problems properly, religious leaders and laypersons have to be in dialogue with environmentalists, scientists, economists, businesspeople, politicians, and educators.

With these qualifications in mind we can then identify three methodological approaches that appear in the emerging study of religion and ecology: retrieval, reevaluation, and reconstruction. Interpretive retrieval involves the scholarly investigation of cosmological, scriptural, and legal sources in order to clarify traditional religious teachings regarding human-Earth relations. This requires that historical and textual studies uncover resources latent within the tradition. In addition, interpretive retrieval can identify ethical codes and ritual customs of the tradition in order to discover how these teachings were put into practice.

In interpretive reevaluation, traditional teachings are evaluated with regard to their relevance to contemporary circumstances. Can the ideas, teachings, or ethics present in these traditions be adopted by contemporary scholars or practitioners who wish to help shape more ecologically sensitive attitudes and sustainable practices? Reevaluation also questions ideas that may lead to inappropriate environmental practices. For example, are certain religious tendencies reflective of otherworldly or world-denying orientations that are not helpful in relation to pressing ecological issues? It asks as well whether the material world of nature has been devalued by a particular religion and whether a model of ethics focusing solely on human interaction is adequate to address environmental problems.

Finally, interpretive reconstruction suggests ways that religious traditions might adapt their teachings to current circumstances in new and creative ways. This may result in a new synthesis or in a creative modification of traditional ideas and practices to suit modern modes of expression. This is the most challenging aspect of the emerging field of religion and ecology and requires sensitivity to who is speaking about a tradition in the process of reevaluation and reconstruction. Postcolonial critics have appropriately highlighted the complex issues surrounding the problem of who is representing or interpreting a tradition. Nonetheless, practitioners and leaders of particular traditions may find grounds for creative dialogue with scholars of religious traditions in these various phases of interpretation.

Diversity and dialogue of religions

The diversity of the world's religions may seem self-evident to some, but it is worth stressing the differences within and between religious traditions. At the same time, it is possible to posit shared dimensions of religions in light of this diversity, without arguing that the world's religions have some single emergent goal. The world's religions are inherently distinctive in their expressions, and these differences are especially significant in regard to the study of religion and ecology. Several sets of religious diversity can be identified as being integrally related. First, there is historical and cultural diversity within and between religious traditions as expressed over time in varied social contexts. For example, we need to be sensitive to the variations in Judaism between Orthodox, Conservative, and Reform movements, in Christianity between Catholic, Orthodox, and Protestant varieties of the tradition, and in Islam between Sunni and Shiite positions.

Second, there is dialogical and syncretic diversity within and between religions traditions, which adds another level of complexity. Dialogue and interaction between traditions engenders the fusion of religious traditions into one another, often resulting in new forms of religious expression that can be described as syncretic. Such syncretism occurred when Christian missionaries evangelized indigenous peoples in the Americas. In East Asia there is an ongoing dialogue between and among Confucianism, Daoism, and Buddhism that results in various kinds of syncretism.[8]

Third, there is ecological and cosmological diversity within and between religions. Ecological diversity is evident in the varied environmental contexts and bioregions where religions have developed over time. For example, Jerusalem is the center of a sacred bioregion where three religious traditions—Judaism, Christianity, and Islam—have both shaped and been shaped by the environment. These complex interactions illustrate that religions are not static in their impacts on ecology. Indeed, throughout history the relationships between religions and their natural settings have been fluid and manifold.

Religious traditions develop unique narratives, symbols, and rituals to express their relationships with the cosmos as well as with various local landscapes. For example, the body is a vital metaphor for understanding the Daoist relationship with the world: as an energetic network of breathings-in and breathings-out, the body, according to Daoism, expresses the basic pattern of the cosmos. Another example, from Buddhism, of a distinctive ecological understanding involves Doi Suthep, a sacred mountain in the Chiang Mai valley of northern Thailand: the ancient Thai reverence for the mountain is understood as analogous to respect for the Buddhist reliquary, or *stupa*.

Converging perspectives: common values for the Earth community

The project of exploring world religions and ecology may lead toward convergence on several overarching principles. The common values that most of the world's religions hold in relation to the natural world might be summarized as reverence, respect, restraint, redistribution, responsibility, and renewal. While there are clearly variations of interpretation within and between religions regarding these six principles, it may be said that reli-

8. See Judith A. Berling, *The Syncretic Religion of Lin Chao-en* (New York: Columbia University Press, 1980).

gions are moving toward an expanded understanding of their cosmological orientations and ethical obligations. Although these principles have been previously understood primarily with regard to relations toward other humans, the challenge now is to extend them to the natural world. As this shift occurs—and there are signs it is already happening—religions can advocate reverence for the earth and its profound cosmological processes, respect for the earth's myriad species, an extension of ethics to include all life forms, restraint in the use of natural resources combined with support for effective alternative technologies, equitable redistribution of wealth, the acknowledgement of human responsibility in regard to the continuity of life and the ecosystems that support life, renewal of the energies of hope for the transformative work to be done.

Just as religious values needed to be identified, so, too, the values embedded in science, education, economics, and public policy also need to be more carefully understood. Scientific analysis will be critical to understanding nature's economy; education will be indispensable to creating sustainable modes of life; economic incentives will be central to an equitable distribution of resources; public-policy recommendations will be invaluable in shaping national and international priorities. But the ethical values that inform modern science and public policy must not be uncritically applied. Instead, by carefully evaluating the intellectual resources both of the world's religions and of modern science and public policy, our long-term ecological prospects may emerge. We need to examine the tensions between efficiency and equity, between profit and preservation, and between the private and public good. We need to make distinctions between human need and greed, between the use and abuse of nature, and between the intrinsic value and instrumental value of nature. We need to move from destructive to constructive modes of production, and from the accumulation of goods to an appreciation for the common good of the Earth community.

There has been much progress in the arena of religion and ecology. Indeed, a new academic field of study has emerged with implications for public policy. This is in large measure due to a three-year conference series at Harvard's Center for the Study of World Religions from 1996-1998, which resulted in ten edited volumes, a large website, and the formation of the Forum on Religion and Ecology based at Yale University. Other milestones include the *Encyclopedia of Religion,* published in 2005. Thousands of people around the globe are now participating in this work, both in the classroom and in engaged projects for a sustainable future.

A School Community Rises to the Challenge

Dexter Mahaffey

In our Sister City of Tamale, Ghana, clean, safe water is a rare privilege most go without. And for the students at Kentucky Country Day School, this means that the children at our two sister schools with whom they regularly exchange pen pal letters are, as a course of living, subject to disease and illness merely by sipping a drink, enjoying a meal with family, or the washing of hands. And so it was third graders hosting a bake sale, middle school students collecting box tops, a walk-a-thon, a pick-up football tournament, and a host of other small actions on the part of this one school that set in motion the raising of enough funds in one year to pay for the construction and installation of water harvesting systems at our sister schools, Dahin Sheli Grade School and Tamale Islamic Science Secondary School.

The latter name strikes a chord of sorts, given the post-9/11 American consciousness and our country's contested treatment of Islam. Yet when it came to water, there was no discussion, no mention of the fact that Louisville and KCD are both majority Christian populations while Tamale is explicitly 95% Muslim. When it comes to water, or the lack of it, this is simply *something you do*. Without question, without hesitation. The interesting thing is that we had no difficulty raising the funds, in the end raising four times our goal. Isn't there something in the context of water that is an absolute, something that political borders, faith lines, gender—all common divisions we create to separate from each other—in the end dissolve when it comes to a belief that every person on our planet ought to be able to drink freely and safely? And it's not an issue of safety, for we regularly allow conflict, violence, injustice, inequality, matters that kill far more quickly than Guinea Worm or River Blindness or Cholera.

For our students, teachers, and families, raising money for the simplest of forms—gutter to downspout to cistern to filter to vessel—came so quickly, so naturally, it was as if they were moved by something other than our requests, something deeper and yet unnamable. For we are a Baha'i, Buddhist, Christian, Hindu, Muslim, Jewish, Secular, and Sikh school, implicitly and explicitly. We do not speak the same language, do not share belief, and yet we found ourselves sharing action without hesitation when it came to water for Rama, Mohammed, Idrissu, Khadija, for those who we know by name and call our own and who in our minds and hearts and finances must not be allowed to go without.

I received the photos from Tamale in an email just two weeks ago. And I and others of us will once again travel to Tamale this year and host friends from Tamale, and despite the waters that separate us, it begins to feel like a communion of sorts, a new definition of that ancient concept.

Biographies of the Contributors

Coleman Barks was born in 1937 in Chattanooga, Tennessee and educated at the University of North Carolina (BA 1959; PhD 1968) and at the University of California, Berkeley (MA 1961). He has since 1977 collaborated with various scholars of the Persian language (most notably, John Moyne) to bring over into American free verse the poetry of the 13th Century mystic, Jelaluddin Rumi. This work has resulted in twenty-one volumes, including the bestselling *Essential Rumi* in 1995, two appearances on Bill Moyers' PBS specials, and inclusion in the prestigious *Norton Anthology of World Masterpieces*. The Rumi translations have sold over a million copies. It is claimed that over the last fifteen years Rumi has been the most-read poet in the United States.

Dr. Barks taught American Literature and Creative Writing at various universities for thirty-four years, and has published seven volumes of his own poetry. The Univ. of Georgia Press published *WINTER SKY: Poems 1968-2008* in September of 2008. In 2004 he received the Juliet Hollister Award for his work in the interfaith area. In March 2005 the US State Department sent him to Afghanistan as the first visiting speaker there in twenty-five years. In May of 2006 he was awarded an honorary Doctorate by the University of Tehran. In 2009 he was inducted into the Georgia Writers Hall of Fame. He is now retired Professor Emeritus at the Univ. of Georgia in Athens. He has two grown sons and four grandchildren, all of whom live near him in Athens, Georgia.

Wendell Berry was born in Henry County, Kentucky, in 1934. He earned a Bachelor's degree from the University of Kentucky in 1956 and continued on to complete a Master's degree in 1957. In 1958, he received a Wallace Stegner Fellowship from Stanford University. Berry has taught at Stanford University, Georgetown College, New York University, the University of Cincinnati, and Bucknell University. He taught at his alma mater, the University of Kentucky from 1964-77, and again from 1987-93.

The author of more than forty works of fiction, nonfiction, and poetry, Wendell Berry has been the recipient of numerous awards and honors; to cite a few: a Guggenheim Foundation Fellowship (1962), a Rockefeller Foundation Fellowship (1965), a National Institute of Arts and Letters award for writing (1971), the American Academy of Arts and Letters Jean Stein Award (1987), the Ingersoll Foundation's T. S. Eliot Award (1994), and the Lyndhurst Prize (1997). His books include the novel *Hannah Coulter* (2004), the essay collections *Citizenship Papers* (2005) and *The Way of Ignorance* (2006), and *Given: Poems* (2005), all available from Counterpoint. Berry's latest works include *The Mad Farmer Poems* (2008) and *Whitefoot* (2009), which features illustrations by Davis Te Selle.

He lives and works with his wife, Tanya Berry, on their farm in Port Royal, Kentucky.

Titus Burckhardt, the son of Swiss sculptor Carl Burckhardt, was born in 1908. His youth was devoted to studies in art, art history, and oriental languages and to journeys through North Africa and the Near East. In 1942, he became director of Urs Graf-Verlag, a publishing house specializing in facsimile editions of ancient manuscripts. He remained there until 1968 when he was asked by UNESCO to help in the preservation of the city of Fez in Morocco. In addition to writing books in German, he has translated many important works from the Arabic. Of his own books, *An Introduction to Sufi Doctrine, Sacred Art in East and West, Moorish Culture in Spain, The Art of Islam, Siena: City of the Virgin, Fez: City of Islam, Chartres*, and a collection of his essays *Mirror of the Intellect* have all appeared in English. The last three, as well as *Alchemy*, were translated from the German by Dr. William Stoddart.

Graeme Castleman is a doctoral candidate at La Trobe University, Bendigo (Australia). He was awarded the 2001 D.M. Myers University Medal as the Faculty's most outstanding honours graduate for his honours thesis entitled "Created to be God: Divine-Human Identity and the Symbol of the Cross in Christian and Islamic Traditions." His work has been published in *Sophia: The Journal of Traditional Studies* and *Eye of the Heart: A Journal of Traditional Wisdom* and has received a number of awards. Graeme's research focuses upon the writings of the Church Fathers and Christian and ancient Greek metaphysics. His doctoral thesis explores the place of *creatio ex nihilo* in traditional Christian thought.

Emma Clark is a garden designer, writer and lecturer specializing in traditional art in general and the design of Islamic Gardens in particular. The subject of her Master's degree (Royal College of Art, 1990, with distinction) was the symbolism of the Islamic garden and garden carpet, later edited and published as a monograph, '*Underneath Which Rivers Flow, The Symbolism of the Islamic Garden*' (1996). Her book, *The Art of the Islamic Garden* was published in the winter of 2004 (The Crowood Press).

Emma is Senior Tutor and lecturer on the post-graduate Traditional Arts Programme at The Prince's School of Traditional Arts in London validated by the University of Wales. Here, since 1993, she has specialized in teaching the principles and criteria of sacred and traditional art, principles fundamental to the great faith traditions of the world.

She lectures both nationally and internationally—participating in various conferences on sacred and traditional art and architecture (e.g. Tehran, 1995 and 1999; Malaysia, 1997; Washington 2001; Jordan 2002; London 2007; Cairo 2009). She has written many articles on Islamic art and architecture, and on the Islamic garden: its history, design and symbolism, in particular the significance of water.

Emma has designed gardens in the United Kingdom (London and Oxford) and abroad. She was a member of the team who designed and planted HRH The Prince of Wales' 'Carpet Garden' (based on Islamic garden design principles) at the Chelsea Flower Show in 2001. This garden has been transported to Highgrove, where, true to its Islamic inspiration, it is planted as a kind of 'secret' garden, behind high walls. (See Chapter 7 of her book, *The Art of the Islamic Garden*). She has designed a Moroccan-inspired garden in Paris (2005) for a Saudi Arabian client and is currently designing gardens in Medina and Jeddah, Saudi Arabia; one in Cairo; an inter-faith garden in the City of London where she is involved with a charity concerned with religious education through the environment; a landscaping project in Manchester; and one in High Wycombe. She has been a consultant on a hospital garden in Guildford, a Muslim Cemetery in East London, and a car park and garden surrounding the mosque at Woking, the oldest purpose-built mosque in the U.K. dating from the 1880s. Emma is currently working on a faith garden in a prison, in collaboration with The Prince's School. She has recently been consulted on a large landscaping project in Lahore, Pakistan as well as to Foster and Partners (London) for a large landscaping project in Abu Dhabi. (2007-8)

She earned her first degree, BA with Honors in History and History of Art (University College, London). Emma worked as a specialist in the Costume and Textile Department at Christie's, London, where she still occasionally acts as a consultant on Oriental and European costume and textiles.

Ananda Kentish Coomaraswamy (1887-1947), described by Heinrich Zimmer as "That noble scholar upon whose shoulder we are still standing", was one of the world's greatest art historians and scholars of traditional iconography and symbolism. He knew thirty-six languages and admitted he did "actually think in both Eastern and Christian terms, Greek, Latin, Sanskrit, Pali and to some extent Persian and even Chinese." While serving as a curator to the Boston Museum of Fine Arts in the latter part of his life, he devoted his work to the explication of traditional metaphysics and symbolism. His writings of this period are filled with references to Plato, Plotinus, Clement, Philo, Augustine, Aquinas, Shankara, Eckhart and the Rhinish and Oriental mystics

He was born in Ceylon, educated in his mother's homeland of England, and then moved to America. He served as curator in the Boston Museum of Fine Arts until his death, having been the first Oriental to make the meaning of Oriental art understood in the West. He played an important role in the collection of Oriental and Persian Art for the Freer Gallery in Washington, D.C. and the Boston Museum of Fine Art as well.

Jeffrey Einboden is a graduate of Magdalene College, Cambridge where he completed a doctorate concerning Ralph Waldo Emerson's translations of Persian poetry (2005). Currently an Assistant Professor at Northern Illinois University, Einboden's most recent publications include the 2008 'Composing a Persian *Letter*: Simin Daneshvar's Rendition of Hawthorne' (*Nathaniel Hawthorne Review*; 34:2); the 2009 'Washington Irving in Muslim Translation: Revising the American *Mahomet*' (*Translation & Literature*;

18:1); and the forthcoming 'Stoicism or Sufism?: Hammer-Purgstall's Persian *Meditations*' (*Middle Eastern Literatures*; vol. 13; 2010).

Rabbi Dr. Aubrey Glazer serves as Senior Rabbi at the Jewish Community Center of Harrison, New York. A native of Toronto, Canada, Glazer holds a B.A. in French Language and Literature (University of Toronto, 1994), an M.A. in Jewish Philosophy (Jewish Theological Seminary Graduate School), and a Ph.D. in Hebrew Hermeneutics (University of Toronto, June 2005). His research is part of a larger commitment to revitalizing Hebrew culture and civilization. His publications include scholarly studies and annotated translations included in: *Hebrew Studies: A Journal Devoted to Hebrew Language and Literature; Kabbalah: A Journal for the Study of Mystical Texts; God's Voice From the Void: Old & New Studies in Bratzlav Hasidism; Ariel: The Israeli Review of Arts and Letters, and Jerusalem International Poets Festival Anthology.* His ordination is from the Conservative movement (Jewish Theological Seminary, 2000).

Aubrey along with his wife, Elyssa Wortzman, and their daughter, Talya Sahara live in New York. Elyssa, an attorney and visual artist, has experience teaching and creating community programming for children and adults in the New York and Toronto Jewish Community. He is on the Fons Vitae Board for the Spiritual Affinities: Judaism and Islam project.

John Grim As a professor of religion John teaches courses in Native American and Indigenous religions, religion and ecology, ritual, and mysticism in the world's religions. His published works include: *The Shaman: Patterns of Religious Healing Among the Ojibway Indians* (University of Oklahoma Press, 1983) and, with Mary Evelyn Tucker, a co-edited volume entitled *Worldviews and Ecology* (Orbis, 1994, 5th printing 2000). In the ten volume series on "World Religions and Ecology," John has edited *Indigenous Traditions and Ecology* (Harvard, 2001). He also co-edited the Daedalus volume titled *Religion and Ecology: Can the Climate Change?* (2001). He is a Senior Lecturer and Senior Scholar at Yale University where he has appointments in the School of Forestry and Environmental Studies as well as the Divinity School and the Department of Religious Studies.

John and Mary Evelyn, Co-Directors of the Forum on Religion and Ecology, together organized a series of ten conferences on World Religions and Ecology at the Center for the Study of World Religions at Harvard Divinity School. They also edited the ten volume series from the conferences distributed by Harvard University Press.

Cecily Jones, a member of the Sisters of Loretto, a congregation of Catholic Sisters, lives at her order's motherhouse in rural Kentucky. Formerly an English teacher at Webster College (now Webster University), an editor of her community's publications, and an activist for justice and peace efforts, she has been writing poetry since her own college years. Currently she is working on a biography of Sister Mary Luke Tobin, also a Sister of Loretto and a noted figure in the post-Vatican II U.S. Catholic Church, and contributing to an upcoming book about Sister Mary Luke and Thomas Merton: *Hidden in the Same Mystery*, Fons Vitae 2010.

Rabbi Dr. Menahem Kallus has spent years immersed in the translation of certain contemplative teachings into a life of practice, as evinced in a vibrant, insightful and deeply spiritual rendition of this classic text included in this volume on water. His annotations broadly contextualize issues involving charismatic leadership; mystical union-*Devekut*; Zoharic-Lurianic unification practice-*Yichud*; cosmic rectification-*Tikkun*; and personal spiritual development. As well by referencing the textual history and provenance of the teachings, this annotated translation serves as a classic guide for further study in the tradition.

Martin Lings is the author of the authoritative biography of the *Prophet, Muhammed, His Life Based on the Earliest Sources*. He has also written *What is Sufism?*, *Ancient Beliefs and Modern Superstitions*, *Shakespeare in Light of Sacred Art*, *The Book of Certainty*, *A Sufi Saint of the Twentieth Century*, *The Quranic Art of Calligraphy and Illumination* and two volumes of poems, *The Element* and *The Heralds*. He is also the author of the article on Sufism in the latest edition of the Encyclopedia Britannica, the chapter on Sufism in the Cambridge University publication *Religion in the Middle East*, and numerous articles for the quarterly journal *Studies in Comparative Religion*.

Dr. Lings was born in Burnage, Lancashire, 1909. After taking an English degree at Oxford in 1932, where he was both a student and friend of C. S. Lewis, he was appointed Lecturer in Anglo-Saxon at the University of Kaunas. His interest in Islam and in Arabic took him to Egypt in 1939, and in the following year he was given a lectureship in Shakespeare at Cairo University. In 1952 he returned to England and took a degree in Arabic at London University. From 1970-74 he was Keeper of Oriental Manuscripts and Printed Books at the British Museum (in 1973 his Department became part of the British Library) where he had been in special charge of the Qur'an manuscripts, amongst other treasures, since 1955. Dr. Lings passed from this world on May 12th 2005 and is survived by his wife.

Dexter Mahaffey is Director of Diversity and Global Studies at Kentucky Country Day School, Louisville, Kentucky.

Thomas Merton (1915-1968) is arguably the most influential American Catholic author of the twentieth century. His autobiography, *The Seven Storey Mountain*, has sold over one million copies and has been translated into over fifteen languages. He wrote over sixty other books and hundreds of poems and articles on topics ranging from monastic spirituality to civil rights, nonviolence, and the nuclear arms race.

Merton was born in Prades, France. His New Zealand-born father, Owen Merton, and his American-born mother, Ruth Jenkins, were both artists. They had met at painting school in Paris, were married at St. Anne's Church, Soho, London and returned to the France where Thomas Merton was born on January 31st, 1915. After a rambunctious youth and adolescence, Merton converted to Roman Catholicism whilst at Columbia University and on December 10th, 1941 he entered the Abbey of Gethsemani, a community of monks belonging to the Order of Cistercians of the Strict Observance (Trappists), the most ascetic Roman Catholic monastic order.

The twenty-seven years he spent in Gethsemani brought about profound changes in his self-understanding. This ongoing conversion impelled him into the political arena, where he became, according to Daniel Berrigan, the conscience of the peace movement of the 1960's. Referring to race and peace as the two most urgent issues of our time, Merton was a strong supporter of the nonviolent civil rights movement, which he called "certainly the greatest example of Christian faith in action in the social history of the United States." Merton had a great interest in and was inspired by all of the world's great faith traditions, as is evidenced by the congresses and books that have appeared concerning his interest in Hesychasm, Judaism, Sufism, Buddhism and soon, Taoism.

During his last years, he became deeply interested in Asian religions, particularly Zen Buddhism, and in promoting East-West dialogue. After several meetings with Merton during the American monk's trip to the Far East in 1968, the Dalai Lama praised him as having a more profound understanding of Buddhism than any other Christian he had known. It was during this trip to a conference on East-West monastic dialogue that Merton died, in Bangkok on December 10, 1968, the victim of an accidental electrocution. The date marked the twenty-seventh anniversary of his entrance to Gethsemani.

Jonathan Montaldo is the Director of Bethany Spring, the Merton Institute for Contemplative Living's Retreat Center in New Haven, Kentucky. He has edited numerous volumes of Thomas Merton's writing including *The Intimate Merton, Dialogues with Silence, A Year with Thomas Merton, Choosing to Love the World: Thomas Merton on Contemplation*, and *Bridges to Contemplative Living with Thomas Merton* (nine volumes). With V. Gray Henry, the publisher, he is the co-general editor of the Fons Vitae Thomas Merton series that examines Merton's interests in Sufism, Hesychasm, Judaism, Buddhism, and the next up-coming volume in the series, *Merton & Taoism.*

Katherine Murray is a writer, chaplain, mom, and grandmother who lives and works in Indianapolis, Indiana. She integrates pastoral earthcare with contemplative writing and publishes two related blogs: *Practical Faith*, about noticing spirit in daily events, and *Narrative*, which explores working with stories in helping professions. In addition to her writing, she facilitates *Listening to the Earth Speak: A Contemplative and Creative Retreat for Artists and Writers* for the Merton Institute.

Christiana Peppard Christiana Z. Peppard is a doctoral candidate in the Department of Religious Studies at Yale University and Scholar-in-Residence at the Cathedral of St.John the Divine in New York City, where she lives with her husband and daughter. Her areas of specialization include biomedical ethics at the edges of life; Catholic moral theology and social thought; poetry as an ethical methodology; and the ethics of fresh water use and abuse. Her dissertation explores moral aspects of fresh water (focusing on scarcity, provision, commodification, and control), and identifies elements for a global fresh water ethic from Christian religious resources, especially Catholic social thought. She is co-editor of the book *Expanding Horizons in Bioethics* (Springer, 2005).

Alexander Price studied Anthropology at Antioch College in Yellow Springs, Ohio. His published writings have discussed such topics as shamanism and the feminist history of religion, and his research interests include ancient Near Eastern hunting traditions, comparative mythology, and cultural exchanges between ancient Mesoamerica and the American Southwest.

Timothy Scott graduated BA (Humanities) from La Trobe University, Bendigo, Australia, with majors in Literature, Philosophy, Religious Studies, and Studies in Western Traditions. He was awarded his doctorate from La Trobe for his thesis, Symbolism of the Ark. He lived and taught Religious Studies in Düsseldorf, Germany, and Oxford, UK. He has worked as an editor in the preparation of the works of Ananda Coomaraswamy. He is a regular contributor to the Traditionalist journals *Sacred Web*, Vancouver, and *Sophia*, Washington DC. His research focuses on the universal language of traditional symbolism with a particular focus on biblical symbolism and the mystical traditions of Judaism, Christianity and Islam. Since 2007 Timothy has been the editor-in-chief of *Eye of the Heart: A Journal of Traditional Wisdom* for the Philosophy and Religious Studies Program at La Trobe University, Bendigo.

John Slater's poems have appeared in various journals in the U.S. and Canada including *Queen's Quarterly, Drunken Boat* and *Brink Magazine*. His poem 'Lost and Found' won the 2007 Foley Poetry Award in *America* magazine. A first collection of his work is forthcoming from *The Porcupine's Quill*. A contemplative (Cistercian) monk, he is currently pursuing a graduate degree in theology at Catholic University of America. John Slater (a.k.a. Brother Isaac) is a monk of the Abbey of the Genesee. The contemplative Cistercian life, with its blend of psalmody and silent contemplation have colored his response to the poems of Hafiz.

Einboden and Slater's co-translations from Hafiz have appeared in, or are forthcoming from, *CrossCurrents*; *WordsWithoutBorders*; *The Dalhousie Review*; and *PN Review*.

Huston Smith is internationally renowned as one of the most eloquent and accessible contemporary authorities on, and teachers of, the world's religions. He is the author of *The World's Religions*, a classic in the field, as well as a number of other works including *The Soul of Christianity, Why Religion Matters, The Illustrated World's Religions, Forgotten Truth*, and

Tales of Wonder. Smith has held faculty positions at Washington University, MIT, Syracuse, and the University of California, Berkeley. In 1996, Bill Moyers devoted a five-part PBS special to Smith's life and work titled *The Wisdom of Faith with Huston Smith*. His book *The World's Religions*, remains a popular introduction to comparative religion. He has received numerous awards, including the Wilbur Award for Religious Communicators, and the Courage of Conscience Award from the Peace Abbey in Sherborn, Massachusetts, for his life long commitment to bringing the world's religions together to promote understanding, social justice and peace. His books have sold more than 2.5 million copies in the United States.

Lisa Starr, an inn-keeper, mother, basketball coach, teacher, and Rhode Island's Poet Laureate, divides her time among a variety of interests, her family, and her passion for poetry. She is a two-time recipient of the Rhode Island Fellowship for Poetry. In her capacity as Poet Laureate, Starr is generating a statewide poetry pen-pal system which creates and then partners writing circles among student and elderly communities around the state. She has also established poetry circles in hospitals, homeless shelters, the state prison, and agencies for children with severe mental and physical disabilities.

From April 19-24, 2009, Starr assembled more than a dozen US State Poets Laureate in Rhode Island for "Poetry for Hope", a series of readings, workshops, and public forums featuring the visiting poets and emerging and established Rhode Island poets and musicians at schools, libraries and cultural attractions around the state. The poets worked with more than 7500 Rhode Islanders during the five poetry sweep.

Starr's third collection of poems, *Mad With Yellow*, was published in September, 2008. She is the author of two other books: *This Place Here* (2001) and *Days of Dogs and Driftwood* (1993). Starr is the founder and director of the Block Island Poetry Project, the nationally acclaimed celebration of the arts and humanities, now in its sixth year. A poet by choice and an innkeeper by necessity, Starr owns and operates the Hygenia House, a ten-room inn on Block Island. The brightest lights of her life are her two children, Orrin (12) and Millie (11) and her dog, Brother. When time permits, she writes her heart out.

Henry David Thoreau (1817–1862) was an American author, philosopher, and naturalist who was part of the Transcendentalist movement. He is best known for his "Civil Disobedience" essay, which he wrote after spending a night in jail for not paying the poll tax; and for his two-year retreat to Walden Pond, detailed in his second book, *Walden, or Life in the Woods*.

Edward O Wilson, Museum Comparative Zoology, Harvard University said, "Thoreau, who rightfully can be called the father of environmentalism, also deserves iconic status in the scientific fields of ecology and biodiversity studies. With the overdue rapid upsurge in public attention to all three of these domains, the study of the Concord Master naturalist and preservation of his memory becomes all the more important in history."

Thoreau may be the most quoted American author. Excerpts from his writings surface in American thought, conversation, even on t-shirts, posters and greeting cards. His words reach out to us across time and inspire us to think for ourselves

Bonnie Myotai Treace is the founder of Hermitage Heart Zen and the Bodies of Water School of Practice. After over two decades in monastic life, she served as the Vice-Abbess of Zen Mountain Monastery and Abbess of the Zen Center of New York City, having received ordination and transmission in the "Dogen style" Zen of the Soto School as well as koan study. Her work in recent years however has been dedicated to the intra-religious, and to bringing environmental protection and celebration into contemplative depth. In her work on behalf of water, she also draws from an earlier career in hydromechanics, as well as a time teaching poetry at the university level, and serving as director/manager of various social justice advocacy projects.

Mary Evelyn Tucker is a Senior Lecturer and Senior Scholar at Yale University where she has appointments in the School of Forestry and Environmental Studies as well as the Divinity School and the Department of Religious Studies. She is a co-founder and co-director with John Grim of the Forum on Religion and Ecology. Together they organized a series of ten conferences on World Religions and Ecology at the Center for the Study of World Religions at Harvard Divinity School. They are series editors for the ten volumes from the conferences distributed by Harvard University Press. She is also Research Associate at the Reischauer Institute of Japanese Studies at Harvard. She is the author of *Worldly Wonder: Religions Enter Their Ecological Phase* (Open Court Press, 2003), *Moral and Spiritual Cultivation in Japanese Neo-Confucianism* (SUNY, 1989) and *The Philosophy of Qi* (Columbia University Press, 2007). She co-edited *Worldviews and Ecology* (Orbis, 1994), *Buddhism and Ecology* (Harvard, 1997), *Confucianism and Ecology* (Harvard, 1998), and *Hinduism and Ecology* (Harvard, 2000) and *When Worlds Converge* (Open Court, 2002). With Tu Weiming she edited two volumes on Confucian Spirituality (Crossroad, 2004). She also co-edited a Daedalus volume titled *Religion and Ecology: Can the Climate Change?* (2001). She edited several of Thomas Berry's books: *Evening Thoughts* (Sierra Club Books and University of California Press, 2006), *The Sacred Universe* (Columbia University Press, 2009), *Christian Future and the Fate of Earth* (Orbis Book, 2009). She is a member of the Interfaith Partnership for the Environment at the United Nations Environment Programme (UNEP). She served on the International Earth Charter Drafting Committee from 1997-2000 and is a member of the Earth Charter International Council. B.A. Trinity College, M.A. SUNY Fredonia, M.A. Fordham University, PhD Columbia University.

Hamza Yusuf was born in Washington State and raised in Northern California. In 1977, he became Muslim and subsequently traveled to the Muslim world and studied for ten years in the U. A. E., Saudi Arabia, as well as North and West Africa. He received teaching licenses in various Islamic subjects from several well-known scholars in various countries. After ten years of studies abroad, he returned to the USA and took degrees in Religious Studies and Health Care. He has traveled all over the world giving talks on Islam. He also founded Zaytuna Institute which has established an international reputation for presenting a classical picture of Islam in the West and which is dedicated to the revival of traditional study methods and the sciences of Islam. Shaykh Hamza is the first American lecturer to teach in Morocco's prestigious and oldest University, the Karaouine in Fes. In addition, he has translated into modern English several classical Arabic traditional texts and poems. Shaykh Hamza currently resides in Northern California with his wife and five children.

Editors

Elena Lloyd-Sidle of Louisville, Kentucky, directs the Spiritual Affinities: Judaism and Islam book series project at Fons Vitae and has been involved in planning inter-religious festivals and congresses since 2005. She co-produced the film, *Death and Transformation: The Personal Reflections of Huston Smith* with Gray Henry in 2006. She has spent considerable time in the Middle East and North Africa as a student of Arabic and religious studies. Most recently she studied the spiritual significance of the natural world in Quranic commentaries in Fes, Morocco with a Fulbright grant. She is currently a Masters student at Yale Divinity School studying religious ethics.

Virginia Gray Henry-Blakemore of Louisville, Kentucky, is the director of the interfaith publishing houses Fons Vitae and Quinta Essentia, a contributing editor for Parabola magazine, a founding member of the Thomas Merton Foundation, and lecturer in world religions. She is both a writer and film producer—among recent films are *Beads of Faith: The Universal Use of the Rosary* and *Death and Transformation: The Personal Reflections of Huston Smith*, Autumn 2006 (co-produced with Elena Lloyd-Sidle). BA, Sarah Lawrence College (Joseph Campbell was her don, 1965), studied at the American and al-Azhar Universities in Cairo (1969-79), MA in education (1981), research fellow at Clare Hall, Cambridge University 1983-1990, currently preparing her PhD at the Faculty of Divinity at Canterbury, Kent.